STOCKHOLM SERIES: 1

CITY OF MY DREAMS

STOCKHOLM SERIES: 1

CITY OF MY DREAMS

A novel
by
Per Anders Fogelström

Translated from the Swedish
by
Jennifer Brown Bäverstam

Penfield
Press

The Stockholm Series:
City of My Dreams
Children of Their City
Do You Remember That City
In a City Transformed
City in the World

City of My Dreams originally published in Swedish as
Mina drömmars stad by Albert Bonniers Förlag, Stockholm, 1960.
Swedish copyright © 1960 Per Anders Fogelström
English translation copyright © 2000 Jennifer Brown Bäverstam
Penfield Press, Iowa City, Iowa
Library of Congress number 00-131059
ISBN 1-57216-088-8

Cover design by Molly Cook
Cover photographs by A. Jonsson, Stockholm, circa 1860,
and by Jennifer Brown Bäverstam

TABLE OF CONTENTS

III

IV

THE AUTHOR

PER ANDERS FOGELSTRÖM is one of the most widely read authors in Sweden today. *City of My Dreams,* the first book in his five-volume Stockholm Series, broke the record for bestsellers. A compelling storyteller known for his narrative sweep, his acute characterization and the poetic qualities of his prose, Fogelström was highly acclaimed even before he wrote the Stockholm Series. Ingmar Bergman made one of Fogelström's earlier novels, *Summer with Monika,* into a film that is now a Bergman classic.

Born in 1917, Fogelström grew up in Stockholm and lived there his entire life. He was a vast resource on Stockholm's history with enormous archives on the subject, and published much non-fiction about the city. He spent his early career as a journalist, and in the 1940s he co-founded a literary magazine. His own prolific writing resulted in over fifty books.

Fogelström's *City of My Dreams* has remained a favorite in Swedish literature among readers of all ages, and he continues to be greatly loved and respected as a chronicler of his people. Fogelström died on Midsummer Day, June 20, 1998, two days before the unveiling of a statue of him at the entrance to the hall where the Nobel prizes are awarded in Stockholm.

THE TRANSLATOR

Jennifer Brown Bäverstam has studied languages all her life. She worked with the Peace Corps in Guatemala, where she trained Spanish interpreters. She went on to do research on computerized translation from English to Arabic through Harvard University.

Ms. Bäverstam holds a degree in French and economics from Georgetown University, and studied Arabic at Harvard University, and translation at the University of Geneva. She learned Swedish while spending time in Sweden and has been a court-appointed interpreter of Swedish for the state of Massachusetts, as well as serving on the boards of several Swedish organizations. Before translating the novels of Per Anders Fogelström, Ms. Bäverstam translated articles from Swedish and French.

She lives with her family in Newton, Massachusetts, and has a second career as a pianist and teacher. She has performed chamber music throughout Europe and the United States.

Translator's Note

Swedish place names are generally one compound word with the proper name at the beginning and the kind of place at the end.

Because most of the place names in the book have not been translated, the following terms explain endings for names of streets, hills, bridges, etc.:

backen: hill
berget, bergen: hill, hills
bro, bron: bridge
gatan: street

gränd: alley
holm, holmen: island
torg, torget: square
viken: estuary

I

CITY
OF
MY DREAMS

In the beginning the city was given its mark and seal: walls and towers along the water.

Protective stone was raised against everything that lay outside, against the enemy and the wind, against the cold and the dark. At one time the city had lain tightly curled, like a hedgehog in a crevice in a hill.

The walls both defended and concealed. Scandal and plague lurked in the dark of the alleys. Those who were protected by the strength of the walls could be killed by their stony chill. Sun and wind seldom got through to cleanse the city. A choking stench rose from piles of fermenting garbage along the shoreline and from the slimy waste of the gutters. In the city there were more alcoholics, criminals, and suicides than anywhere else.

The people outside might fear and hate the city, might talk about the plague hole and the abscess, the giant who devoured human lives. But still many of them sought their way there — and made their mortal sacrifice.

Some of those who came would always long to get out, away from the city, back to life outside the stone walls. Yet they stayed. There was always something that prevented them from leaving, and their children and grandchildren became the city's, and loved the stones. When they said that summer was approaching, they meant they had noticed the heat of the stones and not the scent of the flowers.

The city was dependent on all who were drawn to it by roads and water: without this constant supply of blood it would die. Fewer people were born in the city than died there.

It waited for him, the city that had lain in his dreams for so long.

The evening sun burnished the roofs and towers so they shone, and threw a sparkle of tinsel on the puddles that threaded their way between the confusion of houses. Bare rock rose up on gray hills over the lush greenery of gardens and tobacco fields.

City served on a silver tray, extended like a gift. As if the palace with the green copper roof, the churches with their black spires, the ships in the harbor and the simple wooden houses on the hillsides, as if all were toys. Ready to be taken by eager hands, enticingly close, within easy reach.

Gray smokestacks climbed from the industries along Lake Mälar's shore, bearing witness to opportunities there.

The city waited. Waited for the fifteen-year-old boy who had not yet seen any of its splendor, and for all the others who were coming. It lived in their dreams and offered every opportunity.

But a young boy neither could see nor wanted to see that most were dark ones, that the opportunities for joy and life were far fewer than those for sorrow and death.

The boy dreamed. The city waited.

BRIDGE
TO
REALITY

Late summer evening in 1860, the year of steam.

During the past summer the waters of the city had been conquered by many new small steamboats. And the great revolution was expected soon, when ice's domination would be broken forever and the long period of isolation each winter would come to an end. The railroad was being built, the sound of blasting rumbled from the Nyboda Tunnel.

It was as if he had arrived together with the new era, at just the right moment.

Henning Nilsson had been on the road for almost a week. He'd tried to keep down his excitement to avoid getting too tired. Now and then he had asked people he met about the distance. During the last few miles the answers had gotten more and more exact. Just now an old woman had pointed and said, "When you pass that farm over there you'll see the bridge and the customs house."

The boy slid down the embankment beside a field and took a piece of bread out of his pocket. He chewed slowly while he thought. Earlier he'd had a feeling that the city would welcome him, that all his troubles would be gone once he got there. He began to doubt that now, to feel a slight unease at having left the safe and familiar behind. He almost missed what had so recently been unbearable.

He took off his jacket and brushed away the dust from the road. He tore off some dandelion leaves and tried to polish his boots. They were too big and gave him blisters so he had gone barefoot most of the way. His thin face drew tight while he rubbed the boots with the leaves; the boots were old, already well-worn before he had gotten them.

Everything waited. No one waited. There was no one in the city he knew, no one he could ask for help. He had cut off all ties behind him, there was no going back.

The evening sun struck him in the face and he squinted, wiping the sweat from his forehead. He looked anxiously at his shirt, the only one he had. It had to be kept clean as long as possible.

Beyond the farm he could see the customs house. There the dream would end, and he would walk across the bridge into reality, into a future that waited to be conquered.

He could feel his muscles tense — from apprehension or eagerness to work? He was willing to work and capable of it, even if he certainly knew that he wasn't the largest and strongest of men. But in the city there had to be many kinds of work, including those where other qualities besides strength were valued. While he had toiled under sacks of flour, he had dreamed of sitting at a desk or standing behind a counter. And once in a while, though always with a humble awareness of his own limitations, he had seen himself standing beside a machine — maybe harnessing the steam, prouder than any coachman.

Well, now that the new reality lay so close he shouldn't idle in the ditch any longer. He brushed away a few crumbs and got up. He looked at his boots and wondered if he should put them on, then decided to wait until he reached the bridge. But when he walked into the city he would walk with his boots on.

At first it was a disappointment: the city wasn't there! A long and rickety wooden pontoon bridge led across the water toward some low houses which could be glimpsed through the trees on the other side. Between the houses with their black roofs and chimneys lay an opening, the customs gate. But no city beyond the customs house, just more tobacco fields and gray hills. And clouds of black and white magpies on flat fields.

Though from behind the hills on the Lake Mälar side smoke rose from a few smokestacks at work. And on the other side he saw the new railroad embankment crossing Årstaviken.

Henning grew excited; he half ran down the slope toward the bridge.

As so often this time of year, the water level was low and the bridge had sunk so that it had a steeply slanted approach. The planks of the bridge were still slippery from the morning's rain and the mud from the road, and now when Henning set his boots on them, he slid right down. Far ahead of him a wagon loaded with wood was being pulled along slowly.

The boy was in a hurry now, and he forgot all his self-imposed rules about appearing calm or carrying himself with dignity. He practically ran across the bridge, all the while glancing sideways at the railroad embankment: what if a train came, even though the tracks weren't laid?

At the bridge's connection to land on the city side, he caught up with the wagon which was drawn by a sturdy workhorse. It had been forced to stop there. The bridge's planks sloped steeply upwards. The horse had taken only a few steps forward, but then slid back again. The driver whipped and shouted; he wanted it to try again. But to no avail. It seemed impossible for the horse to pull the wagon up the slope.

Ragged children and a few tired old men from the old men's home had gathered in a little circle. And the boy entered it, looking for solidarity, and found it there.

It soon became evident that neither whipping nor pleading would help, the horse was incapable of more. The discussion became louder and a customs official came over from the guardhouse.

It was some time before Henning dared to make himself heard. He was a stranger, but was familiar with the situation. When farmers had come to the mill with their carts loaded with grain, they often had trouble making it up the last part of the way. That's when they had to block the wheels from behind, taking it a step at a time. Man and beast had managed it together.

At last he dared suggest to the increasingly red-faced driver that they place blocks of wood under the wheels and push at the same time. Old men and children took hold of the cart while Henning positioned the wood and the driver whipped on the snorting, dripping wet horse. Squealing with fear and pain, the animal was at last able to get up on solid ground; with a few tugs the cart followed.

And the driver nodded his assent when the boy climbed up and placed himself beside him on the wood.

That was how Henning Nilsson came to roll into town.

INTO THE NEW

The country road reached far into the city, as if to slowly get the stranger used to all that was new. First the gravel of the road gradually changed over to the rough cobblestones of streets, then fields and hills disappeared and were replaced by the green foliage of gardens and by low houses behind red fences.

The boy twisted around to try to take everything in. He almost fell off the cart when it suddenly jolted over one of the many drainage ditches in the road.

And the houses grew together into stone walls, where yawning gates led to back-yard stables and sheds. Outside the inns stood wagons harnessed and waiting for the travelers who lingered over food and aquavit; in the farmers' quarter, farmers transporting goods and produce mixed with horse swindlers and cattle handlers. Here was the life of the city.

Later he would wonder if he hadn't slipped into town a little too easily and effortlessly, if he hadn't been tricked in some way. The city should have shown its real face right from the beginning — the inhospitable and merciless one. He should have been kicked out, far beyond the customs gates and pontoon bridges, been forced to sneak in time after time until he had gained more confidence and cunning.

But when Henning Nilsson rolled into town, it smiled its sunny evening smile. The wood cart carried him all the way to the farmers' quarter, and the kindly farmhand made sure that the boy got lodging for the night.

He got to sleep in a hayloft above the stable in a house called Noah's Ark. He was lucky enough to be able to stay on there a few weeks, and once in a while a motherly kitchen maid from the tavern gave him a few leftovers.

During the day he roamed around looking for work. He didn't dare cross over the locks at Slussen into the bustle of the inner city because he wanted to be sure he could find his way back to the hayloft and the kitchen maid. Instead he kept mostly to the main street nearby, Götgatan, especially around Fyllbacken, where the workshops lay close together. He wandered between coopers and wagon makers, between blacksmiths and brass foundries. But there were many boys and little work.

In spite of the kitchen maid's care he was usually hungry, and his only shirt grew more and more ragged and was hard to get clean. Sometimes he despaired, wondering if he would find any work before autumn arrived with the cold, and before they got tired of his sleeping in the hayloft.

There were usually many lodgers up in the hay, drunken farmhands and cattle handlers smelling of the barn. Late one evening a small group arrived from Dalarna, a young boy with his sister and his fiancée. Henning gave up his normal spot so the travelers who had come a long way could lie more comfortably. They began to talk to him and listened to his troubles. The young man suggested that Henning accompany them the next morning. Perhaps he too could find work at the candle factory in the area around Danvik's customs house, where the work season was just beginning.

They set off early next morning, Tyrs Olle and Maja, Saros Kerstin, and Henning Nilsson. The girls, with pointed caps in the dress of their parish, shone like dazzling summer flowers between the gray houses of Götgatan. People stared at them, some friendly and almost admiring, but others spat. Those peculiar people from Dalarna took work away from the locals.

Tyrs Olle knew the way and knew the workplace since he had worked there before and was sure that he was welcomed back. Neither he nor the girls had any of Henning's anxiety and uncertainty. They were confident of their worth. Olle and Kerstin, who were to be married in the spring, flirted and joked with each other, and Henning was left walking with the plump Maja, a twenty-year-old girl with bulging breasts that threatened to burst her tight bodice.

She wasn't especially talkative, but she seemed to give off a fragrance, a radiance of newly-baked, warm friendliness. At times she stopped and pulled Henning by the arm, wanting him to press his nose against the shop windows too. There was so much you could buy: French fashion ribbons, herbal pomade for liver spots, pear beer, and Paris shoes. Maja wasn't really going to buy anything but liked to toy with the idea. Again Henning saw the possibilities and impossibilities in the city: anything could be gotten here, but only with the money he didn't have.

Soon the stores disappeared, the houses got smaller, the fences became longer until they ended, and there were cows grazing on the grassy slopes. Henning began to wonder if they were on their way out of the city. But then the houses grew closer together again, and suddenly an opening appeared between two high hills, and before them lay the big wharf with gigantic sheds and rows of vessels on the glittering water of Tegelviken. Still they hadn't arrived, for now the road wound in among new hills.

There it was. A few red brick chimneys rose up over the buildings and warehouses. It was much too early to go in, so Olle led them down to the beach where they could wash up and eat before it was time to present themselves to the foreman.

Enclosed within the picket fence on the opposite shore lay the candle factory, a clump of light-colored low buildings with red and black roofs, completely embedded in the summer greenery. Windmills climbed the hillsides round Hammarby Lake which lay polished by the morning sun, and a rowboat glided out from the dock at Barnängen.

Olle went down to the water, felt it with his hand and grunted contentedly. He waved to Henning, and they went together to the other side of a rise, threw off their clothes and strode into the water. The lake water was lukewarm, but Henning, who had hardly had a chance to wash since he had come to the city, thought it felt nice and refreshing. He had no soap but got himself clean as best he could and dipped his whole head in the water to make his hair lie smooth.

When they came back, Kerstin and Maja were squatting down by the water. Their backs shone white and on the grass beside them lay their blouses. The girls were also washing, making little shrieks when the water ran down their breasts and backs. Kerstin was modest, fiddling with the towel and her blouse, and was careful always to turn her back to them. But plump Maja stood secure, with legs braced, letting the sun shine on her heavy breasts still glistening with water, dried herself carefully, and slowly put on her blouse. Henning tried to look away, but time after time his glance was drawn back to her. He felt his pulse pound and was disquieted.

Olle untied their food sack, and Henning too got a piece of cheese and a crust of bread. They sat in the grass and ate and waited for it to be time to go. Henning felt anxiety before the decisive moment, the fear of soon being left once again to his loneliness and uncertainty. As if she guessed his thoughts, Maja put a protective arm around his neck, and he felt some kind of comfort and maternal longing and would have liked to lean on her and cry. But when he saw the blouse stretched taut, he knew he couldn't. Maja wasn't his mother but a woman. And he could no longer be a child, he had to be a man.

They had to register at the guardhouse on Tjärhovsgatan and then pass through the yard and enter the office in the main building. There had been a few changes made at the factory; the wholesaler Gullberg had become head of production, and young Öhrwall, who had begun as an apprentice some years earlier, had advanced to assistant foreman. That was advantageous for Tyrs Olle's plans for Henning; Olle and Öhrwall had worked side by side and were good friends. Gentle Öhrwall with his enormous sideburns felt that there was always good use to be made of a hired boy, if for nothing else than for the construction that Mr. Hierta and Mr. Gullberg had planned. He went with them himself to the old stone building by the main entrance where the factory workers lived. Two attic rooms were available so they didn't have to sleep in the larger dormitories. The girls got one room, Olle and Henning the other. They would have to fill the mattresses with straw themselves, but blankets had been provided.

From the attic window Henning looked out over the yard and the space which workers had begun to clear for the new factory buildings. He had gotten his first permanent spot in the city. And all around and above him, in the walls and staircases, in the fences and sheds, in the mattresses and blankets, everywhere lay the oily, nauseating stink of candle grease.

That smell stuck to everything during his early time in the city; it would always be linked with the memory of the city of his dreams from his youth.

CLOSE TO
THE WILDERNESS

The greasy smoke billowed out everywhere. Clouds of steam hung thick around vats of boiling tallow and oil.

At the mill Henning had carried sacks of flour. Here he rolled barrels of palm oil and casks of tallow or carts of wood to the constantly hungering boilers.

Tyrs Olle worked as he had in earlier years at the distillery, while the two girls were occupied with the polishing and packaging of candles. There were now almost forty workers at the factory, and over half of them were seasonal workers. Henning was counted as one of the people from Dalarna, even though in truth, he was a native of Södermanland.

He rolled the casks of tallow across the yard between plank bearers and demolition workers. While the work continued in the old buildings, workmen cleared everything for the new site, and Henning's job as hired boy took him everywhere. He looked through the door into the crowded room where the wick braiders sat at their machines while their spindles twisted three strands of Number 32 bleached cotton yarn into a wick. He was where Olle was on the ground floor and saw how stearic acids were pumped into the boilers and after distillation sank down through spiral pipes that were standing in water. And in the casting room, where candle grease was poured into molds, one mold for every candle and ten molds to every "tray." Or out on the bleaching terrace, where the candles were exposed to sun and air for a few days.

But mostly he preferred to be in the hall, where the candles were polished by machine and packaged in blue paper held together by yellow labels. That was the most enjoyable place to be but also the most dangerous, partly because he didn't always have anything to do there and risked being scolded and shooed away. And then there were the girls' giggles and whispers that made him feel both proud and embarrassed.

The days went by, the leaves turned yellow, the sun shone more and more palely over the water of Hammarby Lake. During the rainy October days the mist grew and made the smoke over the factory denser; it spilled over and filled the whole valley between Klippan's and Fåfängen's heights. Sometimes he could hear the cries of the inmates from the madhouse on the Baltic. One night howling woke him: the factory dog had caught the scent of wolves. The wilderness lay close by — the houses along the estuary a last flicker of the city before the great woods and the darkness began in earnest.

Then he felt like he still hadn't gotten farther than the outskirts of the city, and thought how he was counted among the non-locals, among the people from Dalarna. Eagerness and anxiety gripped him, full of remorse he decided never to sneak in again to the girls in packaging and risk being caught there. He had to behave so well that he would be able to remain when the people from Dalarna returned home.

But at the same time his self-confidence grew too: he was paid wages and was his own person. One evening Maja came and asked him to go with her to Götgatan. She was afraid to go alone on the long and dark road: past the shanties by the wharf, through Tjärhovsgatan's endless fences and tobacco fields.

She was going to buy candy, a particular kind. Henning knew how it smelled, it was a part of that fragrance of newly-baked bread that always surrounded Maja, and that he had smelled already that morning when they walked out to the factory. She was constantly sucking on candies, and always the same sort. Now she had two left in her handkerchief and he got to have one. Thoughtfully smacking, he walked along by her side.

Shipyard and dock workers stood in groups around the small taverns, and hungry dogs yelped from bushes and alleyways. A few drunken prostitutes from the hills came roaring out of the darkness beneath an archway, and children with stomachs bloated from potatoes flocked around a soup stand and sniffed with dilated nostrils. Beneath the sparse gas lamps, people stood and stared up at this latest marvel of technology which finally had reached Söder.

Henning suddenly felt grown up. He pulled his visored cap further down over his forehead and stuck his hands in his pockets. And he felt how Maja slipped her hand under his arm, perhaps only to get a little support on the potholed road — but still! Here in the darkness no one could see how young he was, everyone must think that they were a couple, that she was his girl. And it was as exciting and dangerous as when he looked into the packaging room and the girls giggled. Even more.

They reached Götgatan almost too soon. He followed Maja between the stores until she found the right candy. And then he had to ask her if she didn't want to help him buy a shirt, he had taken along his savings from one month's work. Maja was delighted, and she didn't let herself be satisfied by taking just the first one either. No, you had to choose, you had to bargain, you had to say no thank you and leave. He never would have dared do that if he had been alone. At last he got his shirt though, carefully wrapped in paper.

As thanks for her help he would have liked to treat her to something, maybe a lemonade. But the taverns and cafés they passed were hardly the kind that he dared ask her to go into. Most seemed dark and dangerous, a few were too fancy and expensive. Inside under the light he would be exposed, be too young a boy.

But he found a stand where a woman was selling doughnuts and Maja said, "Yes, thanks," and they stood close to the stand's oil lantern and ate the doughnuts still dripping with fat.

Despite Maja's funny, forthright self-confidence at the store counters, Henning still felt oddly the same age as she. She was twenty and he was fifteen. That was a difference that was usually noticeable. Other twenty-year-olds had seemed "old" to him, but now he almost felt older than Maja and thought she talked like a child, and ate like a child: the eternal candies, the contented munching of her doughnut. The sugar powdered her mouth, and the fat made her lips shine in the lantern light. He ate carefully himself and wiped his mouth time after time with the back of his hand.

There was a dance on in some basement premises. Laughter and shrieks wafted out to the street. A few little girls hung in the doorway and looked in longingly, but they still took the time to stretch out their hands and beg from passersby. Their faces were pale, as if powdered with flour, and their gestures had a practiced, worn insolence.

Maja hardly saw them, she had eyes only for the dancing. Her eyes shone, she gripped Henning's hand, talked about the wedding in Dalarna: that would be a real dance!

Maybe she wanted to push her way into the room where butchers' assistants hopped around in their bloody aprons with girls from the spinning mill, and journeymen embraced servant girls amid shrieks and howls. Henning felt a little uneasy about it all. He knew that he wasn't forceful and experienced enough to assert himself in those surroundings. But just as Maja had her nose inside the door, a guardsman let out an abysmal roar when he got a bottle in the head, and a second later a full-blown fist fight was under way. Girls rushed out onto the street, scared out of their wits, and one tripped and fell and was buried beneath her voluminous skirts.

Henning wanted to take Maja with him; this was no place to stay. The police might come or the brawlers spill out onto the street. But Maja was fascinated. She tried to shrug him off and pulled away and wanted to see more. Self-assured and agitated at the same time, she took a place in the ring around the girl who still lay on the street, too drunk to get up. Her legs kicked from inside her billowing skirts, and her stockings shone white above the high black boots.

Finally a journeyman came and dragged her back into the dance hall, where the fistfighters had now been separated.

Maja was bubbling over with her adventures as they walked home. Her fingers went round and round in the paper cone full of candy, and she forgot to offer any to Henning. Just imagine how the men had fought! And how the girl had floundered! What a lovely head kerchief the serving girl had had on! And how much excitement there was in town!

"I like it," she said. "I'd much rather be here than back home. I don't want to go home with them this spring."

Would Henning be staying?

Of course. There was no one waiting for him. He told her about his time at the miller's, about his mother who had died of cholera, and the father he had never known. But Maja didn't listen, it wasn't Henning's past she was interested in, only her own future.

"It's so much more fun in the city," she said, and smiled her child-like smile. "Lots more fun."

But now the noise and the lights disappeared, the endless wooden fences and the dark fields took over. There were long distances between the lanterns that shone dimly into the night. Out here there were only the old oil lamps. Henning led the way for Maja and tried to avoid the puddles of water and the deep wagon ruts.

What fighting there had been! How exciting it all was!

When they were at the darkest spot, Maja suddenly stopped and threw her arms around Henning. And he was pressed into a soft, swelling darkness, she was all around him, everywhere. He felt her lips, slippery with grease and downy with powdered sugar, seek their way across his face, then the smell of candy, and her wide, wet mouth over his.

"I want to stay with you in the city, Henning," she panted. "You must let me stay."

"All right," he answered, although he didn't see how it could happen, although he wanted to shout no.

"You'll let me?" she asked and pushed him away from her a little to search for his eyes in the darkness.

"But I can't get married, I'm too young," he tried.

"You don't want to," she said sulkily and began to walk again.

He didn't answer but followed, caught up with her.

"Watch out for the puddle!" he said and pulled her to the side.

Now the lights were shining from the wharf overseer's house, and they didn't have far to the factory. They went on in silence. Dim lights glowed from the wooden houses that clung to the hillside above.

"You don't want to!" she said again. "No one does!"

No, he probably didn't want to. But he wanted to be kind to Maja, he liked her. So he took her plump hand and patted it quickly, and said: "Yes, I do want to."

"Are you sure?" she asked.

He nodded seriously.

"Good," said Maja and moved on.

He had been afraid that she would kiss him again, maybe pull him up the hill above the road. But she just went along toward home, sucking on a candy with contentment now, excitedly talking about all the evening's events. They nodded to the gatekeeper and walked across the courtyard. Maja asked Henning to wait for her there and stand guard while she visited the outhouse. He sat down on the stone steps and looked out over the barrels and casks that he would be rolling during the coming days and wondered how he would also manage to roll Maja toward a future that he had dreamed of so much.

When she came out of the darkness, she took his hand and said good-night and then went up the stairs alone. Henning stayed where he sat awhile and wondered if he should speak to her brother about the problem or if this was a secret he shouldn't give away. It was probably best to wait and see.

All around him was the stink of candle grease, but he could still smell the scent of candy and newly-baked bread. His lips were sore and felt unpleasantly greasy. As he went up through the dark stairwell, he wiped his mouth over and over and worried about the night ahead, when he would surely dream about Maja.

IN THE DARKNESS

The darkness grew, gnawed at the autumn days that grew shorter and grayer. Candles and oil lamps had to be lighted earlier each day in the rooms at the factory. The trees around the lake stood black and cold, and the carts of the farmers from Värmdö dug deeper into the road that snaked over Danvik's creek and around Klippan's hill.

Henning began to feel at home on the outskirts, what had once been new and unknown soon became familiar. On Saturday evenings and Sundays he roamed around the eastern part of the area, but he seldom dared go farther than Götgatan. On regular weekday evenings work went on too late for him to go out afterward. He was tired and often fell asleep right after the evening meal.

Sometimes he wished he had something to read, but neither he nor anyone he knew had any books. Once when Henning had emptied the trash for wholesaler Gullberg, he had gotten hold of an old edition of *Aftonbladet,* and he had read it, practically knew it by heart.

Olle was out in the evenings. He got together with Kerstin. But when it rained, Kerstin came into Olle and Henning's room, and the couple sat and held hands and whispered till Henning felt he had to go out and leave them alone together. He sat in the dark and cold of the stairs, and now and then he took a look into the dormitories where most of the men lived. But they were drinking and playing cards, and he was a little wary of their company.

He was afraid. And he usually blamed himself when he sat there on the stairs. Afraid to be in with the men, to reveal that he wasn't as experienced as they were, couldn't handle his liquor. Afraid of the girls, of Maja. Was he hiding from her? There had been no more said about their common future, about Maja's staying behind when the others returned. Maybe she had changed her mind. He hoped so, but at the same time he missed something.

Afraid. And because of that he was doomed, would lose. The city was tough, it was no place for the fearful. One had to be daring all the time.

"You have to take risks," he reprimanded himself aloud, still afraid in the midst of his shouting that someone might hear him.

One evening he made himself angry with his self accusations, walked up to the door of the girls' room and knocked. Softly, discreetly, a timid knocking. He heard Maja's responding, "Yes?"

"It's me," he whispered. "Henning."

"Come in!"

He opened the door noiselessly. The room was dark.

"Come in!" she said again.

He walked forward, feeling the way with his hands so he wouldn't trip, groped over a chair and caught hold of something, cloth, clothing.

"Where are you?" he whispered.

"Here."

Whispering, a child's whispering, came from right beside him. He searched with his hands, they glided through her outspread hair.

"Are you in bed? Shall I leave?"

"Sit here," she said and made room, pulling him down eagerly onto the edge of the bed.

He sat there a long time, surely several hours. And she talked the whole time in a low, whispering tone about a party she had been to, about things she would like to buy if she had the money. About everything except what was important.

He couldn't understand her. Why didn't she say anything about their future? She owned it after all, had to say how she wanted it to be.

Finally, when he had nodded off a few times and noticed she had fallen asleep, he left her as softly as he had come.

Eventually the cold and snow arrived. Hammarby Lake froze and a black hole in the ice lay in wait close to the ice-covered stream which ran under Danviken's sewers and across the spit toward the Baltic.

Over a number of days, the connections to the city were broken. The snow lay in giant drifts, and it took some time before horses and men made the road passable again. In the factory yard Henning shoveled away the worst of it, and he exchanged his cart for a sled. And Olle, who saw this piece of equipment, got the idea to ask the foreman if they could borrow the sled some Sunday.

They set off one morning when the sun made the endless blanket of snow shine whiter than the whitest candles just out of the polishing machine. Henning and Olle took turns pulling the sled while the girls, in their sheepskin jackets, trudged after. One hill gave way to another. They walked upward the whole time. They weren't going to take just any hill. Olle knew of a particular slope up in the White Hills; it began at the very top and didn't stop until the farmers' quarter by the winter customs house.

Gray wooden houses crouched under their weight of snow, and children with runny winter noses stared out from drafty sheds and lopsided gates. At the top the hill was cold and empty, as if the wind had swept away all the soil and prevented bushes and trees from growing there.

The way down looked dizzyingly steep. And from here they could see the candle factory's smokestack sticking up in the east. Closer at hand they had beneath them the cluster of houses surrounding Barnängen's factory. Beyond the lake the great woods took over, a dark background of pines.

They had to squeeze together on the sled to fit between the four posts, which were useful when pulling wood but were mostly in the way now. Olle first, then Henning between the two girls. Henning wasn't afraid now; despite the enormous slope in front of them, he only felt the joy of adventure. And nearness to people. The nearness of warmth and companionship, and women. The pressure of Kerstin's back and thighs, the feeling of Maja's soft padding behind his back.

They pushed off with their heels first. The sled moved forward heavily and with resistance, slowly it began to glide, picked up speed, and then it flew! They clung tightly to each other so as not to fall off;

the girls screamed like sirens; the snow swirled up in white clouds around them. Olle shouted some words that they couldn't make out, and for a moment they were close to tipping over. Then the speed slackened and they were down. Laughing, dazed, covered with snow, still filled with the thrill of speed.

They went time after time, panted up the hill and flew down. Henning felt he could go on endlessly. Perhaps mostly for the joy of feeling how daring he was, how wonderful the adventure was once he had thrown himself into it. And more guiltily: to feel a girl so close. And the girl wasn't Maja.

But in spite of everything the girls began to get cold. And Olle had new plans: they should go to a tavern on Stadsträdgårdsgatan, all the way down by the winter customs house, and drink hot toddy.

The way there was well trampled, and outside a few ragamuffins stood and counted to see if they could scrape together enough coins for a stiff drink. Henning hid the sled in a shed in the yard and hoped it wouldn't be stolen. He felt he was responsible for it. Then he followed the others in, unafraid now that he was in their company.

The girls drew back at first from the darkness, the stench, and the buzz of voices. But they soon got used to it, and at least it was warm inside since the tavern keeper had treated them to a fire. Some bearded farmers delivering goods sat in a corner and quarreled over a bottle. At the zinc bar two longshoremen hung about and tried to sing a ribald sailor song for the barmaid.

There were some empty chairs around a table in a corner, and Henning found a barrel to sit on. The barmaid was able to tear herself away from her attendants long enough to get them their hot toddies. And soon they were sitting there feeling good in the warmth and obscurity, engulfed by the buzz of voices, feeling their cheeks grow rosy with the heat, loosening their jackets and sweaters. And purses.

"It's not often that we let ourselves go," Olle said when Kerstin watched a little pensively how their household money filtered out of the purse and was turned into arak liqueur. Maja got a piece of crisp bread with lard and a grilled salt herring. Olle didn't want to give her more than the one toddy to drink. Though he made an exception when Henning treated them to another round.

Again there was talk about the wedding that would be celebrated in the spring. It sounded as if Maja had no doubt that she would be there. Had she changed her mind? Henning didn't know if he was sorry or glad. He would be left all alone, but also without responsibility for anyone but himself.

It was Kerstin who was the centerpoint of the little party. Kerstin with the dark hair that hung down over her thin face, the eyes that shone, the quick smile that could be happy and melancholy at the same time, the hands that animatedly and lightly played around her hood, around the edge of her leather overshirt, around the circle of her glass.

Kerstin was the most alive, the changeable one. Olle sat there fair-haired and secure, Maja heavy and sucking on her candy, Henning himself thin and shy. All as if frozen, the way they always were. But Kerstin shifted the whole time. She was also shy, but her shyness attracted, played hide-and-seek. Henning grew more and more envious of Olle. Just like Kerstin ... so slender and yet so round, so soft and yet so firm, so shy and yet so easy to approach. He listened to her every word and was made happy by her tone and gestures, felt himself loosen up, finding that finally someone listened to him: she could listen too. He was enchanted, could have sat there forever. But Maja was yawning and Olle had drunk too much.

They broke up, went out into the dusk that had spread a light blue film over the snow. Luckily the sled was still in the shed, and Henning pulled it with a rather unsteady gait up Meijtensgränd, past the hill they had flown down so recklessly a few hours earlier. On the other side they were able to ask the girls to sit down and be pulled along the winding roads down toward Danvik's customs house. As they walked the darkness descended rapidly, the lamplighters made their rounds, and small lights flickered from behind the houses' dark panes.

Henning followed the others, who had already gotten a little way up the stairs. In the dark someone stood and waited for him. It was Olle.

"Sit and talk to Maja a little," Olle said.

Maja wasn't especially talkative.

"We can talk while I lie down," she said.

She lit the little lamp which threw flickering shadows against the walls. Henning hung about the window and looked out into the darkness while she got undressed.

When he heard the bed creak he turned around.

"Come, Henning," she said and yawned. "Come and sit a while."

He sat himself carefully on the edge of the bed.

"Blow out the lamp," she said.

He blew it out.

In the darkness he thought about Kerstin, felt how her body had pressed against his, saw her eyes shine. And felt like he couldn't touch Maja. It wasn't really Kerstin he wanted either, but someone who was like her and didn't belong to Olle. Suddenly he felt afraid of Maja and wanted to go.

"Lie down a little," said Maja, and he didn't dare do other then obey.

She drew him close to her, held him as if she were holding a child, and laughed a low, contented laugh.

Then the door opened and a light fell into the room. It was Kerstin. She carried a small lantern, must have been out in the yard. Henning sat up hastily.

"Are you coming in now?" asked Maja. "We were lying and talking in the dark."

Henning said good-night and left. And felt that Kerstin was watching him the whole time.

Perhaps it was the fear of Maja that drove him outside when, the following evening, he went walking aimlessly in the darkness and the wind for a long time. When he got back to his room, Kerstin slipped out quickly.

Olle was solemn.

He didn't know if Henning had understood. But in any case Henning must be told.

And he learned how Maja was an overgrown child, a giant child in darkness. She would never be any more than a child, not be able to take care of herself. Olle had promised to watch over her, make sure that she came home unharmed.

Henning now understood what previously he had only sensed. He knew why he had felt so grown up in her company. And suspected why he had gotten along so well with her: together with her he had also been able to be a child. Now the game was over.

Henning was able to reassure Olle that nothing had happened. What he now knew would make him very careful, he would help Olle take care of Maja.

It was easy to promise, and good to save himself by making a binding promise. And he told Olle what Maja had said that evening when they had walked back together from Götgatan. But the words came with a sense of shame, in spite of everything he felt like he was betraying Maja.

Still, he slept peacefully that night. Maja no longer came to him, even in his dreams. But he tried to catch hold of a girl that looked like Kerstin, and fell off the sled and rolled over and over until he awoke on the wooden floor.

THE REAL STOCKHOLMER

Henning stuffed the cloth sample deep into his pocket and set off. As so often happened, he was out on an errand for the wholesaler, Gullberg. It was whispered that Hierta, the manufacturer, complained about Gullberg taking advantage of the employees for his private interests. But the arguments of the great are not for the small to concern themselves with, they only follow orders.

He pulled up his coat collar, stuck his hands in his pants pockets, followed the path through the snow. He jumped from the boat dock down onto the ice. In the winter the way to the dyer's was short and easy.

Henning felt gloomy, gray as the sky that crawled heavily across the hills. Instead of making friends and getting into the life of the city, he had become even more alone. He couldn't talk to Maja like before. It didn't work now that he knew. And Olle and Kerstin had enough with themselves and each other, so he couldn't demand that they make time for him as well. The other employees were decent and friendly enough, but no one became his friend and confidant. Maybe he hadn't tried to get close to them either, but most of them were going to leave the city soon and return to their homes far away.

It was a lonely, dark figure that moved along in the white snow parallel to the shoreline. He rounded the point with the manor house and Barnängen's factory on it, where the thumping of the looms could be heard far out onto the lake.

Close to the old winter customs house lay the long green and red wooden buildings of the dye-works which partially surrounded a courtyard opening toward the lake.

The dyers had lived and worked alongside the lake for centuries;

the water was seen as suited to their work. But gradually they had been crowded out and now there were only a few left. The largest of the dye-works was the one called Dyer's Yard, owned by old man Wanselin.

A boy Henning's age stood and chopped a hole in the ice. Beside him he had a sled with an empty water barrel. Henning had exchanged a few words with the dyer-boy before, when the boy had come to the candle factory to get candles for his employer. Now it was Henning's turn to ask his way, for he wasn't sure who it was that was to receive the dye sample.

The dyer-boy left off chopping and caught his breath. A wiry, dark-haired fellow with a funny, pointed nose, and with the quickness of the city in his movements and facial expressions.

"You'd better give it to the master's old lady," he said.

That answer didn't make things any clearer for Henning, and he had to ask again.

"Madam Wanselin, of course," said the dyer-boy. And pointed with a hand that was missing a thumb toward the red-painted dye house.

"You're not from Dalarna?" he wondered.

"No."

"But you're not a real Stockholmer either."

That was harder to answer. Henning hardly knew what he was. He wasn't a country boy anymore, and he hadn't had time to become a Stockholmer.

"I'm newly arrived," he answered. And felt the need to talk about his situation, how he wanted to put down roots in the city, become one of those real Stockholmers. But that he didn't know how he would succeed since he'd only found work for a short time.

"Then you have to get to know this place," the dyer-boy said decidedly. He was a good local patriot and felt that he had suddenly been given a mission in life: he was going to reveal the city's, the neighborhood's, mysteries to this shy country bumpkin.

"People call me Thumbs," he said, and stuck out his thumbless left hand, grinning broadly. "What's your name?"

"Henning Nilsson."

"Say, Henkan," said Thumbs, "come on down to the corner outside the joint tonight. We'll find something to do."

Henning was happy to go along with that. Filled with anticipation he went on toward the dye house, hopped from the ice up onto the washing dock and entered the yard.

"If that beast gives you trouble just give it a good kick!" yelled Thumbs. Not until the dog came rushing at him did Henning understand the words of warning. But the dog only barked and let the visitor go in, unaccosted, to the little cubbyhole where Madam Wanselin received visitors.

Ture Lindgren, called Thumbs, was waiting outside the tavern as he had said. Thumbs wasn't the type to spend time waiting standing silently, he was in constant motion. Looking in and talking with the girls at the counter, helping the tavern keeper lift a keg of aquavit, watching two farmhands fighting out in the yard. He always wanted to be in on it, know what was happening. Got involved or kept himself out of it with the same assured smoothness. It was child's play, a game, he followed the figures and performed the steps as if he were a ballet dancer or a bullfighter.

When Henning got there, Thumbs was standing and talking to a barmaid who was sweeping away the snow outside the door. Thumbs quickly broke off an icicle from the roof gutter, stuck it inside the girl's blouse, took a few quick steps to the side to avoid the broom, grabbed Henning by the arm and made off with him.

"We don't have time this evening," Thumbs shouted to the girl, "but another day you can treat us to a drink."

"Come on, Henkan," he went on eagerly, "haven't you been across the locks at Slussen yet? We really have to begin thinking about your education."

While they walked into town Thumbs talked incessantly, relating stories and explaining things. There was so much that Henkan had to know if he was going to stay and live in the big town. About police and guardsmen, about apprentices and schoolboys — the battles between them — and coachmen and innkeepers, prostitutes from the hills and cigar shop girls. Henning understood far from everything, and at times Thumbs just hinted at things, skipped over things too quickly. Besides, he used so many new words, the idiom of the true Stockholmer.

They came to Stora Glasbruksgatan, a narrow gutter that dropped down toward the town across the hill on Söder. Inmates from the Dihlström workhouse clomped along here in their enormous shoes. From the Wallmanska, dance hall music could be heard and from inside taverns, beerhouses and whorehouses came the buzz of voices and shrieks. But Thumbs took Henning farther down across the windy square by Slussen, where the statue of Karl Johan XIV stood between gas lamps in front of the new yellow bazaar building.

For the first time Henning entered the city itself. There were neither rocks nor fields here, only the narrow gutters of the streets between tall buildings. Now they had to thread their way along between groups that had collected around stands and doorways. Coachmen plowed carefully through the multitudes, and through the coach windows they could see aristocratic ladies and gentlemen on their way to parties. Grim policemen in leather coats and black helmets shook their clubs at hooting apprentice boys; streetwalkers dressed up in ragged finery came tripping in a flock from one of Österlånggatan's many nests.

Henning felt insecure and clumsy. There was so much to look at, and at the same time he had to constantly watch out. He was jostled, and he stepped on people's heels. Now he understood why the real Stockholmers walked like Thumbs did, they had to be able to glide, to float. In the city you couldn't tramp along like a peasant.

He decided to observe Thumbs, learn the style, the talk and the walk. But he wondered if he would ever get the self-assurance too, he really doubted that.

Suddenly Thumbs was gone. Henning looked around helplessly in the crowd. A fat matron squeezed by him and a young girl with skirts that filled half the street. Some dogs let out a yelp and took off after a cat, a string of small boys plowed after them.

He could probably ask his way back to Söder. But he stayed where he was, waiting. He would never be able to find Thumbs here by himself, but if Thumbs wanted to, he could certainly find Henning. And sure enough he came along with a paper cone full of cake crumbs in one hand. With the other he held onto the ear of a whining twelve-year-old girl.

"She'd better stop peddling her wares," said Thumbs bitterly. "She knows very well it's not the soaps the old men are paying for. Now we'd better drag the kid home."

Slowly they pushed their way through — back toward Söder. Thumbs held the girl in a firm grip, and she sniffled and tried to protect her wicker basket with the three soaps in it. When they emerged from the alleyways Thumbs dared let go of the girl. Her sniffling gradually ceased. She walked more and more contentedly between them and ate some of the cake crumbs.

"She's my cousin," explained Thumbs. And he told how the girl lived with his parents and that nobody forced her to run around in taverns with a wicker basket.

Henning still didn't understand why Thumbs was so upset.

"Who do you think buys her soap?" said Thumbs. "People who want to get clean? It's none of that rubbish. No, the dirty old men don't pay for the soap. They're paying to get their hand under her skirt."

The girl sneered. That irritated Thumbs and he pinched her arm.

"Everyone else …." she said sulkily. "And it's not so bad."

"Try again and I'll see that you get a good whipping," threatened Thumbs.

They had reached the long, low row houses beside the dye-works. Thumbs shoved the girl inside. Then he came back to Henning, made a tired gesture and said, "I know it doesn't help."

He stood a moment and leaned against the lamp post. The pale oil lamp shone down over the thin, boyish faces, the rough clothes.

"In France they tried to have a revolution at any rate," said Thumbs in a low voice, "but here we don't do anything. We toil and grind and get a measly sum for the work, and when it's not enough to live on, we beg or starve. And think that's just the way it is when every other factory girl takes to the streets, and even little girls go out and sell themselves."

Henning couldn't answer. Everything was so new to him, he didn't know anything, didn't have any opinions.

"The old people are already worn out," Thumbs said. "They don't dare, they just hide and hope that the rich will at least let them live. My old man was there in '48 ... threw stones at the soldiers and cheered for the republic. Now, he shuts up and just drinks. But you and me, Henkan, we're going to have a revolution."

And Henning saw the quick smile, the nod, the smooth gait when Thumbs turned and headed home.

"Stop by in the morning," shouted Thumbs.

Henning walked home across the ice, filled with the newness of it all. The city, the people, the revolution. He'd suddenly been torn loose from everything familiar. He didn't know if he was afraid or happy, if he wanted to flee or prepare himself to join in. Yes, he wanted to be in on it. He'd follow Thumbs wherever it all led. Thumbs who knew everything about city life surely understood all about the revolution too.

FAREWELLS
AND
ARRIVALS

Spring came and the city shook off the shackles of winter. Heavy, dark barges filled with excrement were towed out to the Fjäderholm Islands to be emptied of the winter's wastes. The snow melted, and in ditches and gutters everything lay exposed that had been thrown into them on dark evenings. The swollen corpses of dogs and cats spread their stench, dung-heaps outside stalls and barns thawed, the roads were transformed into muddy ditches.

Men from the workhouse were sent out to clear the yards and streets of all the trash that had collected. But most of them were able to sneak away from the few supervisors. They sat on the steps of taverns and on the grassy slopes which were still yellow, fiddled with their bottles, and grinned at the sun. All around them swine rooted, and hens pecked contentedly at the garbage piles.

The ice gradually disappeared on Hammarby Lake too, and Henning had to take a longer and more difficult route when he went to meet Thumbs at the dye-works. But usually they met at other places, such as in among the sheds on Nytorget or on Söderberg's steep stairs.

Henning now knew names and streets and felt that he had gotten a little of that gliding style he sought; he began to learn how to "float" around. He would glide into the yards behind the slaughterhouses where cows were bellowing disconsolately and pigs squealing like children. He went down via the stairs toward Stadsgården, where grain bearers and meat packers bent double under their loads and the taverns stood wall to wall.

Blood and filth, sweat and aquavit. The city offered a rank drink.

But those that were thirsty drank.

And both Henning and Thumbs suffered from an unquenchable thirst, that of awakening and discovery, of youth. They were constantly on the lookout for anything new. The old also had much to offer that was new for Henning; it was mainly Thumbs who saw the signs and directed their expeditions.

One April day they stood on Götgatan and saw the water spraying from the first fire hydrant. The water flew out in a giant stream and the whole street was suddenly rinsed shiny and clean. Henning watched it as if it were fireworks, an experience for both eyes and ears. But Thumbs dreamed about the power welling forth and clenched his fists to check the desire to run forward, lean on the spray and direct the stream toward the nearest figure of authority.

When they walked home he was excited, spoke with zeal in a low voice, swore with great relish.

"It's up to us to do it," he suddenly burst out. "It's us, Henkan!"

But soon after, they were stretched out lazily on one of the grassy slopes in the White Hills, poking around in last year's dry leaves and talking about the girls and the silk mills at Barnängen.

There was so much they were going to do — to have the time to do. And the free hours were meagerly few.

Henning had worries. He tried to cover them up under brave talk as long as possible, didn't want to ruin his time together with Thumbs. But finally he had to talk about them. The season at the candle factory was coming to an end. Soon the last of the people from Dalarna were going to return home for the spring plowing. It was possible that Henning could get work as a helper in the construction at the factory, but it wasn't for sure.

Thumbs calmed him: summers weren't so hard, one could always get by, and the work opportunities were more numerous than in the spring. Helper at a construction site wasn't the worst thing, if it came through.

But even if work were taken care of, there still remained the ques-

tion of living arrangements. No one was allowed to stay over the summer in the old stone house with the attic rooms. Henning had to find
something else, at least a bed or a sleeping space. Thumbs, who knew
people in the houses of almost every neighborhood, promised to think
about it.

"Everything will work out," Thumbs assured him. That was the
real Stockholmer's motto: Everything will work out.

And in hopes that Thumbs could take care of everything, Henning
forgot his troubles in order to celebrate the last day in town of his
friends from Dalarna.

Alongside the shipyard lay boats, rowed by women from Dalarna,
which took care of the traffic between the Danvik district's industries
and the island of Djurgården's amusements. A few travelers had
already seated themselves, so the four from the candle factory didn't
have to wait long for the women to put out and start rowing. The boat
glided out slowly, rocked on the gentle waves from a steamboat on its
way to a more distant destination.

They couldn't see the factory from here, everyday life nestled down
and hid behind Fåfängan's hill, festively clad in spring green. Soon the
inner city dwellers would be moving out to their summer places
alongside the hill and the main channel. It wouldn't be long before
summer was here, but that was when Olle and the girls would be
home in Dalarna again, and Henning would be alone in the city.

That's what they said. Still Henning knew, with a feeling of happiness, that he wasn't alone anymore. He had a friend. But out of
friendship he agreed with them, upon their departure he would be
alone, and he would miss the three of them.

A Sunday in May with sunshine, could they ask more of the city
as a farewell gift? The glitter of the waves and the flag that shone from
the red tower of the little castle. Multitudes of steam launches and
rowboats, the place was crawling with people between the wine cafés
and the market stands on the fields of Djurgården. Punch and Judy
shows and acrobats. And the horde of people in front of the picture

showing the guardsman Göthe's horrible murder of the shopgirl on Hornsgatan.

The four stuck together, country folk afraid to lose each other in the crowd. Kerstin reached out her hand and Henning gripped it, held her small, wiry hand almost anxiously. Kerstin had somehow become his dream of a girl, of a woman. She was the first with a face of her own. Now he knew it was her face that he would remember and miss the longest.

Maja carried a basket with food and drink that they eventually set out on a grassy space. Here they ran into another group of Dalarna natives from the factory, and soon they were all playing the game "last couple out" together. Giddy from the beer and the frenzy of the game, Henning ran to save Kerstin from being caught by Olle, caught her in his arms, felt her tremble from exertion and laughter.

In the dusk they made their way down to the boats again, soon took their seats and watched the water slowly turn to silver, the evening and the city to blue. And they didn't get much sleep that night, there was talking and laughter all over the old stone house. Knapsacks and birch bark rucksacks were packed; newly-bought goods from town were shown around, then carefully wrapped in clothes and paper; money was counted, and bottles went from mouth to mouth.

Early next morning Henning followed his friends across the island, took the route he walked with Thumbs, down Stora Glasbruksgatan and across at Slussen. He followed them all the way to the bridge, Norrbro, where the bazaars still hadn't opened. They said good-bye, Henning stood at the end of the bridge and watched the three grow smaller and smaller, get farther and farther away. Maja ambled along heavily, but with determination. She was eager and wanting to get home now, had apparently completely forgotten that she had talked about staying in the city. Olle was a little tired after the night's merriment, he stumbled from time to time, was weighted down by the stuffed knapsack. But Kerstin turned around several times and waved, and although she was far away now Henning knew exactly what her facial expression was. He waved back and thought that he would never see her again, that it would probably feel empty without Kerstin.

He turned back to the everyday life of the city. But he walked with confident strides, he knew the city, he knew the way.

Thumbs had found a place. Not the best he admitted. But cheap. And it was hard to find a bed, every place was filled with people, there was someone living and sleeping in every nook and cranny.

They went together to one of the sagging houses in the vicinity of the dye-works that evening. They walked through the back yard between the stable and the outhouse. Piles of manure and broken carts almost blocked the way in. A few dirty children, who were playing between the garbage heaps, interrupted their game to stare at the new-comers.

The man who rented out the apartment was a coal bearer. Big and black, he stepped forward to meet them. The hand that grasped Henning's was black-furrowed and rough. The coal bearer was called Bigsack and was the pride of his work team, the man who, without collapsing, could carry a two-hundred-kilo sack of coal from the barge to the scales and stand there unperturbed while man and sack were weighed.

He pushed open the door to the dark room. Henning's eyes slowly got accustomed to the darkness. He saw the fireplace blackened with smoke, the small windowpanes that were broken and mended by placing more glass right over them. The stained wallpaper that was peeling, two beds, a few mattresses, and piles of rags on the floor.

"The old lady and I sleep in the inner bedroom with the youngest children," Bigsack said. "You won't be more than seven in here, so it's not so crowded."

He told Henning who his roommates would be. Two workwomen from the textile mill shared one of the beds. The other was rented by a dyer that paid extra to get to sleep alone. On one mattress and rag heap slept Bigsack's two oldest children and a foster child. Henning would get another mattress all to himself.

He probably had gotten spoiled during the time he'd shared the attic with Olle. Before that he had, of course, lived under poor and crowded conditions at the miller's. And the most important thing was that he had some place to sleep.

Henning paid for the first week and was invited to enter the bedroom where the little children were already asleep, one on a few blankets under the table, and the smallest in his parent's bed. Bigsack's wife opened the door to a cupboard and brought out a bottle and some cups. Henning's host poured and said: "We'll have a drink to that."

The deal was closed.

When Henning came back alone later in the evening, all of his new roommates were in except for one. The workwomen from Barnängen sat on the edge of their common bed and conversed with the dyer's apprentice, who was already lying down. Bigsack's eleven-year-old boy wrestled on the floor with a girl of the same age, the foster child. Bigsack's fifteen-year-old daughter hadn't come home however, she was a barmaid and worked late on the evening shift but got to sleep in in the morning.

He went around and introduced himself. The dyer stuck out his hand, tired and indifferent, and said his name: "Johansson." The older of the two workwomen, a little, stick-thin, middle-aged woman, introduced herself as Mamsell Tornberg. The other was young and plump, she smiled broadly and said: "My name's Klara."

He had to satisfy himself with a nod to the children on the floor, they didn't have time to say hello. They tumbled about and didn't stop the roughhousing until Bigsack roared at them from the room next door. At that they crept silently and hastily under the blankets and sacks and lay like two frightened animals in their holes, eyes reflecting in the light of the oil lamp.

Henning got one of the four drawers in the bureau. He opened his knapsack and pulled out the drawer and placed in it his few possessions. The old edition of *Aftonbladet* came in handy now. The drawer seemed hard to get clean so he lined it with the paper.

Mamsell Tornberg had disappeared out into the yard. Klara loosened her hair, sat and combed it in front of the glass pane. The dyer lay and watched her, an interested and grateful spectator. The girl was unperturbed by her audience. She was too used to it. For three years, since she was fifteen, she had been living with men and women on top of each other in the same room. At first she had crawled into a corner, tried to get away from the men's eyes and hands. Now that was just the way it was, and some nights she earned a little toward the rent by moving over to the dyer's bed. Every bit of income was welcome, the mill work was so badly paid.

"So you know Thumbs?" she said and turned to Henning, letting the comb stop in her hair. She sat in her nightgown, had taken off her dress, corset and petticoats, and the short, white sleeve made a small opening showing white skin and the little tuft of hair in her armpit.

Henning nodded. Klara gave a few more tugs of the comb and then pulled a short, tight sweater over the long nightgown. The children on the floor listened quietly. From the bedroom next door came huge snores, Bigsack had fallen asleep. The girl on the floor giggled but then grew uneasily quiet when the next snore had another more threatening, growling noise.

"If the Tornberg lady absolutely must lie against the wall she doesn't have to sit in the outhouse half the night," said Klara bitterly. "There's no reason for anyone else to go to bed before she does."

She took a few steps across the floor, as if to inspect Henning's sleeping spot. The dyer's apprentice stared jealously and twisted in his bed to keep an eye on her.

"If the kids don't fool around too much you'll lie all right here," she said knowingly. "You don't feel much of the floor draft this time of year."

Finally Mamsell Tornberg came back with a white nightcap over her wispy hair. Like a thin shadow she slid in against the wall and down under the covers.

Klara yawned, went over to the oil lamp. Stood there a moment so that, with the light coming through, the contours of her body could just be distinguished as a darker shade of grey against the nightgown. Then she blew, and the light and the picture disappeared. She slapped automatically at the dyer's groping hand, the bed creaked when she got in. She and the Tornberg lady bickered in whispers about getting enough space. Then all was quiet.

Henning lay in the dark and looked at the window's one little pane that was lighter. The first hissing, sleeping noises from the dyer were soon heard, then Mamsell Tornberg fell in with a gentle whistling, and from the room next door Bigsack's snoring could still be heard. He could make out the boy and girl on the floor as shadows. The girl's bare arm lay outstretched across the floor, the boy was apparently still awake, his eyes shone in the weak light from the windows and the spring night.

This day had been a day of farewell. Henning had said good-bye to the first friends he had made in the city. And at the same time, he had entered further into the community of the city, become one among the others more tangibly than before.

Somewhere in a corner a rat gnawed, but Henning didn't hear it. He had fallen asleep and was sleeping soundly.

SUMMER
IN
YOUR HAND

The sun had barely had time to peek over the edge of the ridge to the east before the small houses along the lake were teeming with life.

Bigsack's stocky wife threw up the bedroom windows and let out the musty night air which was replaced by the still-bearable early morning stench of the outhouse and the garbage piles. The four-year-old, who had been sleeping under the table, crawled in against the wall and sat there, eyeing her parents' feet warily. In the morning rush it was best to protect oneself; she had been trampled enough times to know.

Now everyone in the two rooms had to wake up and get up, except for Bigsack's oldest daughter. Those weeks when she had the morning shift, however, found her already gone when the others woke up, to get to the tavern in plenty of time. It opened at five o'clock so that the workers on their way to their daily labor could make it in and get their morning schnapps. But today Annika didn't begin until twelve o'clock, she slept undisturbed by the noise and the jostling.

Mamsell Tornberg lay against the wall farthest from the bedroom but was still always the one that caught the morning signal first. She crawled over the sleepily groaning Klara, took her pile of clothes in her arms and hid herself in the darkest corner. Once she was dressed she became loud and wakened the others. The children on the floor shot up like rockets and fought over the clothes that they had jumbled together in their sleep. The dyer sat up half-awake. When he had assured himself that Klara was still in bed, he sank back onto his pillow and waited for her to get up. The girl resisted waking up. She gradually allowed herself to be driven out of bed by the Tornberg lady's fretful clucking and the inevitable advance of time. The dyer gazed at Klara devotedly as she drew out her white legs and freed herself from the bedclothes and spilled over the side of the bed. She was the joy of his evenings and mornings.

The children disappeared quickly into the bedroom to be fed before their long workday began. Before them lay twelve hours of hard work, but they had gotten used to it. They had been at it for several years now, were workers who had picked up their older companions' jargon and mannerisms. But the little they had learned of reading and writing they had almost managed to forget.

Annika still lay asleep in the middle of all the hubbub and commotion. Now and then she grimaced and wrinkled her forehead, her mouth puckering as if she wanted to spit. In the corner inside her sleeping, area she had suspended a string between two nails, and there hung her pride and joy: her clothes. They would help her build a career, help her to a position in a better tavern, maybe to a husband who wasn't a laborer..

In the crowd and the din she was alone. And this aloneness was in preparation for flight, as soon as she could she was going to leave the darkness and the poverty. She knew that there weren't any common escape routes. The masses were condemned to live as miserably as they did. But in the middle of that poverty she owned some capital: her body, her youth. And this capital she took care of and received interest on. In secret she had learned the possibilities afforded by cosmetics and learned the rules of the game of love. But in her sleep, dissatisfaction also dug small, ugly wrinkles around her mouth.

Henning had gotten a few hours off in compensation for working the night before when the big new steam boiler had been installed in the new building. Still, he woke up when he usually did, from all the disturbance around him. First he felt a jolt in his body and sat up; he took it for granted that he had to hurry too. Then he remembered, stretched contentedly, and stayed where he was. Augusta, the eleven-year-old foster daughter, came and looked for a hair ribbon that had disappeared somewhere in the mess between them. She thought Henning had overslept and nudged him a few times until she found out what the story was. Then she sighed enviously.

One after another they all disappeared. Bigsack walked out, heavy and in a bad morning mood, to go see if the day would lead to anything in the way of work and income. Klara finally got her dress on and ran out after the Tornberg lady, who had stopped nagging and hurried on ahead. The dyer was also ready now. Bigsack's wife closed the young children in the bedroom and went out to buy skim milk from the cow man at Stadsträdgårdsgatan. But Henning couldn't go back to sleep, and instead lay and looked around, sometimes at the ceiling, sometimes at Annika, who wasn't lying more than an arm's length from him if he stretched out his hand.

His gaze wandered, from the girl's fuzzy hair and bare arm to the ceiling, from the ceiling's water stains and spider web across the tattered wallpaper down toward the corner where the clothes hung on their line. She had such lovely clothes, Annika. High-topped shoes well whitened with chalk, and light-colored cotton stockings. Several white petticoats. And some funny tubes with lace on them, like two halves of men's long underwear, only embroidered and made fancy. Neither Klara nor Augusta used such clothing, they kept themselves to a layer of skirts. But Annika was different, he understood that.

Now the sun was shining through the small windows; the dust hung in the air. It was a shame to lie inside on such a beautiful morning. The free hours could be better spent. He felt like bathing, could almost swim now after Thumbs' Sunday lessons.

While he got dressed he felt someone watching him. He turned around and saw Annika lying there with her eyes open. She smiled quickly and said, "I just woke up. Did you oversleep?"

He told her about his morning off and the beautiful weather, and she raised herself up on one elbow and looked toward the window thoughtfully.

"Perhaps you're right," she said. "May I go too?"

Of course she could.

"Wait outside while I get dressed," said Annika. She wasn't shy but wanted to be left alone. Maybe because she had a different schedule from the others, and wasn't used to having others there.

Henning left obediently, sat on the stairs outside and waited. Smoke rose up from the dye-works, where probably Thumbs was very busy. Lately he had been working in the laundry, where all the cloth was washed before it was dyed.

Maybe that was Thumbs now carrying out one of the large, woven baskets that were used to drain the water out of the newly-washed woolen yarn. It was too far away for him to be sure, but he recognized the baskets.

Then Annika came, and it was a lady who stepped out of Bigsack's black lair. At least Henning thought so. Annika herself wasn't at all satisfied with her finery.

She wanted to go somewhere where she wouldn't get dirt on her newly-chalked boots. It wasn't easy when all the roads were dusty and slush overflowed from the ditches and gutters. He understood that they couldn't go down to the lake, the bathing would have to wait. Besides, he certainly couldn't bathe together with Annika. Instead, they went up toward the hill's grass-covered slope. She had brought a bit of cloth with her and spread it on the grass in the shadow of a tree, smoothing her skirts carefully before she sat down.

He threw himself down beside her, pulled out a blade of grass and stuck it between his teeth. Felt shy, chewed instead of talking.

Beneath them lay the cluster of red houses along the lake, an idyll when seen from a distance. But Annika screwed her face into a discontented grimace and said: "I hate it. I have to get away."

That was just the way he had felt sometimes when he was at the miller's. He had wished himself away from the mill to the city — here? And Annika longed to get away — where?

"Why?" he wondered.

Didn't he understand? Didn't he feel it? That they lived like animals, penned in, full of lice, filthy, poor. Had he ever seen the charity ladies that came riding along, who were so nauseated by the stink of poverty that they couldn't even get out of their carriages?

Yes, he knew. And he borrowed a few of Thumbs' words: the revolution, the uprising that had to come.

Annika laughed at him. Henning was as dumb as her father was when he had drunk too much: believed that anything could be changed, that the world could be made better. There had been rich and poor from the beginning, slaves and masters. It was the law of nature. Those once condemned to poverty, labor and misery, they were doomed. For life. Any attempt they made at that revolution he spoke of would be crushed. The rich possessed power and opportunity. What could the poor do? Nothing!

No, revolution was just a foolish dream. But there was one opportunity for a few.

For a boy it was almost impossible to succeed. But a girl that could take care of herself in the right way: many fine gentlemen had married waitresses or dancers, or at least taken them as mistresses.

While she spoke he glanced at her out of the corner of his eye. Annika wasn't anything like her parents, had none of their unwieldy force and abruptness. She might possibly develop it later, but she was still only fifteen. Yet almost uncannily adult in her way of speaking and moving, so aware of the monetary worth of her womanliness. She had grown up hurriedly and turned rigid, become hard.

"But is that right?" he asked.

She sniffed disdainfully at the word: right! The poor had no rights, and therefore had the right to do anything to escape their poverty.

And Henning recollected what he had heard about the fire at the poorhouse back home. How the old and the sick had climbed over each other to get out, how they had knocked each other down. What mattered was to save yourself, the one who didn't trample was trampled. There was no right in that case, no law.

Was that true among the poor as a whole also? But he had never found his existence to be as unbearable as Annika obviously thought it was. He worked hard and was paid little: he ate badly, slept in cramped conditions on the floor, and had no fine clothes. He possessed no security and no promise of a better tomorrow, but he lived. And life was still an adventure.

Annika had found a tiny little spot on the lace edging of her petticoat. She scraped and rubbed, becoming more and more annoyed. It was as if that little spot spread and smothered the sun and the summer. She finally became completely disconsolate, red with fury. How could that spot have gotten there? Who was it that was trying to ruin everything for her, pull her down into the dirt? Maybe Augusta had been fingering her petticoat, that child had her fingers into everything, was so impossible.

Suddenly Annika began to cry. About her losing once again, about the dirt that crawled over her. She sacrificed everything, every penny to be clean and refined. Henning couldn't imagine what it cost her, in money and humiliation. She was constantly in a battle against her parents, had to lie about what she earned. She had to be obliging to sticky old men, floury bakers and blackened chimney sweeps, to earn as many tips as possible. She had to use every free moment to care for her clothes, her face and her hands, since her appearance was her only opportunity, her springboard. And there was no one she could talk to.

She hated, hated, hated.

And wept.

Fumblingly, Henning tried to console her. There was so little he could do, he felt so young, so awkward. He listened, shared, but could that bring her any happiness?

"The spot is so little," he said and held the lace-trimmed ruffle in his hand. "You can hardly see it, just a little water, a touch of soap. Then it'll be gone."

She ceased her crying and wailing as suddenly as she had begun. Looked with interest, maybe it wasn't so bad. That would probably work. Now she held the edge of the petticoat in her hand too, she really had to look carefully, convince herself that the spot really was so insignificant. And at the same time as he moved his hand, hers shot out; they both went to scrape at it with their fingernails at the same time. Hand reached hand, it was as if her fingers just glided in under his palm. And she let out a little embarrassed laugh and turned her hand so that it was pressed against his, palm to palm.

Henning felt himself grow red with confusion and excitement. He didn't dare move his hand but felt as if it rested against hers, as if body to body.

"What I have just said to you I haven't told anyone else," said Annika. "Funny, isn't it? We have hardly spoken a word to each other before."

He only nodded.

"People can to talk to you," she continued. "They feel it without knowing you. It's strange, but that's the way it is."

She laughed again and seemed to have completely forgotten the spot.

Then her hand took his and turned it over, slid the tips of her fingers over his palm, and he shivered from the sudden tickling sensation.

"You have such a nice hand," said Annika softly. "You shouldn't work and ruin it."

But work waited for him. He had to go soon.

He had to carry bricks that day. His back ached, and his hands became red and rough and scraped. As he carried he thought about Annika in her light-colored dress and white high-topped shoes, her soft skin and shining hair, the scent of perfume and freshly-ironed clothes. And while he felt the weight of his loads, he thought how he wanted to work hard, struggle on to better pay and a better life. A life so good that he would dare to ask Annika to share it with him.

But as the hours passed and he became more and more tired and his arms and back grew sore, the certainty dawned on him that his drudgery would never yield a dividend. That Annika was right when she said that those condemned to poverty and labor were doomed forever. Then he realized it: no one grew rich from hard work. No, you only grew poorer and poorer, even more worn out, tormented, destroyed. He looked at his older work companions all around him and saw how tired and ragged they were, how harshly sentenced. And the revolution was only a far-off dream.

While he bent under the weight of the bricks, he saw Annika disappear into a world that he would never be able to reach. In a light dress with a twirling parasol, she wandered among the rich and distinguished who didn't have to work because they already had everything they could wish for: power and rights, slaves and property. She could mingle with them because she had something to sell: her beauty, herself. Carefully, and at the same time audaciously, she would bargain and barter until she got the greatest value. She would win everything they had, escape from the poverty and the stench, the cramped living conditions and the dirt. But she would lose something too. Wouldn't she?

Tired, he staggered up the laid-out planks with his load, walked as if in a trance, lost all sense of time and space. He carried, put down and staggered on — carried — carried till he could have screamed from exhaustion — carried again — carried till he was too tired even to scream. Finally evening arrived, and he didn't know how he was going to make it home. Now that the compulsion to work was gone, he just wanted to collapse, fall asleep in his tracks. He forced himself into the usual tavern to get something to eat but couldn't manage to get down the food he'd paid for, just felt like vomiting. Only after he had lain in a crevice up in the White Hills did he have the energy to continue home to his room and the mattress on the floor.

But then his hands still bled, and his back ached so that he couldn't fall asleep despite his fatigue. When Annika came home from the tavern, he still lay awake. He watched her move through the room that was softly lit by the summer night, ethereal and light like a vision from another world. He lay quietly, closed his eyes, looked up again and saw that she was standing in her long nightgown straightening out the clothes that were hung over the line.

When she went to lie down she saw him, saw that he was awake, and reached out her hand to catch hold of his. But she drew it back hastily and examined her hand in the dim light from the window.

"Be careful," he whispered, "otherwise you'll get yourself dirty."

"You're bleeding," she said, and wiped her hand off on Augusta's blanket.

She got back up and searched among her clothes, slipped over beside him and carefully knotted a handkerchief around his bleeding hand. Then she stroked his cheek, and for a moment he felt her fingertips stop, press lightly, as if they pressed a kiss on his lips.

Annika was gone again. But he didn't have the energy to watch her go, instead he felt himself fall away into unconsciousness and sleep, felt how joy and bitterness were mixed together in an all-obliterating darkness.

LONG, HEAVY
WORKDAYS

He had chosen his load himself. Brick carriers earned more than hired boys, and when an opening had come up on the brick carriers' team, Henning had accepted the offer to come aboard. He needed the money that heavier labor brought; his clothes were falling to pieces, and he needed to eat more than he had been.

The wooden catwalks were laid out over the whole construction site and led up to the upper story that was just being laid in brick. With the "bundles" on their backs, the carriers raced over the swaying boards, raced for their wages and their team.

Henning came down the plank, swinging the strong brick rope in his hand. The next load already stood and waited on the wooden scaffolding, carried there by one of the men who took care of transport to the first story.

A bundle was twelve bricks and weighed around sixty kilos. It stood stacked up on the trestle, and Henning twisted the rope around it, turned his back to it, lifted, ran up the plank. He almost collided with the mortar woman on her way down. The large woman jumped clumsily aside, and the empty wooden buckets swung from their yoke.

The brick carrier and the mortar woman were the mason's attendant and supplier. Ölands-Kalle, who received his working materials from Henning and Mortar Maria, was well aware of his importance. He was the expert here, the artist. His long hair blew in the wind, and his visored cap sat at an angle. The soft, red lips under the little mustache twisted into a sneering smile. While Henning ran and Maria lugged her buckets, Ölands-Kalle leaned against the wall he had just built and took a long swig from his bottle. He was a hardened alcoholic, but his hands still obeyed him, they flitted, almost danced along with the trowel.

Before, Henning had carried the farmers' grain, now he carried the bricks of the city. One burden like the next perhaps, but the city had a quicker pace, and contract labor's extra weight.

Often he was so tired that he felt ready to give up, didn't believe he could get up after his break and start all over again. He no longer had the energy to get out and walk with Thumbs. Instead they lay down by Hammarby Lake on the summer evenings and dozed. Henning tried at least to go there to get to talk to his friend and to wash off all the brick dust. He came directly from the site, with the large, wide-brimmed felt hat, the brick carrier's top hat, on his head. The mat that he wore over his shoulders during work stayed back at the site.

The knight of the hat and mat, a man among men, no longer a hired boy. If he had been capable of it he would have been proud, the youngest on the brick carriers' team, accepted. But above all he was tired, and whenever Thumbs talked about the revolution, Henning had to wonder if Annika wasn't right after all. How could those who worked and therefore were the down-trodden, have the strength to revolt?

He asked his friend. Would they be capable of anything other than sinking even deeper into their misery? Ölands-Kalle, for example, the man who was successful, the upper class at the building site? Worn-out, capable only of drudgery and drinking himself even lower to the bottom and the end. Or Maria, old yet not much over thirty, broken by pain. Like most of the mortar women she tried to pad her wages by prostituting herself. For a few öre or a schnapps, anyone who wanted to could lie with her between the piles of planking or in some rocky crevice. Boozers and whores, cripples and coughing consumptives. Why shouldn't they capitulate for a schnapps or a few coins?

But Thumbs rubbed his sharp nose and smiled as if he had a well-kept secret.

One evening as they sat on the washing dock and dangled their legs in the water, Annika came along. She had had the morning shift at the tavern and was free that evening and was carrying clothes she was going to wash. She'd put on an old, outgrown dress that made her look childish and simple, a completely different Annika from the usual.

They lay back on the gray boards of the dock and watched while she worked. She snapped at them a little angrily when she was scrubbing her underclothes: it wasn't proper for them to lie there and watch. But Thumbs didn't make the least effort to move, so Henning remained where he was too. He figured that what Annika said wasn't all that seriously intended.

She rubbed, red in the face with the effort, inspected the garment, muttered dissatisfied, wetted it and rubbed again.

"You're a lousy washerwoman," said Thumbs. "Make way for the expert." He shoved Annika over so that she almost fell off the dock, took hold of the garment, took a good-sized chunk of soap and began to work with sweeping motions. Now he'd really show how a professional launderer did it.

Annika protested weakly: he should be careful with the delicate, expensive clothing. As if he didn't know! He had washed the finest silk in Venetian soap. Had Annika ever tried that? And silk yarn: you had to hang the yarn on rods and turn the rods unceasingly so that all the pieces of the yarn were boiled equally, otherwise the silk got all tangled up. Yes, indeed, silk yarn was so delicate that sometimes you even had to sew it inside cloth bags and boil the whole bag, stirring continuously. He had done that, and she didn't believe that he could wash a few shifts!

Thumbs worked like a machine, garment after garment came clean. They had never been washed so well before. And so quickly. As thanks she promised to treat them to coffee, would go right home and prepare a picnic basket.

While it grew dark they sat on a hillock down on the beach and enjoyed the coffee and the bread that Bigsack's wife had baked. It was Saturday evening and lively on the lake: small lanterns shone from a few rowboats, naked bathers splashed under cover of darkness, and from some of the gardens rose singing and bellowing. Lights were lit in the low houses, and all the work noises of the day were silent.

Thumbs knew someone who owned a rowboat. He slipped off into the darkness to borrow it. Annika and Henning stayed sitting where they were, shyly silent now that they were alone. She gathered up the cups and placed them in the basket. When she sat back down, she moved closer to Henning, leaned against him. She smelled so clean, so unfamiliarly clean and fine. He wondered what Thumbs would have done in this situation. Maybe he would have put his arm around her and kissed her.

But Henning wasn't Thumbs, he just sat there and felt fear and joy, the uneasiness and the pleasure of closeness.

Then suddenly he remembered something he had to tell them. It was just a year ago that day that he had come to the city. He was celebrating his first anniversary as a real Stockholmer, and could he have celebrated it in a better way?

But once Thumbs came back and they had rowed out on the lake, he began to feel the tiredness and weight of everyday living again. He lay down in the boat and looked up at the stars ... and fell asleep. When he awoke, the boat was scraping against the dock and Thumbs and Annika were laughingly bending over him. Thumbs had his arm around Annika's waist and tickled her a little so that she laughed even more.

They walked in the dark on the way up from the dock, Annika in the middle, Henning carrying the basket. Annika held the arm of each of her cavaliers, talked so quickly and assuredly — was used to bandying and playing with words. Thumbs had the same manner, the same ability. But for Henning the words eluded him and despite his closeness he still felt a little outside. In some ways it felt good to get home when their walk was over.

Annika disappeared toward the outhouse, Henning went on into the room. The children and the Tornberg lady slept, and Klara had moved over to the dyer's bed. Henning fell asleep immediately, before Annika came in. Even in his sleep he felt his back and hands ache, the weight of his workday life and the pressure of his hat and mat.

Autumn came and Henning still carried bricks.

His thin legs felt like round, heavy logs. His shoulder blades ached after hours of rubbing against hard stone. There were pains in his chest and his arms felt numb. The wind blew inside his unbuttoned shirt, slipped in at his back, which was wet with sweat.

Ölands-Kalle took the bricks and transformed them into a wall, constantly requiring more. Mortar Maria puffed along with the buckets and stole envious glances at the mason's warmth producing flask. But he was uninterested, knew he was a handsome fellow who could get the company of nicer girls when he wished. Why would he spend his aquavit on Maria?

But Henning could have a drink if he wanted to, or rather because he didn't want to. The boy was strangely afraid of schnapps and didn't even take a swig at lunch break. With these ways he would never become a real brick carrier. The boy was too weak, without being an artistic type like Kalle himself. The boy was just fumbling and timid, and out of sheer deviltry he decided to offer Maria a drink after all, so that she would get ahold of that coward and put him to shame. Kalle enjoyed himself with that thought for a long time and was in a good mood, such a good mood that he forgot the reason and let Henning go in peace.

One cold November day, Henning carried the last load. After that the bricklaying was finished and work done for the season. He received his salary, and the construction manager invited them for drinks and sandwiches. He didn't dare refuse, so he drank. He felt how the loads of many months weighed on him and didn't know whether he felt despairing or exalted. Without work and without a load. Henning understood that he wouldn't have had the strength to continue much longer, but he could get by without work even less, and the cold and hungry winter was coming, when chances would grow fewer and fewer.

"Drink and sing, you good-for-nothing boy!" screamed Ölands-Kalle, and the mortar women laughed and lapped up their aquavit greedily.

He drank but without song. And Ölands-Kalle suddenly became genial and generous. He placed his arm around Henning and explained that this was one of the quickest and best brick carriers he had ever had, and that they should drink to him.

Round-Julle, who usually led the songs when they prized big stones to clear for the foundation, began a stone-prizing song:

> "Oh ho! So we'll prize this one away — hey!"

The other's joined in:

> "Yes, he'll willingly come away — hey!"

Round-Julle sang:

> "Yes we'll blow in his rear end — hey!"

And they answered:

> "Yes, now he'll willingly go — hey!"

And the schnapps went down.

He stumbled out of the tavern, ready to vomit and half-crying, exhausted, wondering how he would get home. But he had to, he had to. It was too cold to be lying outside now, and he couldn't get sick — what would happen then? He heard the door open behind him, that someone — more than one? — followed him. Thought how he'd hidden his money so well inside his belt and was glad now.

Giggling, whispers. They came closer and he didn't have the strength to resist, nor to flee. Someone pulled his hat down over his eyes, someone took hold of his arms and held them in a deadlock. And someone, another person, undid his belt. "The money!" he thought. But the unknown hands slid past it and further, undid his pants groping for his member. The hand was hard and rough but still he knew that it was a woman's hand.

He began to kick out of desperation, heard someone cry out, the hold on his arms loosened, he took a few steps but was ensnared by his pants and fell. He got up, pulled his hat up off his face, got his pants up, ran while he held onto the waistband, ran without looking around.

He heard laughter behind him, farther and farther away.

When he had gone a reassuring distance, he sat down on some steps and caught his breath, straightened his clothes, felt if the money was still there.

Comrades, he thought, Ölands-Kalle and Maria. The oppressed and the oppressors. And through them the revolution would come, tomorrow would be won? Wasn't Annika right? Wasn't fleeing from them the only possibility?

Once again he felt his solitude. He had been cast out, degraded; those to whom he had been closest in his work had violated him.

Tired, he got up, leaned against the wall of the house and threw up. And began the difficult walk home to the room with all the people—to days without secure work and pay.

When he came home, the lamp was lighted, and there was much commotion. Mamsell Tornberg, who for a long time had complained of chest pains, lay dying, and no one knew what to do. They couldn't get a doctor to come at this hour and from so far away. Or could they? But the skinny little Mamsell quickly closed the discussion by giving a few gasps, then lying there dead and gone. Don't trouble for my sake: that had always been her motto.

Bigsack carried her out to the shed and hoped the rats would stay away. Klara refused to lie in the bed where the Mamsell had just died, and the dyer was in no mood to offer her a place beside him. So she crawled onto the floor between Henning and Augusta and lay hiccuping with sobs and terror. Henning, who had himself cried so recently, now had to do what he could to console her. He fought off his tiredness and tried to whisper soothing, friendly words.

At last he fell asleep, before or after Klara he didn't know. The next morning there was no Mamsell Tornberg to waken them, but Bigsack's wife was up earlier than normal and banged around more than she usually did. When Henning woke he had Klara's cheek near his and her naked arm lay across his back. The dyer sat bolt upright in bed and stared at them with hostility.

Henning carefully moved her arm away, shook Klara awake. She sat up and looked around wonderingly, then she remembered why she was lying on the floor and shed a few more tears over her old bed and bickering companion who lay cold and quiet in the shed.

Mortar Maria's rough hand. Klara's soft cheek. And Mamsell Tornberg. Everything came so near, and the nearness both frightened and warmed him. He didn't know if he wanted to flee or come closer to life and people.

On a day at the end of the week, Mamsell Tornberg was buried in the paupers' graveyard beyond the Skanstull customs house. A hauler took care of her transport. The Mamsell didn't have any living relatives, and so that she wouldn't have to make the last journey alone, Bigsack's wife asked Henning, who was out of work, and Annika, who had the evening shift, to go along with her to the grave. They walked after the wagon with the coffin, which rattled over the ruts and stones along the roads and streets. Out to Skanstull and to the graveyard close to the execution site.

After a few days, Klara got a new bedmate, she had picked her herself. She was a young girl from the spinning mill named Matilda, who looked at the world with big, childishly round eyes. Klara took, with the right of the first-born, Mamsell Tornberg's old place against the wall, and the dyer had his morning and evening enjoyment doubled. It was really only a cat that missed Mamsell Tornberg: it no longer found the usual little saucer of skim milk that used to stand just inside the shed door.

JUST DESSERTS

When winter came and the boats didn't get through, Bigsack had to go without work. The first few days he tried to enjoy his free time; he sat by the open fire in the bedroom and drank. But when the money ran out worry took its place: here he was, big and strong, with his enormous powers, and he couldn't support his family. Now it felt good that they had so many boarders and that the children worked. But Annika irritated him. She went around dressed like a countess while her parents and younger siblings almost starved.

He went over to the corner with the clothesline, stood there and stared: this was too damned much. Look! That kid had lace! And legs on her underwear! Was the girl completely mad? You didn't need those kinds of signposts and billboards for the guys to find their way to a piece of tail, for that's what she wanted. He called for his wife. She took her time, then he roared so that the old wooden house shook.

She came hurrying, saw the huge man standing there pointing with a large, accusing finger.

"Your daughter dresses like a whore!" he roared. "Burn up this evil! Yes, those there, those legs there. And if I catch her buying any more monstrosities, she'll get it so that she has to crawl on her knees the coming weeks."

His wife scurried anxiously away with the sinful cloth legs. It was really bad of Annika to have bought them and even worse that her husband had noticed them. And just now, too, when he was so easily irritated, when he just looked for the chance to break out with blows. They had had two foster children before Augusta, and he had beaten them senseless. The boy, Johan, had finally run away. He never complained, that boy, not even when his leg had been broken by his foster father. It healed crooked after that, so that Johan limped when he walked. And Hanna, poor thing, she moved away from home as soon as she could. She still carried the marks of all the beatings she had received.

But the last few years had been better. Better for work, better for temper. With his own children he was kinder, if he wasn't crossed. And Annika had a remarkable talent for staying out of his sight; she seemed just to evaporate, was never in the way.

But this was too much, why couldn't Annika be more careful, hide her clothes under the blankets instead of hanging them up as if on display. She knew how her father got irritated with everything.

Burn them up, he had said. Of course, of course. But surely that was a pity, such fine and embroidered garments. She should be able to hide them somewhere where he'd never find them. Not that she wanted Annika to go dressed like that, but it was wrong to destroy something which had been paid for so dearly.

Bigsack's wife climbed up onto the kitchen chair and hid Annika's pant legs in an empty pot far back in a seldom-opened cupboard.

Klara came home with the rumor: tomorrow the event would certainly and finally take place. She had heard it from a most reliable source, a girl whose sister went out with a caretaker's assistant in the old courthouse. There was no doubt about it. She and Matilda had already requested and succeeded in getting half of Saturday off.

Bigsack who had gone on muttering all day said my, my and well, well, one should go out and watch, of course. Gradually he was drawn into all the talk and speculating and relating how it had been before. He had been there certainly, but with this cold weather one had to be sure and take along plenty of schnapps. Not least for the girls' sake, if they thought about it. For it wasn't really any women's entertainment.

Henning didn't have any work that waited, he could go along. For a few days he had been down picking up at the candle factory, cleaning after the construction work, but now he was free.

He decided to talk to Thumbs first before he made plans with the others. While they were discussing it, he took his cap and went out into the sleet. He followed the street that had shrunk to a path in the snow.

The apartment where Thumbs slept with his parents, siblings, cousin and boarders wasn't as badly overcrowded as Bigsack's. There was actually a corner there where they could sit in peace.

Yes, Thumbs had also heard the rumor. Master Wanselin had even said that those who wanted to could get time off for a cut in pay. Partly because it could be good for them to be there and see it, and partly because it was better that they take the time off rather than try to sneak away by every conceivable means.

As they usually did, the two friends walked a little before they separated, following the street up to Nytorget and strolling around a while among the farmers' snow-covered sleighs and closed-up sheds. Drunken farmhands bellowed from the pubs, somewhere a girl screamed, but it sounded as if she was drunk too. A small figure with large wind-filled skirts struggled onward alone. It was Annika, and they hollered to her. She stopped and waited, glad to have some company during the last, dark part of the way. She squeezed between them to be as sheltered as possible. Small and seeking shelter, but at the same time plucky, so assured and saucy.

But in the dark and cold vestibule her mother was standing and waiting for her. Thumbs and Henning each went their way, and Henning slipped discreetly past mother and daughter, who obviously had something important to talk about. And something that made Annika angry and dangerous, he could hear that by her tone. But Bigsack's wife prayed and implored, and warned.

She did what she could, as she always did, with such little success. Annika wasn't to lose her temper and begin to scream for her clothes, then there would be a big scene this very evening.

But the girl was seething with rage. Those clothes that she had worked so hard for, sacrificed so much for. That he even dared touch them with his big, black paws. Suddenly she saw her father as one of the many ruffians who had to be slapped and put in their place. He had dared mess with her clothes; he had gotten into something that was none of his business!

Annika had been spoiled. Bigsack had a weakness for his beautiful daughter, and had taken much from her that he never would have taken from her mother.

She pushed her mother aside and strode in. She saw her father sitting in the outer room talking to the dyer and the two girls. Pretty drunk, like so many of her customers. Without saying hello, she walked past, went into the bedroom and slammed the door behind her.

Bigsack watched her go. The package she was carrying. Her way of walking, the contempt that could already be distinguished in her movements. Well, so now the countess has arrived and has bought more finery while her father can't even buy any schnapps. She's slammed the door, so now we're putting on airs. We're not good enough for her anymore. In that case the countess is going to hear who it is that's in charge in this house.

He got up heavily, began to reel, and caught himself against the wall. The mill girls and the dyer watched him wonderingly; they had been in the middle of a conversation. The children on the floor crawled carefully backwards. Bigsack opened the door to the bedroom, slammed it behind him.

His wife stayed where she was in the vestibule, cried, and collapsed when she heard the door slam. Didn't know where to turn. Not into the bedroom, she could do nothing there now. Not into the room to the strangers that lived among them. Only the vestibule remained, and there she stayed, trembling with cold.

Silent, frightened, the boarders stayed where they sat. Waiting.

They heard them quarreling inside the bedroom. Annika's small, shrill voice. Bigsack's low, almost heavy tone. Annika so angry that she was practically screaming with fury. And then a roaring that made Augusta hiccup with terror and move all the way in under the dyer's bed.

They crouched, felt the blows. Matilda looked at the door with wide-open eyes, suddenly placed her hands over her ears, fell down across the bed and shook with sobs. Klara held her soothingly, herself in a mood of despair mixed with a strange joy over Annika's degradation: a fugitive brought back to their common cell. The dyer squirmed uncomfortably, unbuttoned his shirt at the neck, looked around, got up and went out. And Henning sat and looked at the closed door, wanted to rush in and say "Stop!", wanted to defend Annika, but couldn't move.

Annika howled in there. Now there was none of the rage left, only the pain, despair, fear. Sometimes a word escaped from the howling, a "please, Father," a "forgive." But the blows continued to rain down.

Finally he was finished, now they only heard him panting to catch his breath and Annika's wrenching sobs. And like an echo Augusta's crying came out from under the dyer's bed, from Matilda who had burrowed down among the pillows and blankets, from the vestibule where Bigsack's wife had sunk down on the stairs.

The door to the bedroom opened. Bigsack came out, sweating and red with rage. Without looking at anybody, he closed the door behind him, walked across the room, opened the door to the vestibule, swore at his wife whom he tripped over, disappeared out into the night.

Shaken, the boarders remained in their places, not really knowing what they should do. A family scene wasn't exactly what one should get involved in. And at least the girl was still alive, they could hear her still crying. The door from the vestibule opened carefully, the woman who had waited out there slipped past them. She opened the door to the bedroom, and they heard the crying more loudly from inside: Annika's abandoned sobbing, the four-year-old's anxious, childish wailing. Then the door closed again, and they could sense, rather than hear, how the mother calmed and consoled, how she got the child to quiet down and the girl to sob more softly.

The dyer who had kept watch from behind a peephole in the outhouse saw Bigsack leave and now came back in silently. He undressed quickly and crawled into bed, pulled the blanket over his head and showed that he was unavailable for conversation. For once he denied himself the girls' evening ritual. It was a small loss. They huddled together almost completely dressed, hid themselves from their existence and their surroundings. Matilda was still crying, and Klara held her as a mother would.

Terror also drove the children on the floor closer to each other. Bigsack's son and foster daughter rolled themselves up into knots, tried to make themselves so small that they would be forgotten and not annoy anyone. Henning sat and looked at them, two frightened animals, trembling like newborn puppies. At last they fell asleep, Augusta still sobbing in her sleep.

Henning roused himself, got up and went to put out the lamp. Found his way back carefully in the dark, pulled off his jacket and boots, and lay down fully dressed under the blanket. He was still cold. Lay and heard the others toss and turn. Until the dyer apparently fell asleep. And then Klara. But Matilda still lay tossing.

What could he have done, what should he have done?

The crack of light under the door to the bedroom disappeared, they had put out the lamp in there. The door silently opened. It must be Annika coming. She stumbled forward toward her place on the other side of him, collapsed on the mattress in the corner, let out a whimper, tried to find a way to possibly lie down.

He reached out his hand, wanted somehow to show his solidarity. He reached her hand, stroked her hair. But Annika recoiled from him, hid herself in her shame.

When he awoke in the morning, she was already gone. And the line where the clothes had hung was empty. For a moment he wondered if she had run away from home, but then he saw that something was left, white clothes under the blanket. The rest she had apparently hidden in a safer place.

From the bedroom could be heard Bigsack's snoring and his wife's careful hushing of the little ones so they wouldn't waken him. He was dead drunk. And everyone in the apartment crept carefully so as not to waken the mighty attack bear in whose den they had come to live.

The streets and roads were bubbling with life, people were pushing their way through everywhere, tense, expectant.

Thumbs stood and waited for Henning. The two boys struck up company with Klara and Matilda, who had succeeded in escaping the dyer's attentions. Klara laughed and hung onto Henning's arm, but Matilda hadn't been able to sleep off yesterday evening's experience. It was hard for Thumbs to get her to thaw despite his efforts. Finally Klara felt she had to explain what had happened. As Klara explained it, it didn't sound so remarkable: a father had given his daughter a beating and such things happened daily everywhere. Thumbs didn't appear to take it so deeply.

Gradually even Matilda was caught up by the atmosphere, the excitement. There was something of a festival in the air. Small streams of black figures came from houses and streets, flowed together to mighty rivers that made their way toward Götgatan. Eager boys ran to get there in time, panting old men struggled along, girls giggled, all jittery. When they reached the smaller streets parallel to Götgatan they had to make way to let the sleighs that were coming pass by. With shouts and warning cries, those who rode tried to get through on the side streets so as not to be blocked by the throngs on the main street. They had to hurry if they were going to get to see anything. People had placed themselves everywhere. Klara picked up the pace. Because of this they almost managed to reach Skanstull before the buzz grew louder, before the shout was heard: "He's coming!"

There came the cart rolling along, followed by people running to keep up.

They got up the hill a little way before the cart passed them. They stood pressed against a wall and stared: where was he sitting? Yes, that must be him, beside the man in the uniform, riding backwards. Across from him was a priest and some civil servant. He didn't look like the wild animal they had imagined, just an ordinary, pug-nosed peasant boy.

And now the cart was close to its destination, the end of the line waited. Soldiers from the garrison had built a V-formation around the wooden platform. An official read something, they couldn't hear what, but presumably it was the sentence.

Everyone climbed and clung to things to get closer. A few wagons were taken over by curious onlookers; some climbed up onto the roofs of sheds and small houses; grape clusters of boys hung from the bare trees. Some women who had little children with them screamed and scolded; the children were squeezed together and whining.

An angular figure with sharply chiseled features freed himself from the group. It was Johan Fredrik Hjort, the prisoner chosen to become an executioner. A shiver ran through the crowd, a cool breath of fear. Hjort gave an order to his men, checked all the preparations one last time, well aware of his public's demands.

Now the wagon had driven up to the V-formation. The priest and the other two officials stepped out. The condemned man, guardsman and woman slayer Göthe, stood up quickly. He took a few quick steps. Then he was standing on the scaffold. He looked around bewildered, bowed. He pressed the hand of the preacher and of one of the officials; one of the spectators claimed that it was the prison director.

A muffled growl rose up from the mob, someone hushed them in hopes that the condemned would speak to the people.

Guardsman Göthe removed his cap and coat and placed them on the railing set up around the scaffold, took off his vest, undid his long, white scarf, fumbled with his hands at the back of his neck. The shirt was buttoned in back, and he yanked at it so that the buttons flew off and the shirt split open. The preacher who had taken his scarf took a step forward, apparently to tie it as a blindfold around the condemned man's eyes. But the guardsman shook his head, and the priest moved back again.

Klara's fingers dug into Henning's arm. And he felt how the terror and aversion of the day before came back, wondered why he had come here, if he should look or close his eyes, stay or flee. But he stayed there and watched, as if transfixed, as bound as the evening before.

Matilda had buried her head in Thumb's chest, hid, wanted to go. But now it was impossible to squeeze through the sea of people.

The guardsman walked forward to the executioner's block and fell on his knees. The preacher followed him, now to lay his coat over the almost naked back. While the priest read the blessing, the condemned adjusted his head, fitted his throat into the groove on the block.

Once again a murmur arose from the silence. The executioner had raised his ax. Then there was a gleam of the winter sun on the edge, like a flash of lightening. Some women cried out, a boy fell out of a tree.

Two streams of blood spurted out from the headless neck, colored the snow, were united in a slowly swelling stream.

A howling arose from the sea of people, the cry of a wild animal. The joy of the tormented at seeing another's torment. Someone had suffered and made their own suffering a little less.

Matilda shook with sobs. But Klara stood fascinated and watched, as if she wanted to imprint every detail on her memory.

The performance was over. The executioner's assistants heaved the body into the basket where the head already lay. The executioner inspected his ax and wiped off the blade.

All the taverns were filled, everyone felt they needed a bracer. They toasted Göthe, and the skillful Hjort, who with a single blow had rid society of one of its worst criminals.

THE BEAUTIFUL SPRING

Henning would always remember the spring when he turned seventeen as the beautiful spring. The bird-cherry blossomed white against light green leaves at the corner of the red row houses, and on the other side of the lake, the fields around Hammarby Farm glistened a new-plowed black. And in the evenings the city lay wrapped in the spring sky's light blue tulle, a beautiful city that was washed clean by the spring rain and still didn't have the damp odors of summer.

With the spring came increased work opportunities. Bigsack was fully engaged down at the coal yard beside Danviken. Annika became a waitress at the café at Strömparterren. It was a big step on the way to another world.

Henning got temporary work in construction at the candle factory again. Now that the cold had released its grip they had begun with the interior. He was paid less than what he had received as a brick carrier, but the work was lighter, and he had the energy to be alive on his time off. Together with Thumbs he wandered around the city for longer periods. They got into the habit of finishing off the evening by picking up Annika at Strömparterren and accompanying her home. It was late before they got to bed, and the hours for sleep weren't many, but the light spring evenings weren't there to sleep away.

They arrived in plenty of time to meet Annika, the Norrbro was the right place to wait. There was always something happening there, and there was so much to see. Here was where the town's dandies and beauties went strolling, all the celebrities walked this way. In Bonniers bookstall window, inside the bazaar building, hung posters you could look at. And they saw smelt fishermen pulling their catches out of Strömmen, and listened at the same time to the music of the wine café's orchestra. They hung over the railings and looked down on Annika as she served, as she gave a sharp swish with her full skirt. Although she wasn't more than sixteen, she already had an accomplished way of dealing with her male public. She stood at the table with an empty tray like a silver shield against her stomach, leaned forward and flashed her smile. They didn't hear but could imagine her quick replies, see the gentlemen's pleased and admiring expressions. One day she would surely capture one of them, disappear from Henning and Thumbs' world of poverty.

There were many girls who smiled that spring thought Henning. Butterfly-light smiles and images as fleeting as the wind, sometimes a pressure of the hand. Not much more. Oh yes, a darker and more burning image.

Annika. Their habit of accompanying her home created a new habit: she and Henning went to bed at the same time. And even if there was a scrap of curtain hanging in front of the window, the light still came through. They were close to each other, only separated by the sleeping children who lay head to foot between them. The habit eased away their shyness. Often they continued some conversation they had begun on the way home, whispering while they undressed. One evening she told him she had to run away from home, couldn't bear it any longer.

"I will never forgive him," she hissed. "Never. I still have the marks on my back."

And she pulled off her nightgown. "Look!"

He hardly dared look and still he looked, still he would never forget the picture. The white skin. And the dark, oozing sores, the marks. She shivered as if she were cold, huddled up. She cried quietly while he stood there and didn't know what he should or dared do. Wanted to take her in his arms and console her, but her nakedness stopped him, he couldn't. He just let his hand glide over her back, felt the roughness of the scabs, followed it with his finger.

Annika put on her nightgown, sat on her heels with her knees under her chin.

"If only you had money," she said. "If only we could take off together."

He didn't have any answer to give to that.

"But one day I'm going to disappear," she said, "because I can't bear it here any longer, because I don't intend to let him beat me to death." And she shook her fist at the bedroom, in the direction of Bigsack's snoring

Henning fell asleep holding onto the image of her white skin, her slender back.

He had the feeling that Annika regarded him as a brother while she thought of Thumbs in a completely different way. And also that Thumbs was interested in Annika. That was really why they had begun to pick her up from work. It was too bad, for he could sense that Annika still would never give up her plans for finding someone to carry her out of poverty. Thumbs didn't fit into her future.

And for Henning: was Annika a sister? No. He dreamed about her sometimes, dreams that he was ashamed of when he was awake. He could look at his hand that had stroked her back and recall the feeling. But he wouldn't have wanted to marry her even if he'd had the money that he lacked. Annika wasn't at all like Kerstin. And it was someone like Kerstin that he thought about, daydreamed about.

Perhaps Matilda. Her big eyes reminded him of Kerstin and he liked Matilda a lot. But still, she wasn't really the right one.

Annika was almost always tied up with her work. So it happened often that Thumbs and Henning got together with Klara and Matilda.

This spring Klara had taken it into her head that she was going to spend the night before Trinity Sunday at Uggleviken, and the others were also interested. It was a long way there, but it was just this once, and it was the night before a holiday. Bigsack's wife helped them put together a picnic and Thumbs supplied a sturdy basket for carrying drinks. But Klara had to stay out of the dyer's way. He went around watching out of the corner of his eye, suspecting something was being plotted but too proud to ask.

The steam launch came chugging up Tegelviken, full of people on their way to the evening's amusements. They managed to squeeze onto a long bench that went all the way around the boat and sat and looked down into the machinery and felt the pulse of the motor. They had to admire the crewman in charge of landing. He grabbed hold of or shoved off with the boat hook, made fast or untied, threw coke into the boiler, sold tickets and collected tickets again when they got off. He was all the crew that the captain had to command, an admirable and estimable Jack-of-all-trades.

At Nybron they disembarked and the launch continued on toward Djurgården. Berzelii Park was turning green among the slender trees behind the stone wall, and small cargo boats were crowded in along the wooden quay in front of the Artillery Yard. Everything was new for Henning here, but he wasn't able to stand long and look. Thumbs led them with sure steps up the street toward Ladugårdslands Church. And soon they were outside the city, had passed the dark hills of Tyskbagarbergen and Lill-Jans park where the gatekeepers' houses stood between budding fruit trees and greening gooseberry bushes. A curtain of dense pine woods sheltered them from the northerly winds.

Unfortunately Pentecost, the poor people's season for celebration and merry-making, wasn't what it had once been. The governor had not only forbidden accordion playing in the streets, but also dancing in public. Angry critics asserted it was done with thought for the police's profits, people would drink and not dance. The police received their salaries from the tax on aquavit and the fines for drunkenness went into the police pension fund.

But the four of them hadn't been to Uggleviken before and could make no comparisons. There wasn't any lack of people. They felt like it was crawling with them everywhere: youths who frolicked and danced on the sly without music, staid couples who settled themselves on the grass with their picnic baskets, drunken guardsmen who sat with giggling girls on their knees, sweaty old men and groaning old women who shoved their way to the spring to drink of the ice-cold water.

They played tag, creeping through the bushes in the gathering darkness, and had to look out that they didn't tread on sleeping drunks or lovers. When they had run themselves breathless and thirsty, they threw themselves down on the grass and opened the picnic basket. Klara pulled out one of the large, wide cakes and declared laughingly that it was big enough for two. Immediately Thumbs bit in from the other side, and Matilda and Henning had to take a cake and do the same. Henning wondered what they would do when they got to the middle of the cake and glanced sideways to see how Klara and Thumbs managed it. They kept up till they were almost eating out of each other's mouths, and Henning realized that he and Matilda would be obliged to do the same. But when they bumped noses, Matilda took the piece that was left and stuffed it in his mouth.

It was morning when they wandered back. From the meadow by the spring, they could still hear the cries of fighters pummeling each other and of girls who were being squeezed too hard by fumbling hands.

They walked two by two. Thumbs and Klara, the girl leaning heavily on him. She had been in a bit too much of a hurry to get at the contents of the bottles. Thumbs supported her and laughed, pulling her into the shade of a large tree and pressing her against the trunk. Henning and Matilda walked on, pretending not to see. They were too shy, mostly of each other. Henning wondered if Matilda wanted him to do what Thumbs was doing to Klara. Matilda was anxious in case he thought she wanted him to. But she wasn't afraid of Henning, he couldn't scare her. She just carefully loosened the hand that he had placed around her waist, took it in hers, walked and swung it. Then he began to laugh, and she joined in.

They couldn't wait for Thumbs and Klara. They tried, but the two moved farther off, disappearing into the pine woods beside Lill-Jans park. With that Matilda and Henning went on alone, now that they could find their way on their own.

The city slept, pale and silent in the first morning light. No steam launches had begun to ply the waters yet. Some policemen patrolling watched the young couple suspiciously but let them pass by. A drunken girl sat on a stoop and cried.

When they walked past Jacob's Church, the clock struck four. On

Strömparterren the chairs stood piled on the tables, and the sun began to shine in the windows of the bazaar building. At the statue of Gustaf III, they had to sit on the circular steps and rest a moment. Matilda leaned on Henning's arm, and he felt happy at having her so near. To just sit like this, nothing more, and feel that the world could be soft and pleasant.

She was seventeen years old, the same as he. She had worked at the mill for several years but still earned so little. She knew that many of the other girls padded their income, like Klara. But Matilda didn't want to, had said no to the dyer even though he had promised her a whole dollar, a sum which otherwise took her two days to earn.

Look! Matilda pointed out over the water. Like silk! And she talked about the cloth she wove, about the silk which was so soft and fine, the cloth which was made from her labor and which she would never be able to afford. She liked cloth, would probably actually have wanted to become a seamstress. What did Henning want to be?

Once he had wanted so much. Now he had to weigh his will against his judgment, the knowledge of what was possible.

"Being a brick carrier is a good job," he said thoughtfully, "as long as you have the strength for it."

Yes, he liked Matilda. Would gladly talk with her, walk by her side. But it didn't go much farther than that. Once in a while he could wonder: why? Perhaps because the right opportunity never came along, their common barrier of shyness was too high during the time they lived in the same room, so near each other.

It was different with Klara, she didn't build barriers. She could be lying in the dyer's bed and wink conspiratorially at Henning when he came home late. She could lure Thumbs under a tree with her in the woods at Uggleviken Spring, or was it Thumbs who had lured her? She could sit on the edge of the bed and pull her skirts up too high, she could come along and gaily smack Henning on the backside when he had hidden to change his pants.

Still she wasn't fresh or unpleasant, he thought. She simply was

and took the world such as it was. Kind and usually happy, there was-
n't much that could get to her. She made faces at the dyer's bad breath
and filthy smell, but thankfully accepted the twelve shillings she
received; he never offered her a whole dollar.

You didn't have to offer Klara so much, she had gotten used to
being grateful for a little. That Henning wasn't impolite and unpleasant was more than enough, she took it as politeness and a compliment. If he had stroked her cheek, she would have thought he wanted to sleep with her and made herself ready for him.

For this reason he never dared do more than smile at Klara. And
she smiled back, broadly.

The boys lay on the grassy slope and watched the boat being rowed
out to Sickla by women from Dalarna. The little steam launch that ran
on the lake had been taken in since the water had gotten too low.
Thumb's cousin had thrown herself down beside them on the grass;
she lay flat on her stomach and tickled Henning with a blade of grass
and listened to every word they said.

Anna-Kajsa. Thirteen years old and a little beast, curious and
intrusive. Thumbs sighed about her and snapped at her. But at the
same time he was fond of the girl. Good material, he said. But even
the best material can be misused and turned into, practically speaking,
just about anything.

Anna-Kajsa hung on Henning's heels especially, had discovered
that he was easy to conquer, easy to tame. He never snapped back. No
matter how much of a nuisance she was, he still talked to her like a
person. Thumbs treated her more like a dog. He whistled when she
was to come, and even if he didn't kick, he still pushed her away if he
had grown tired and wanted her to go.

"Get lost," said Thumbs now, "we're going to have a swim."

After a little whining she obeyed, crawling down the other side of
the hill. But they had gotten no farther than the water before she came
flying back and jumped in. She flailed her arms and shrieked, splashing water on them and pulling Henning by the hair. She was a naked

little troll child, with a slight hint of breasts, a wiry child, all elbows and without inhibitions.

"Get lost!" said Thumbs angrily. "Aren't you ashamed to jump around naked that way?"

"Bah," she said, "it's only you two. And you're just as naked — so there!"

She let her arms swing like scoops and the water flew about Thumbs' and Henning's ears. Then they dunked her and she fought back, snorting, but didn't scream.

However, when they went ashore she crept carefully around to the other side of the rise and got dressed there. She lay behind the bushes, spying, and didn't come out until the boys were dressed.

She followed them a little way along the road, but then there were a few hens to be chased from the garden plot and some cowslips that had to be picked. Besides, she had grown tired of their endless dumb talk.

She was the meager springtime, thin and undeveloped, audacious and full of pranks. Long after she had disappeared between the fence and the bushes, they could hear her mocking laughter.

BOAT ROCKER
SUMMER

On a day in the beginning of June, the new building at the candle factory was completed. A few days later old Wanselin at the dye-works decided to cut back on operations; he had been in poor health for a long time.

So both Henning and Thumbs were out of work. They hunted for more work together and took extra jobs wherever they could find them. At last an opportunity presented itself through an uncle of Thumbs by the name of Beckis. He had been a pitch burner in his youth but was now one of the few representatives of the old boat rockers' guild. For the time being, he was lying at home with a broken leg; he had been run down by a flock of schoolboys on Sista Styvern's Stairs. He let himself be talked into convincing his workmates to let the two ambitious youngsters with spotless reputations take his place.

In the same way that the rich get to inherit companies and official positions, the poor should be allowed to inherit a trade, Beckis said, once he had made up his mind. That was why Thumbs could give it a try. And if Thumbs wanted to have his good friend with him that was just as well, inexperienced and scrawny as they were, there would be two of them, and they could work for the pay of one grown man.

They met with Kalle Hump and Kikus who were the oldest in the trade. The older men were anxious to impress upon the boys that even though the boat rockers worked in the harbor, they weren't just ordinary, simple longshoremen. The profession had fine traditions in its guild, and they didn't accept just anybody into the corps. But the recommendation from Beckis meant a lot, and new talent must be had. The first few days Kalle Hump would see that Thumbs and Henning learned the basics with Kikus. Once they had learned the hand holds and duties, they could take care of themselves.

The boat rockers had their meeting place at Fiskarhamnen, the harbor by the locks at Slussen. The harbor was made up of a floating dock that together with the walkway on the land side formed a rectangle. On the six-meter-wide dock the crews of the fishing boats had to get along with the dock workers and the fishwives.

It was bustling and full of life all day long. The fishing boats came and went; catches were brought ashore in big wooden crates and auctioned off. Old women in shawls and kerchiefs stood behind their stalls under flapping awnings. They cleaned fish and tried to attract customers. And on Fiskargången, the walkway alongside, rows of shops and beer parlors beckoned.

Above Fiskargången, hooves clattered and wagons rattled past. From the Iron Pit the ferrier's clanging was heard. Along Stadsgården's narrow wooden docks, the dock workers were squeezed together with the inhabitants of the dismal houses that huddled beneath the precipice.

From the outskirts of the city Henning and Thumbs had come to the confusion and throng of the hub. The first day Henning felt completely dizzy, felt like he was going to be run over and pushed into the water, wondered how he'd find the way to his boats.

Kikus was a little, cross-eyed, wiry old man with arms like a gorilla. He didn't say many words, preferred to point. But he was particular when he taught the fine art of his trade, demonstrating and repeating. He tied the rope around himself and pulled the huge stone that weighed close to a hundred kilos. The stone was terribly heavy to put in place. But later it was what would do most of the work.

They climbed aboard a boat from Åland that had come in with fish at dusk. The fish would not be auctioned off before tomorrow morning. It was the duty of the boat rockers to keep them alive by keeping the boat in motion the whole night so the water would circulate.

A rope was fastened high up on the mast where the fork at the end of the main boom was attached. The stone, which had a hole drilled in it, was fastened to the lower end of the rope and was meant to dangle from a hook a little ways up in the air. Another piece of rope was attached to the stone, and Henning had to pull on that until the stone swung like the clapper of a bell. It took a while until he got it to an even and steady tempo. Kikus swore up and down when the angle wasn't right: was he thinking of splitting the mast? And if he didn't get up any speed, that meant it needed bigger swings. More and more until the whole boat rolled.

Henning struggled and pulled. Even pulls, he remembered, large, even pulls. Oh ho! Oh ho! He should sing along, maybe a stone-prizing song. But Kikus seemed not to be the sort that sang or appreciated song.

Finally the old fellow was satisfied. The stone swung evenly and well, the boat rolled in time. That was that. Now Henning only needed to give the stone a push now and then or pull on the rope. He could half-lie with his back against the mast, take it easy. But he had to beware of falling asleep.

He lay and watched the enormous stone swing back and forth over his head. What if the rope split, or if he hadn't fastened it properly, or if the hook didn't hold? But the stone swung calmly above him in a steady beat, back-and-forth, sleep-inducing strokes of the pendulum.

"The skipper will take care of the midnight meal," Kikus instructed. "That's included in the pay. But schnapps and beer you'll have to pay for yourself."

Henning thought of saying he didn't want any schnapps; that if he had any, he might fall asleep instead of perking up, as was the objective.

He never got a chance to say anything. Kikus had thought further on the subject: "We arranged for you to get a meal — so I'll pay for your drink too."

Kikus disappeared inside to see the skipper to settle it. During the training period Thumbs and Henning weren't going to receive a cash salary, that would be paid to the masters who taught them.

Henning couldn't leave the stone now, hardly dared take his eyes off it in case it should go off beat or change directions so that the mast was endangered. But he could still see how the women folded up their awnings, how the evening turned even more blue, and the last streaks of pink disappeared in the west.

A few more boats began to rock slowly, one boat rocker after another fell into the rhythm. The waves slapped against the sides of the decks, and the small boats alongside the wharf began to rock in time. Night fell and it grew cooler. Henning buttoned up his coat, thought how he'd get himself a sack or some sort of pillowcase to fill with straw to provide more support and something soft to lean on.

Shortly after twelve the shipsboy came with two substantial sandwiches, a bottle of beer and the promised aquavit. Henning asked the boy to take half of the aquavit. And that he did even before he had time to get over his astonishment, and so quickly that he almost choked on the liquor.

"You said it, so suit yourself," sputtered the boy and wiped the tears from his eyes with his coat sleeve. Henning nodded but didn't answer. He listened, wondering if it was Thumbs who was rocking the boat closest to Fiskargången.

The night wind played over the water, blew small, light cross waves that were broken by the swells from the rolling boats.

The morning and the light arrived; the first rays of sun warmed the rockers that sat and half-dozed, as if chained to their masts. The crew members awoke, pulled up buckets of water and washed the sleep out of their eyes. Henning braked the stone's swinging, getting it to stop. A crew member helped him get it off the hook while Henning panted and lifted and then carefully put the stone down. With a net Henning and the crewman began to take up the fish from the tub in the boat and fill the large wooden crates that stood ready. On the wharf the buyers were gathering and waiting for the skipper to proceed with the auction. While Henning and the crew member fished with their nets and carried fish, the bidding began. Part of the fish would be transported to the bulk buyers. For that purpose there was a special group of fish carriers. Then those who bought smaller quantities would have their loads delivered. Today Henning was going to go as far as the

Three Rummers on Regeringsgatan.

The transporting crate, which was called the drum, was placed on a two-wheeled cart and Henning rolled it away. The cart bounced and jolted against the cobblestones. Going along the water at Skeppsbron, he was met with sails drying and snapping in the wind, smoke rising black from the steamers' high smokestacks. The city awakened, teeming with life everywhere, the workday had begun. But for Henning and Thumbs it was soon time for rest and sleep.

On rainy days Henning slept on his mattress at Bigsack's. While Henning worked at night, his landlord had taken on a temporary lodger, it would be a pity and a shame to let the space remain empty. This new roommate, Wagtail, who slept the other shift in his sleeping place, was a girl who fit into the looser category. Bigsack's wife went to great lengths to get her out of bed so that Henning could have his sleeping place on time. Sometimes Wagtail only rolled over, half asleep, to the pile of clothing beside her, and went on sleeping while Henning, a little irritated, tried to turn the mattress over to avoid the smell and the warmth she left behind.

If it was passably good weather and warm out, Henning preferred to sleep in the bushes by Hammarby Lake. Thumbs went there also, it was too hot and noisy at home. They made their way in under the shady branches and slept with one arm as a pillow. Sometimes they were awakened by the lapping of the waves or noise from the lake, children who had free time swam and splashed. The two boat rockers also took a dip to feel wide awake before they went off to their night's work.

After the first few nights they got to work together. At times they helped each other raise the heavy stone. Sometimes they worked with another system: they fastened a weight on the boom instead, and then lay there at leisure on their backs and swung the boom with their feet.

They shared their bread at the midnight meal, sometimes ordering an extra portion. Henning declined the schnapps while Thumbs took at least one: you had to stick to the traditions of the trade.

While the boat rocked, they talked softly, about the day's work and the money that they divided after Thumbs took care of collecting it. About the many small tasks which they competed for to see who could get the most. About the peculiarities of the skippers and the girls selling on the dock. And about the maids and the elegant wives from Skeppsbron who came down to shop.

And about Annika. They could no longer go to meet her, and it was seldom that she went down to Fiskarhamnen on her way home. Once Thumbs had seen her with a flashy and horrible snob. Striped pants with skinny legs, a monocle and high hat. Papa's boy, probably, one of the crown princes of wealth. And Annika was actually dumb enough to believe that she would be accepted.

Thumbs kicked the boom so angrily that the boat almost lost its rhythm.

"One day we'll hang those swine from the masts," he hissed.

Thumbs took both shots of schnapps with his midnight meal. And Henning let him sleep while he, himself, watched over the weight on the boom and saw that the fish down in the tub got what they needed.

No, Annika didn't come. But sometimes Klara and Matilda stood on the floating dock and laughed at them. Then it seemed as if Thumbs had completely forgotten Annika, he could toss out impudent remarks that made Klara hiccup with laughter and Matilda blush. But despite Thumbs' assurances that their rhythm would be much better if the girls climbed on board, they never really dared let them do it. The skipper would surely not allow it.

On light evenings in June, they saw the city swept in a fine gray-blue veil. The night was just a mist on the water. From out of the mist they could hear voices: the sailors on a boat that had come in late, the last late-nighters reeling home from one of Stadsgården's many taverns.

One evening in July steamboats came loaded from Djurgården. Sharpshooters in uniform, finely dressed ladies and portly shopkeepers returned from the Poltava demonstration at Cirkus. They had protested against the tsar's trick of canceling all victory festivities except those in honor of the Battle of Poltava. It was an insult to the Swedish nation and now there would certainly be a collection of funds across the country in order to erect a statue to the Swedish hero-king. They were still grumbling about it; fists were raised, and someone whistled the march of the Björneborg Regiment.

And August: the nights turned black, the lamplighters came ever earlier and, as they made their rounds, one little blossom of light after another burst into flower. The stones swung in the dark, the wind became cooler, black water slapped against the sides of the boats.

Henning and Thumbs began to feel at home; they had come to the harbor, and there they would remain. It was no supervised workplace: they were a part of the harbor rowdies, the dock workers, despite what the old boat rockers imagined. They might hear that the harbor folk were a bunch of beggars and thieves, that the police could draw straws on who to detain without risk of making a mistake — no innocent could ever be hit upon.

The harbor life was tough, poorly paid, looked down on. But still there was a freedom that the factories and workshops couldn't offer. And despite all the filth, all the drinking and poverty, all the meanness and drudgery, there was adventure at hand in the harbor. Boats came from foreign cities; sailors told their stories; every day was a lottery where one man starved and the next one slaved.

They lay on a rolling boat full of fish and talked. They were no longer boys, they were men who had chosen their places in life.

II

THE PROMISE

The promise had been given: the door to a new era would open.

In the darkness of the December evening, crowds of people poured through the city streets, buzzing and cheering. The soldiers who had been called out were transformed suddenly from enemies to friends, and they were embraced and clapped on the back. Every person was now a friend and brother.

When the king came from the theater, they all rushed forward to unharness the horses and pull the carriage to the palace. But King Karl bawled out that he wanted his horses left where they were, so they sang the king's song instead and told how he loved his people so much that he didn't want any Swede doing slave labor for his sake. And they cheered again. All the windows of Operakälleren café were thrown open and many panes were smashed. The crush was as great inside as out, money was passed in through the windows, and bottles of arak liqueur lifted out. Speakers stood on the café tables and screamed praise-filled speeches without being able to make themselves heard. Until there was a shushing and the buzzing died down: *August Blanche is going to speak!*

He stood there, the peerless occasional speaker, round like a toad with his huge, bobbing belly, white wisps of hair fluttering around his shiny, florid face. Smiling and teary-eyed, assured and yet faltering in his gestures, the words tumbling over his lips. Hardly anyone could actually understand what he said, but it was something about Engelbrekt's fight with sullen noblemen and overbearing prelates. And the people, noble and unspoiled, who had been victorious that day. Blood would have run in the streets if the privileged hadn't given up their opposition. For the first time radical agitators and republicans wanted to propose a toast to a king.

They clinked glasses and cheered and dragged the speaker out with them; now they had to pay tribute to the founders of the reform with singing and cheering outside their homes.

Hoarse and tired, people slowly began to turn homeward, still transported by the wave, the sense that the time was young, that flowering promises would soon be turned into nourishing fruit.

A few young dock workers continued to sing on their way toward Söder, as if afraid to come down from their high.

But bitter opponents of reform hid from the shouting and jubilation, wondering if riff-raff and madmen would seize power now that the country was sinking down into democracy's deepest mire.

Some wondered perhaps why they cheered so wildly. What had actually transpired? Maybe the domination of lineage and title had been exchanged only for one still harsher: that of money. The door would open, but the threshold might be so high that only the well-to-do would be able to climb over it to participatory democracy.

Two dock workers stood beside Hammarby Lake and cheered one last time before they parted. They were young and their time had given a promise. It was enough that night.

DOORWAYS TO
THE EAST

The harbor was a dark archway opening onto a lighted stretch. The hillside rose over those who worked there, steep and black, and dilapidated wooden stairs climbed up toward the light. Warehouses, taverns and small industries pressed against the edge of the hill to make room for the jumble of goods and garbage on the wharf. Pens of swine and hens were piled between coffee bales, bundles of leather, and barrels of herring. Mounds of horse manure were heaped outside the public outhouses, and every night the city's waste was loaded onto latrine barges at Lokatt's Stairs. Small cargo boats lay tightly packed alongside the docks and wooden piers. Stevedores and sailors crowded together with oarswomen and washerwomen. From cookhouses smoke arose, from taverns clattering, from pigpens shrill screams, and from hatches the cries of foremen.

But beyond all the darkness and crowding lay the water, and it shone in the morning sun, a light blue and open thoroughfare to foreign lands and adventure.

A stench rose from the harbor. But the winds that always swept across the blue surface, that darted among Djurgården's green trees and Söder's dark stones, fanned away the worst of it and cooled the sweaty dock workers who toiled with their sacks and bales.

The harbor had awakened after a winter's sleep to the enormous rush of springtime. It hadn't been more than a week since the first boat had made its way in through the ice of the archipelago. Day after day the dock workers had gone out on the hill to look out. Wasn't spring coming and prospects for work? Day after day the downhearted men had to return to temporary work, hungry children and despairing women. No, not yet. And their women had begged in the shops for just a little more credit. Soon the boat, the work had to come.

And then it came. And the ugliest old hulk of a ship was a beautiful sight if it happened to be the first to arrive.

The foreman, who was called Heathen Dog, didn't have to go out to scan the horizon. He lived with his wife and dog up on the hill in an old summer house made of stone that was reached by an extension from Sista Styvern's Stairs.

Heathen Dog had four windows in his eight-sided house, and through all of them he could see out over the city and the harbor. From one of them he saw the sea approach, and that was where he sat during the early spring days and waited for a ship.

When the first boat came, and he'd had time to ascertain that it wasn't an optical illusion, he rushed down the stairs and hurried to the stevedore. Heathen Dog saw it as his particular mission to announce spring's arrival to his employer.

Suddenly every alley teemed with life. Now they were done with surviving on crumbs. The old fellows who had spent the winter at the workhouse, Träffen, hastily checked out and hurried to report to their foremen. Work crews were put back together, and one or another dock worker who had earlier had only piecemeal work could fill in the vacancies left by those who had died or disappeared over the winter. Those who no longer had access to the workhouse's beds tracked down the tried and true holes where they used to sleep: under the wooden quay and the stairs, in sheltered nooks on the hillside.

During breaks and stolen moments, they met once again at the many taverns, drank a glass for One-eyed Frasse who had died of drink and for Double-Olle who froze to death in a woodshed.

As was his custom, Heathen Dog put out a bottle and invited everyone on the team for a welcome drink.

For some years now, Henning had been part of the team. He and Thumbs had never become full-fledged boat rockers. Beckis had returned soon after and the craft had been too near dying out to give newcomers enough opportunities for work.

Henning was now twenty-one years old. He was still rather skinny; he was clearly never going to be anyone of great size and build. But his hands were weathered from heavy work, the sinews tough and durable, the muscles hard. Now he knew his work, his comrades, the city. As before, he still spent most of his time with Thumbs, even if they hadn't managed to get on the same team. He was still living at Bigsack's and sleeping on the floor, but now in against the wall where Annika had slept before she left home.

He nodded, shook hands. Here was his team, his comrades: Big Pain, Gränges, Fearsome, Grab-hold-here, Piglet and the others. No beauties exactly, tousled and ragged, full of lice and dirty. Lovely ladies and well-dressed gentlemen went out of their way to avoid coming too close. But comrades, people, brothers in the city and the world of the poor.

Now, when the ice's power was broken, the boats came close together. Spring and autumn were the harbor's peak seasons, that was when everything came to life. Now it wasn't a question of finding work, rather of keeping up with it.

The stevedore himself, the powerful Konrad Lundström, came down to urge them on.

"Work hard, you rascals, and you'll get a schnapps!" he bawled.

"Then we should get two," yelled Fearsome in reply.

"Go for it!" nodded Lundström. Time was valuable but aquavit was cheap.

Henning picked up his pace. During this shift he had a good job: strapping sacks. He drew the strap around the sack, slid in the hook, gave the signal that it was ready. He saw the sack above his head and hoped that they had a good hold up there, then threw himself onto the next one.

Often it happened that Henning paired up with Fearsome, a fifty-year-old dock worker, not at all as bad as the name implied. It was actually only his voice which instilled fear. Fearsome was especially favorably disposed toward Henning, not just because he usually got to have Henning's liquor. He liked the boy, and they also had an acquaintance in common: Klara. The girl had changed both career and residence. When the work at Barnängen became even more scarce, she had become a cigar maker and lived in the same house as Fearsome now, a ramshackle wooden house on Nytorget.

Fearsome heaved the sacks over, and Henning strapped them. The hours went by until it was time for a meal break. Fearsome wiped the sweat from his forehead and came out with an unexpected question: did Henning feel like coming to his wedding which would be celebrated at Pentecost?

Actually, Fearsome thought it was a damned nuisance. His woman, who was a washerwoman, worked for a clergyman sometimes as well. The priest's wife had figured out that Washer-Johanna wasn't married to her man, even though they had four children together. That had to be rectified. And Johanna didn't want to run afoul of the priest's wife. Klara and the other girls, as well as the guys for that matter, had been beside themselves, of course, when they had gotten such a fine reason to put together a party. Since women were so plentiful in the house, Fearsome thought he had better invite along a few more men. Otherwise they ran the risk that the women would fall on each other when they became drunk and horny, and start fighting over the men.

"Klara has nothing against you," said Fearsome, and gave Henning a nudge. "Although," he said, and wrinkled his forehead, "you'd better be careful."

Henning left work late that evening. Thumbs sat and waited on top of some sacks. Both of them felt rather tired out; the pace had been hard, and they still weren't quite used to it. Slowly they climbed Söder's stairs, and the city fell farther and farther away beneath them: cargo boats and steamboats, Skeppsbron's houses, the Citadel's towers, and the evening-pale water.

Up on the hill Klara and Matilda stood and waited. Their wide, heavy skirts flapped slowly, and the wind played among their shawls and hair. As soon as the girls caught sight of Henning and Thumbs, they began to walk away, pretending that they had just been passing by. But the two dock workers quickly caught up with the girls, and together they climbed down to the path in the valley between the hills.

Klara hadn't completely abandoned them even though she had moved. Perhaps she came mostly for Matilda's sake. Klara was kind in her careless way. At times she remembered Matilda and showed up unexpectedly, took Matilda out whether she wanted to go or not.

It was also good to be two. A girl alone was a challenge, an invitation. Two was an adventure, a game. And Klara liked to play, thought it was fun when they had gotten a little string of boys after them. She also wanted Matilda along when it came to teasing the dyer. But Matilda never wanted to do that, she felt only afraid of him. Since Klara had moved out, the dyer's apprentice, Johansson, had become even more insistent in his attentions. Matilda had trouble protecting herself. His eye was always there in the light, his hand in the dark.

Klara wanted to talk to Henning about the wedding. Matilda and Thumbs weren't invited, of course. Henning had to pay his share ahead of time, as they were going to pool their resources for the party.

They walked behind Thumbs and Matilda, and Henning saw how his friend who had so recently been tired and sluggish became enlivened by her company. Thumbs' hand closed over Matilda's, he almost lifted her over the sewage ditches. Suddenly Matilda laughed and Henning thought how he had never heard her laugh before. He liked hearing it and felt simultaneously a pang of envy; it was Thumbs who made the girls laugh.

At the same time he was happy for Thumbs' and Matilda's sake. Thumbs had gone on missing Annika for a long time, had become bitter. Annika had disappeared, had never come home to Bigsack. From Strömparterren Café she had moved on to the Pohlsro on Djurgården. Where she had gone then, they didn't know. Perhaps she was still waiting on tables somewhere, perhaps she had succeeded in becoming some rich man's mistress.

In any case, Thumbs had been abandoned. Annika hadn't wanted to condemn herself to the miserable life of the poor for his sake. Henning didn't begrudge Thumbs and Matilda the laughter and happiness they could get.

For an instant he felt a little envious, he would have also liked to joke like that with Matilda. But now he walked with Klara, and she placed her hand resolutely under his arm and led him as if she were making off with the loot.

That wedding was one that nobody who attended would forget.

Fearsome had borrowed an old frock coat from a coachman. Washer-Johanna had been done up in a white veil over her black dress. And Fearsome told all who wanted to hear what remarkably delicate things she wore under it. Johanna had borrowed from the gentry's clothing she had as laundry. It had been a little difficult to put together appropriate witnesses, none of their friends had suitable clothes. Finally Johanna had even solved this problem with the help of her washing. Klara and the young daughter of another washerwoman in the house had been rigged up according to the same recipe. Klara ran around and tried to find mirrors that were big enough.... She felt sorry for herself: it was just her fate not to get to see how beautiful she was the one time in her life that she had on a gentlewoman's dress.

Oh, Klara was a dream, assured Washer-Johanna. The crinoline that swayed like a cloud around her, lustrous, foamy blue. She could borrow a fine little shawl to lay across her bare throat. And washerwoman Malin's daughter all in white! Good Lord, who would have guessed that the girls were so beautiful! But as soon as they came home, they had to be good and take off the finery again. They couldn't eat or dance in the borrowed feathers, for who would be able to replace them if they got ruined?

The bridal couple and the witnesses paraded off, and the others made everything ready for the party. The sun shone over the back yard that lay well hidden by sheltering houses and wooden fences. Luckily the weather was so fine that they could set up tables outside. The keg of aquavit stood on a table by itself, the beer kegs on sawhorses. They placed a whole barrel of splendid herring in the middle of the table. Cumin cheese and smoked sausages were brought out, lard and plenty of bread. They weren't going to hold back on anything. The cigar-maker girls watched across the table while the dock workers placed planks on sawhorses. The musician lay on the grassy slope and rested up before his approaching labors. The bridal couple's children scampered between the tables and tried to sneak food, but were driven mercilessly away.

The couple took their time. The priest had certainly had many admonishing words for them. Now, finally! Followed by a caravan of curious onlookers who had filed out to see the pomp. Did they really think that old Washer-Johanna was going to make herself available for a more thorough showing of the bride?

The bridal couple and the witnesses rushed in, and the bridegroom was obliged to hurry and lock out all uninvited well-wishers. There wasn't that much food and aquavit! A few pounded on the door, others climbed up to see over the fence. Angry voices answered back that this was a completely private affair.

The chosen ones welcomed the center of the festivities with cries of joy and music. Henning stood there in the crowd, waved at Fearsome, was amazed by Klara's elegance. But he looked mostly perhaps at the girl in white, Washer-Malin's daughter. A small girl, dark and slender, almost hidden behind the prancing Klara. He thought he'd seen her before some time, yet he knew it was the first time.

"Now you have to change your clothes, girls, before we start the party," said the bride, motherly and authoritatively. The little washerwoman's daughter slipped away quickly, but Klara protested.

"We can surely wash the dress if something happens," she said.

"It is washed," declared the bride.

Klara had to content herself with one last turn around the yard, strutted round with swollen sails, lifted the thin shawl and looked admiringly at her breasts arching out from the low décolletage, and sighed.

"Pull in your skirts on the stairs!" called out the bride anxiously. And Klara made a grand farewell gesture and wandered up to the attic room to become herself again.

There was a line in front of the aquavit keg, one little bleach measure had to do as a schnapps glass for twenty people. Beer was drunk from cups and scoops. The herring was grabbed with their hands from the large cask on the table: the skull twisted off, one finger disappeared into the dark entrails and hooked onto the innards that were ripped out. After that it was only a matter of eating it right up and spitting the bones under the table.

They ate and drank, were in such a hurry that they began before the witnesses had had time to change. Then the washerwoman's daughter came down the stairs and looked around for a seat. There was a space beside Henning. He had ended up a little on the fringes.

The girl slid across the board and sat down.

"This is free, isn't it?"

He nodded. "Shall I get you a herring?" he asked.

He took one with his fingers, like the others, and placed the herring before her. He saw a fork hidden somewhere on the table and gave it to her. She smiled gratefully but wondered if he couldn't find a knife as well.

Her name was Lotten and she was eighteen years old. She worked in a glove factory. She was no longer a dream but, the reality was also beautiful to look at: the girl in her simple dark skirt, the white blouse.

"Now we ask them to dance, boys!" bawled out Fearsome.

Henning hesitated, he was a bad dancer, had only done it a few times.

"We can at least try," said Lotten. And soon the dust from the gravel stood like a cloud round the dancing couples and the table with the leftovers and half-empty plates.

They danced that night. Danced as long as the poor musician could manage to saw on his fiddle. They danced past that point too, then they had to sing along themselves.

One after another, the guests dropped off, sank down on the grassy slope and snored. Someone threw up in the archway to the street; someone turned on the tap for aquavit one more time; someone built up their thirst with yet one more salt herring. Someone groaned desperately in the privy; someone passed water behind the woodshed. The bride stood in the attic window and surveyed the battlefield, unlaced the corset she had borrowed, tucked in the children. Fearsome rubbed a spot on his frock coat, and Klara sat on the knees of two heavy-handed longshoremen who pinched her bottom and squeezed her breasts while she shrieked with laughter.

Lotten began to be worried. She had been to parties in the yard before and knew that most of the participants got drunk and crazy, that some wanted to fight and others to rape. She could go upstairs and try to lock herself in, but the latch would give at the first powerful tug. Actually, she didn't want to go in either, she and Henning had had such a nice, quiet time together in the midst of the din.

"Shall we walk a ways?" Henning dared ask.

She nodded.

They walked along the narrow Nya gatan in among the White Hills. Small houses slumbered between bushes and rock outcroppings, in the east the sky began to glow with the sun. When they stood silent they could hear bellowing and shrieks from the yard where the wedding was held.

Henning helped Lotten up onto the edge of the hill, kept her hand in his after they got up. Looked at her furtively, thought how beautiful she had been in that white dress. She was pretty now too, and he knew now why he imagined he recognized her: she resembled Kerstin from the candle factory. Or at least his memory of Kerstin.

When they got back to the house at Nytorget, the brawling had died down. Henning threw open the door and made way for Lotten. She took a step forward, but then they both stopped. On the gravel between the barrels and the table, on the grass slope, everywhere, people lay on each other and slept. The herring barrel had overturned during the dancing, and the brine still dripped down onto the gravel. A joker had stuffed a big herring inside Klara's unbuttoned blouse, it peered out like a sharp-nosed rat. The tap on the aquavit keg stood open; the keg had long since been emptied.

The sun shone cruelly and mercilessly down over the yard, and Henning and Lotten stood in the archway and looked at the havoc, the grandiose misery of the festivities of the poor. There was no reason to stay here; the first thing that would be heard upon someone's awakening would be the cry for more aquavit. Whoever had an öre would have to sacrifice it.

"Let's go," whispered Lotten.

They walked down to Hammarby Lake and borrowed a rowboat. With sure strokes Henning rowed out into the sunshine, rested on the oars, listened to the refreshing rippling round the bow. They went ashore on the Sickla side, pulled up the boat and sat on the edge of the beach.

"You were so beautiful in that white dress," he said and looked at her. "Didn't you like it?"

She shook her head.

"I only felt afraid," she said. "I didn't want to wear it. What if whoever owned the dress had seen me. You should be who you are and not pretend."

"You're just as pretty like this," he hurried to say.

Then Lotten laughed and lay down in the grass.

"Let's go to sleep now," she said.

But he lay there a long time and looked at her and thought how strange it was: he hadn't even known her twenty-four hours and already it felt like they were old friends. Now she lay here and slept securely beside him.

At last he drifted off to sleep, too. When he awoke he was alone. He flew up, looked around, took a few steps in the direction of the boat. Then he saw her, framed in a bower of greenery. With carefully drawn up skirts, she was standing at the water's edge wetting her feet.

QUARTET AND SOLO

The angry bite of a bedbug woke him. Henning scratched himself automatically and sleepily. His glance wandered around the room in the morning gloom. It was caught by a light glimmer from the corner by the door: white nightgowns, bare arms. The insufferable heat had made Matilda and Augusta, Bigsack's foster daughter, throw off their blanket, those two lay in the same bed now.

Someone watched over the sleepers, as if his eyes were glued to them. The dyer was awake.

Henning lay silently and observed him, watched over the watcher. Ever since Klara had moved out, there was no longer anyone who willingly and gladly crept from one bed to the other. Astonished, the dyer had to acknowledge that Matilda said no even to what he thought were dizzyingly inflated sums. The dyer had been forced to go in search of Wagtail, who had long since moved out of Bigsack's lodgings. She received visitors in the bushes out on the hillside, it was both uncomfortable and unworthy of an established man. Besides, it was risky. It was true that Wagtail was responsible for check-ups and was examined once a week at the bureau, but sooner or later she would be infected and would end up at the sanitorium. No, he really missed Klara.

My girls, thought the dyer sorrowfully as he sat up in bed. He had seen Augusta grow up. She was only six or seven when he moved in. Now she was sixteen. Before she had certainly not been shy of him, that child. The other one though, Matilda ... whined when you poked her, sneaked off with her rags of clothing like that holy Mamsell Tornberg.

In the newspaper he had read that various experts on immorality said that hardly any girls from the lower classes were chaste, that practically speaking all of them could be bought. Lies, he thought bitterly.

My girls .... He leaned forward carefully, with a finger he brushed aside a few strands of Augusta's hair. Then he got up and slipped outside to relieve himself on the front porch. The morning was lovely, the girls lovely. Still, life was dreary.

Henning had been so occupied with the dyer's morning business that he had almost forgotten his own. It was, of course, Sunday and plans had been made far in advance. He flew up from the mattress, pulled on his pants. Padded across the floor, shook Matilda carefully. She woke up, groped with her hand after the missing blanket.

"Oh, it's you," she said. And the blanket was no longer as important. She sat up in bed. Augusta also opened her eyes and blinked, half-awake.

"Has the old guy gone?'" wondered Matilda.

"He's standing on the steps," Henning answered. If they listened they could hear the sound of his stream on the gravel and the grass just outside.

Matilda got quickly out of bed, wanted to take the opportunity to get dressed if possible while the dyer was out. But Augusta, who didn't have any pre-arranged meeting, pulled up the blanket and lay down again. She watched the other two a little enviously. She wondered what she could find to do. She had not been allowed to keep one penny of her wages this week either. Just the opposite, her foster father had complained over her not having full-time work at the factory. He thought she should get herself an extra income.

As soon as she stepped inside the door, he was reaching out his hand and taking her purse, counting the sums. He threatened with beatings. She'd had her ears boxed a couple of times before he accepted her account of how many hours she had worked that week.

Augusta shook off the memory, crawled under the blanket and hid. The dyer came in, stealthily as always. Matilda, who stood with her back to the door, noticed him too late and didn't have time to move before he touched her. Displeased, he grunted at the silly girl who so clearly took offense.

Henning and Matilda came out from the gloominess of the room and the vestibule into the sunshine and stopped, blinded. It took them a moment before they saw Thumbs who stood at the gate to the street trying to spit at the hens that wandered past.

None of them owned a watch, which was why meeting times could never be that exact. It was morning, afternoon or evening; it was early or not too early, or late or not too late.

Lotten was to watch through the window of the old wooden house on Nytorget. Already from the distance they saw her, and before they reached the gate she had made it down to the street.

Henning listened for the sound inside him. Every time she arrived it was as if something clicked inside him. He could feel it, couldn't it also be heard? He never quite figured out what it was, just that when it made itself felt, it was too late for him to listen for it.

"What luck we're having with the weather," Lotten said. Henning looked at the sun and the cloud-free sky one more time and nodded: they were lucky. He was lucky. How had he managed, clumsy and shy as he was? It had just suddenly happened that Lotten was his girl, that they met, went together. Without anything really being said, anything that made it official. At times he felt gripped by anxiety, wondering if she would disappear as quickly as she came. Shouldn't he bind her to him, or at least come down to a clear decision: yes or no? But he was so afraid of a no that he didn't dare ask for a yes.

Thumbs had naturally arranged the day's program. He had a unique and expensive habit: every day he bought a newspaper. Usually it was *Dagens Nyheter,* which was cheapest, it cost five öre. Henning could borrow the newspaper. Mostly it never happened, after the day's work he felt like he didn't have the energy to read.

Thanks to the newspaper, Thumbs became something of a news bureau. He knew of everything that happened in town and had ideas and opinions about almost everything. He talked about the liberal workers' organizations, but thought they seemed too spineless, or about the parliamentary elections which had come into being after the old system of class representation had ended. But that was a mockery since the line was drawn to include only the wealthy, and the poor didn't have a chance to make themselves heard. He'd talk about the Civil War in America and the dangerous Scandinavists who wanted to throw Sweden into war, and on *internationality, forward progress* and *revolution.*

Or perhaps he would talk about the whale that they should see; you could walk through a lighted room inside the whale. And they should also try to catch a glimpse of the Chinese, the people with real yellow skin that were guests in town and were staying at the Rydberg Hotel. But the big industrial exhibition that filled the whole park at Kungsträdgården, and was the real reason for the whale's and the Chinese people's visits to the capital, they couldn't see that no matter how badly they wanted to. The entry fee was way too high, a whole two dollars per person.

Their Sunday outing would consist more of the whalefish and the Chinese. Perhaps also a Lapp woman and a tame "sealdog," if they could afford more than the twelve shillings that the whale cost. Both the misshapen Lapp woman and sealdog were pictured in the newspaper. Thumbs showed them the advertisements so they could pick and choose.

They walked through the city that was still wrapped in its Sunday morning slumber. They passed Slussen and glanced sideways at the gloom of Stadsgården with its memory of workdays. They followed Västerlånggatan where the girls had to look in so many windows and where heavy odors were already beginning to rise from the gutters.

They were on their way and a long day off awaited. The sun shone, they were young. Forward progress, thought Thumbs. He put his arm around Matilda's waist, and she felt a little awkward at first — what would people think? But she didn't see anybody who would think there was anything wrong with it, so it felt all right and she may have even leaned a little closer to Thumbs.

Henning saw them, felt the pang of envy again: Thumbs dared. He wanted to force himself to be just as daring. But he satisfied himself with taking Lotten's hand in his, and she held on willingly, and hand-in-hand they walked past Norrbro's bazaars.

By that time the dyer had already sat for a long time on the edge of Augusta's bed. Couldn't he very carefully feel how soft her skin was? Like a little cat: kitty, kitty. The damp hand slipped under the blanket. The girl shuddered but didn't dare scream. Tried only to get farther away until the wall stopped her. Then she was stuck. "Nothing bad," he whispered, "nothing at all." And she would get a whole twelve shilling piece, just because he liked to stroke the little kitty.

Tears streamed down, and she bit her lips to not cry out loud. Otherwise her foster father might come and beat her because she didn't want to earn an extra income.

The dyer wasn't sure what Bigsack would think and say. He wondered: could he ask outright? The girl was only a foster child. But it was probably safest to keep quiet for now.

Then he heard that they were awake in the bedroom, that the windows were being opened. Quickly he pulled his hand back. Got up, wiped his sleeve across his mouth, disappeared to the outhouse. On the way back he ran into the girl in the vestibule, she was dressed but still red-eyed. The dyer remembered his promise and pulled the large purse out of his pants pocket. The promise had to be kept if he was going to renew it.

After he had gone, Augusta stood there, looked through the fog of tears at the coin. Even though she hated the dyer and wanted to throw away the coin, she understood it would help make it easier for her the next time she was held accountable.

Augusta rubbed the coin so it shone and went to find a really safe place to hide it until she had to report her earnings.

They were out way too early for the city's amusements, nothing opened until after the church services. But they had planned on spending the morning on Djurgården, and there they found a sheltered slope where they could spread their blanket. They half lay among the bottles and sandwiches, small streaks of sun slipping through the oaks' greenery. Thumbs had found a blade of grass, sat bent over Matilda and stroked it across her cheek. She tried to free herself, but he held her, looked into her eyes until Matilda cast down her gaze and blushed.

"Come," he said, "I'll show you something down at the beach."

He held out his hand, pulled her up, Henning watched them. Before the trees hid them, Thumbs had pulled Matilda to him and kissed her. And Matilda didn't let it just happen, but was going along with it so clearly, answering back.

Confused, Henning looked at Lotten, wondered how he would dare, what she must be thinking.

"Shall we walk a little, too?" he asked.

She looked up, smiled. A little slyly?

"Why not?" said Lotten.

He helped her up, as Thumbs had helped Matilda. But he didn't get his arm around her waist, and he didn't stop and kiss her. Instead, they came rather quickly down to the beach, obviously far ahead of Thumbs and Matilda. Lotten felt the water and wiped off her wet hand on his cheek. That couldn't go unpunished, he had to find some way to get her back. He wet his hand too, but then she ran away and he had to hurry to catch up with her. Between the trees she had trouble getting through with her wide skirts, and there he caught her and suddenly she was just in his arms. He held her but she turned her face away and his lips grazed her ear.

When she resisted she was hard and angular. Now she became unexpectedly soft. The arm that had kept him away came around his neck, the hand that had pushed him off pulled his face closer.

They met. Mouth to mouth, hand to hand, breast to breast. Everything was so natural, as if it had happened before, as if no fear or uncertainty existed. And at the same time so new, so untried and fantastic.

"Lotten," he only said.

"We," she said, "we will stay together."

And he felt that we, that jubilant we. Like when he met Thumbs, the joy of togetherness. Then it had been friendship's, now it was love's. Life wasn't poor, he didn't have to be afraid.

"Are you sure you want to?"

Lotten nodded seriously.

"I wanted it the first time we saw each other. If you had ... yes, if you had wanted to kiss me then you could have. Though I hardly knew you."

"Would you have wanted that?"

She thought a moment.

"I'm glad you waited," she said. "Till we knew for sure. Otherwise I might have thought you did that with all the girls."

He kissed her again. Trembled when he felt her against him, when he could feel her body, soft and alive under all the clothes.

"They may be waiting for us," said Lotten and smoothed her hair. Her cheeks glowed red and she was breathing rapidly.

They walked back to where they had eaten. Thumbs and Matilda hadn't come yet. Lotten sat with her back against a tree trunk; Henning lay down with his head in her lap. They sat that way until they heard steps, then they moved a little away from each other.

Thumbs and Matilda came. And Matilda was strangely red too and Thumbs unusually quiet. He helped Matilda sit down, he fussed with the picnic basket.

Then Thumbs looked at the other three, and burst into laughter. And suddenly they were laughing out loud, all four.

Arm in arm they walked back toward the city. Now it wasn't really so important to see the advertised wonders, the greatest wonder was inside themselves. But the program was meant to be followed, and maybe it was safest to.

They didn't begin to wend their way back toward Söder until twilight began to fall.

The street lamps gleamed between the trees at Strömparterren. Henning thought about the time when he and Thumbs had stood here in the evenings and waited for Annika. And how he and Matilda had walked here after that night on Uggleviken, since Thumbs had lingered in the woods with Klara. Henning might have had plans for Matilda then. He liked Matilda. But he loved Lotten. Difficult, new words. He hardly dared think about it, it was too big, too happy. As if he could lose everything in a moment's recklessness.

But Thumbs told the story about how Strömparterren got seltzer arak liqueur. They happened to distill it when the current was going upstream. The girls may have heard the story before, but they laughed willingly.

At Nytorget they parted, Henning was going to see Lotten home. When he said good-bye one last time, he crossed the street and stood there until he saw her wave from the window.

Then he walked, light as a feather, without a thought for tomorrow's heavy sacks and strenuous labor.

Back home in her room, Matilda was going to bed, her bare arms and white gown shimmered in the dusk. The dyer snored slowly. On the floor lay two dark shadows, Bigsack's son and a new boarder. Augusta had apparently not come yet, otherwise everyone was in their place.

It had already gotten late before Augusta came. For several hours she had sat hidden in the woodshed, wanting to be sure that everyone was asleep.

Now she no longer had the strength to cry and brood any longer. She had stood for a long time down by the lake and thought she would drown herself, that it would be easiest that way. But she hadn't had enough courage. Crying, she had crept back to life.

Why hadn't she gone farther off this morning? She hadn't thought that she had anywhere to go, had felt herself miserably alone. Just walked up on the hill and sat there, trying to hide herself in a crevice. Then the dyer had come. Anxiously she had drawn away, didn't dare do what he wanted and didn't dare refuse either. Perhaps he had misunderstood her. In any case, he had come closer while he increased the promised compensation. He had gone up to a whole riksdaler before he couldn't restrain himself any longer, and she hadn't had the strength to resist anymore.

Afterward Dyer Johansson had seemed afraid. Afraid of what he had done and of her crying. He had given Augusta his soap and asked her to wash herself very carefully, and forced the money on her.

She hadn't dared to die. She hadn't even thrown away the money.

Shaking, the girl huddled in bed, tried to console herself by thinking she would avoid a beating since she had money to pad her wages with in a couple of weeks. And for a moment she thought: I'll get more money, the worst is over, and maybe I'll avoid beatings if it continues.

Still, she hated her snoring benefactor, would have liked to sneak into the bedroom, take the large carving-knife and stick it into his breast. But she didn't dare look at him. She fell asleep, sighing.

Heavy with fragrances, with dreams and weeping, the summer night rested over the small houses along the lake.

AUGUST WASHING

Before the clock had struck two and before the first hint of daylight could be seen, the laundresses got up so as to have time to do their work. Washer-Johanna groaned with the effort when she went to get out of bed without crushing the children to pieces, her chest heaving like a bellows. Anxiously she eyed the children, was always terrified that she may have lain on and smothered one of the younger ones. But they slept on peacefully and didn't seem to have suffered any injuries.

Washer-Malin in the room next door had an easier time of it. She didn't have any of Johanna's formless flesh to carry but was instead small and thin. Besides, they were only two in her room, and they had paid for the luxury of each having their own bed. Lotten could sleep undisturbed when her mother got up; she still had a few more hours of rest.

Malin lit the oil lamp, turning it as low as possible. In the dim glow she saw her daughter's face. The girl was so young and unspoiled still. Of course, she toiled and had hard work, didn't get to eat what she needed, didn't have clothes to make her beautiful. Malin hadn't forgotten how well that borrowed white dress had suited her at Johanna's wedding. Whatever might happen, Lotten would surely have a white dress when she was a bride. Craziness, of course. Customs that didn't suit poor people. But when Malin had seen Lotten in white, she had made up her mind, and ever since carefully put aside a few öre now and then. The money that she couldn't pretend to have when hard times came.

Lotten. Her mother went a step closer, shone the lamp on her. Without her daughter saying anything, Malin knew that the girl was happy now, that she was in love. Love was a rare gift to the poor, it was as if they couldn't afford to accept it. Most often it was just circumstances and a moment's deplorable hunger that drove people together in the darkness. People lived under such crowded conditions and

young men could grow so impatient, that at times the girl had barely
had time to wake up before it was over. Overworked and tired, the
girls lacked the power to resist; the boys lost their feelings of responsibility. And the confusion in the living arrangements of the poor
drove everyone close together, all shyness disappeared, children became audiences for the adults' coarse necking and impoverished sexu-
al acts and imitated them as best they could. She had seen Washer-
Johanna's and the cigar maker's children in the courtyard, how they
had tumbled about between the currant bushes.

Malin had wanted to protect her daughter. She had carried double
loads so that they could get their own room. She had tried to keep the
girl healthy and clean and free of lice, had taken Lotten with her to
work when she was little, tried to keep her from the children in the
yard. But you never could know. Perhaps Lotten would become a leaf
in the wind, she like the others.

But now the girl was happy. And the mother stood with the lamp
by her bed, glad and anxious at the same time. Happiness always caus-
es worry, happiness and sorrow are so close to each other. Only the
person who has once been happy can become truly unhappy.

That boy, thought Malin. She knew his name, knew what he
looked like. A longshoreman. The trade wasn't the best, if one listened
to what people said. But she knew many of the men from the harbor
and most were honorable and decent even if they drank a lot. What
man didn't? And he, Henning, had been one of the few sober ones at
the big wedding.

No, she couldn't stand and ponder while work waited. She should
go out, and she might manage to save a few more öre for that dress.
Lotten's wedding. Would it be Henning? One should hope so since
the girl obviously wanted it. Hope, a mother could do no more. But
the person who remained unmarried probably had it best, that person
avoided a lot of cares.

The two washerwomen had already borrowed a wheelbarrow the day
before and carted the wash down to the washhouse at Stadsgården.

They'd had to make a couple of trips, Malin had pulled and Johanna pushed. The sun had been shining and Johanna had perspired so that her whole dress had turned dark. Now the heat of the washhouse awaited them.

Malin took out the bread and the tall, one-eared stone jug. She made sure that she had a string to hang the jug by, that the granulated coffee was in the bottom of the jug and that the sugar cubes were in her apron pocket. She opened the door and knocked carefully on Johanna's door. She was ready, and she rolled out through the door panting strenuously, even though work hadn't yet begun. Luckily it was downhill most of the way to Stadsgården.

Soon the fire was blazing under the wash cauldrons, steam shrouded the house in a white mist, rows of laundresses stood stirring, each surrounded by her own washing. Malin poured water in the stone jug and lowered it down into the vat. It didn't take long before the coffee boiled, and they could each have their first cup. It was coffee that held them up, that gave them the right to small breaks in their work, cheered them, made life worth living.

Around dinner time they took the laundry out to the beating dock. Johanna swore and quarreled with a boat skipper who had anchored too near. But the skipper just laughed and the washerwomen had to crowd together, trying to find a free space. They swung the wooden paddles in time. Both were known for being good laundresses and, careful of their reputation, they never let anything go half-clean. The genteel ladies wouldn't need to complain: the wash would be clean.

In the harbor all around them the longshoremen labored. The stevedore bosses screamed their orders; measurers and weighers called out their measurements and weights to customs men and bookkeepers who sat with their books. Drovers hollered at stray cows; herring packers pried open barrels of herring to take samples of size and quality; bacon packers nailed down the lids of crates of bacon where the salt shone white.

A team of stevedores from the Lundström firm was in the process of unloading cane sugar from a large West Indian sailing ship. The vessel was too big to pass through the locks and make its way to the sugar refinery on the south shore of Lake Mälar. So the cargo had to be brought ashore to be put on barges later. The sugar was packed in enormous chests, longer than a man's length and weighing up toward two hundred kilos. The men fastened large hooks around the chests which were then hoisted with winches out of the cargo hold.

When it was time for the dinner break, those who had the shift in the cargo hold came up, among them were Fearsome and Henning. They passed by the washing dock where the women lay and pounded and sweated in the sun. Fearsome stopped to say a few words to his wife, Johanna. Henning lingered a little way off, satisfied with saying hello from a distance.

Washer-Malin looked thoughtfully at the boy. She had never done more than say hello to him. At the wedding he had sat far away from her, and she had gone up to her room early, much too worn out to participate. Later she had seen him standing and waiting for Lotten, from the window she had seen how he and Lotten walked off together.

She should know something about her daughter's choice.

"I would like to speak a few words with him," said Malin and nodded toward Henning.

He started, became nervous. Did she want to forbid him from seeing Lotten? Maybe she thought that a longshoreman was too common?

"I'll take an extra little break," said Malin. "And I'll offer Nilsson a cup of coffee — that way he won't have to go into that dirty tavern." Malin got up nimbly and left Johanna to guard the wash. And Johanna nodded and understood, she had also seen Lotten and Henning together.

"She should be glad if someone like Henkan chooses her daughter," grumbled Fearsome. Johanna hushed him, he shouldn't get mixed up in this. The very least a mother could expect was to speak to her daughter's suitor.

"If she doesn't talk nicely then I'll be damned if I don't speak up too," said Fearsome.

The skinny little Malin walked first to the washhouse. Henning followed her, he had to practically run.

"Wait a moment," she said at the door. "I'm just going to lower the bottle where someone's washing."

He wasn't familiar with her methods of boiling coffee and didn't understand what she meant but stayed obediently. She only took a minute, pulled him by his shirt sleeve and said: "We can sit on the steps while the coffee's boiling."

"So, Nilsson likes Lotten?" she began, and observed him the whole time.

"Yes," he said and looked her squarely in the eye to assure her and to fight back any eventual opposition.

"And both are in agreement, he and Lotten?"

"Yes, we're in agreement," he said and wondered if she had asked Lotten too.

"Is he all alone?" the older woman continued.

"Yes." He told her about his life, his years in the city. In just a few words, as briefly as possible.

"He has work," she said and it wasn't exactly a question, she knew after all. He told how he was permanent on the stevedore team, it wasn't just a temporary job but guaranteed work.

"Then I'll get the coffee," Lotten's mother said and got up.

It wasn't until a few days later that he saw Lotten. The usual foursome was going on a Saturday outing.

Thumbs had gotten some rope. They had learned: a longshoreman's girl had the right to swing. A man who carried a lot of heavy loads developed muscles and really knew the art of swinging a girl. Now it was time to let Matilda and Lotten know just whose girls they were.

They met at the clothes beating dock by Barnängen. Thumbs with oars, rope and a bottle. Matilda and Lotten with food and blankets. Henning with the beer basket. And a guitar that he had bought cheap from a bird catcher. Would it work? Henning wondered, the man was probably a swindler: he supposedly caught sparrows, painted them yellow and sold them as canaries.

Henning had felt a little tense before his meeting with Lotten. The conversation with her mother had meant that everything was decided, that he was accepted. Now they were one, their future in common. They should probably get married. That's what her mother wanted, otherwise it wasn't unusual that people were satisfied with just moving in together. But that was a formality and not what really mattered.

Lotten looked at him. As if in complicity? Her mother had told her, of course. He could see by her look. He must get hold of Lotten's hand, press it, feel how she pressed it back.

"Was mother difficult?" she whispered.

He shook his head.

"She liked you," said Lotten.

But Thumbs was waiting with the boat.

They glided between the yellow-green shores of August, between lily pads that slowly rocked around the boat. Music and song could be heard from the islands. Lotten let her hand trail in the water, small eddies played between her fingers.

They found a point that was free of people and glided in. The girls set up the picnic in the grass while Henning and Thumbs looked for the right trees for the swings: two mighty oaks with enormous branches. And then the girls got to swing till their skirts stood like parasols around them, and they screamed like sirens.

By then it was already becoming dusk. Evening was a dark, warm blanket that swiftly spread over them. Thumbs pulled some stones together. Henning broke sticks and made a pile. A little fire glimmered from out of the darkness, lit up their faces.

The water lapped dark and soft along the edge of the shore.

"Let's go in," said Thumbs.

They stood at the water's edge, all four. Lotten felt the water with her hand, it was warm.

The boys went behind some bushes and undressed, jumped in. They saw the girls like white spots on the beach: billowing shadows, large white skirts and camisoles that were pulled off. They swam out, not wanting to disturb them. But they turned when they heard splashing and calling. They swam closer, saw the girls' faces shining like light-colored balls on the dark water, sensed the light-colored bodies under the water's surface. For a moment they glided into each other, were happy together in the evening's warmth and the water's coolness.

"You can swim out while we go ashore," commanded Lotten. Henning and Thumbs obeyed without protest and went out a distance one last time before they slowly turned back to shore.

They fed the fire with new sticks and it caught on and warmed them after their swim. Still, it felt good to sit huddled together, two and two. They pulled the blankets that the girls had brought around them. And their love dwelled in the small tents they raised, while they whispered softly to each other, love found its way.

Silently the boat moved forward toward the small lights, glided in toward the pier. Silently they walked to the house. They stopped: somewhere far off some people laughed and shouted in a boat. And suddenly, close by them, someone started screaming in distress.

Thumbs took a few hasty steps. Yet it was Matilda who got there first, stood in front of the couple who were wrestling on the grassy embankment.

"Augusta!" she cried.

The wrestling ceased quickly. The girl got up, shaken with sobs. The dyer got up also, confused and fumbling, searching for explanations. But he didn't have a chance to say very much before Thumbs had taken hold of him and thrown him like a sack over his back. He carried the struggling and protesting man out onto the dock, heaved him over his shoulder so that he went down in the water with a giant splash.

"I can't swim!" screamed the dyer.

"Put your legs down and walk to shore," snarled Thumbs.

Matilda took care of Augusta. The girl cried all the way home, told how she had gone along with the dyer's suggestions for a while but that she now neither wanted to nor could do it any longer. She understood that she had committed a grave sin. Before she might have been able to claim ignorance, but not anymore. The feeling of sin had driven her to the mission house up on the hill. She had let herself be converted. Now she had wanted to explain this to the dyer, get him to leave her alone, perhaps influence him to convert. But he had become enraged and tried to rape her.

The four of them stayed outside and whispered in the yard after Augusta had gone inside. While the dyer crouched shivering in the bushes and wondered how long it would take until he could go in the house and get out of his wet clothes.

A couple of days later he moved out. Bigsack tried to question him but didn't get any clear answer. Wondering, he glared at Augusta, as if he suspected some connection. Week after week Bigsack had to grimly declare that neither threats nor blows could induce the girl to get the extra income she had apparently had for a while. She was obviously tricking him somehow. He growled furiously at her martyred expression, and when he found out that she had become a pietist, he was so upset that he first threatened to throw her out, and then he went out himself to get drunk at the tavern.

He hit her a lot during the following weeks. Until his own son, Augusta's foster brother of the same age, slammed a frying pan down on his head. The boy disappeared the same evening, and Augusta too. They didn't come back. Now there were only the two youngest children left at home, and Bigsack's wife went around crying to herself. Then she got mad, snapped and let fly at her husband. Bigsack fingered the lump he had received and felt misunderstood and wretched. He complained about the new times, children had no respect for their parents anymore. It didn't help to make an effort, to try to bring them up. Just as well to drink and shut up.

So he drank.

REFUGEES

The last vessel had disappeared from the harbor, fled for the winter. Slowly, the dock workers left labor's joy and curse, lingering as long as they could at the taverns, bidding farewell to their comrades, to fixed wages, to daily routine. At Träffen a small line formed of those who wanted to register for the winter.

In the house beside Hammarby Lake, Bigsack sat in front of the fire where the remains of some wooden boards smoldered. The enormous man trembled with anxiety. Now while he had plenty of time, he looked for and watched the small signs nervously. He knew the rule: a coal bearer never reaches more than fifty years of age. Then he dies, worn out, destroyed.

Bigsack was already fifty-seven, had been given seven years of grace. He was also a strong man of unusual dimensions, could not be worn down so quickly. But during this past autumn, he'd had a harder and harder time of keeping up. He had been short of breath and his hands had shaken. Of course, he had been drinking heavily, the same as the others. Neglected himself, maybe. But wasn't that what you had to do to cope with living?

He was losing hold of his powers. Really, he was losing hold of life. Children and foster children moved away from home, friends and old work colleagues died. Liquor no longer gave joy nor oblivion.

He sat there and grew anxious over loneliness and death, and dying alone. He listened to hear his heart beating, to assure himself that he was still alive.

The fear of death was the hardest. Then that thing with his daughter, Annika. In some ways she had been his dream: she would succeed and find happiness and her happiness would give him life and keep death at a distance.

It was out of fear of losing her that he had struck her, he thought. It was like when he forced himself to take the heaviest sacks, the sheer weight had made him feel that he was alive. In the same way the blows

were supposed to have made her understand that she had to stay. He
had wanted to strike her to bring her to him, not drive her away. Strike
down what was coming between her and her home: luxury, a dream
of something different. It was different with the foster children, with
one like Augusta who had gone and become a pietist. He had given it
to them because he thought they deserved it; children had to be
brought up. He had certainly had to learn his lesson in his day, and
he'd been no worse for it.

But with his Annika it had been different. If only she would come
back, she would get to dress as she pleased. If she felt like going
around in long johns, then why not. But she hadn't even sent a message, not given one sign of life. And he knew that she hated him.

Only tatters. Everything was falling apart. The rats were gnawing
in all the corners. Of course, it was foolish of him to have kicked the
cat to death, just because it had happened to get in his way. But he
needed someone, something to kick.

Bigsack got up, went into the room where his many boarders were
crammed. Most of them were out now, only two soot-blackened, lice-
infested coal bearers lay in a common bed and slept off their inebria-
tion.

Before, he'd had a truly fine and pleasant collection of boarders.
Pretty girls and the old and proper Mamsell Tornberg, and the dyer
who had paid so well. Now they were all gone, not more than two of
the "old ones" left, Henning and Matilda. The rest were scum, he had
to admit that. Coal bearers, factory girls who drank and prostituted
themselves, the newspaper-selling cripple who smelled of rotting flesh,
the muddle-headed crone who made brooms. People who quarreled at
night, got everything filthy, lay in bed like pigs whole Sundays.

Henning and Matilda had complained, talked about moving. That
had made Bigsack take notice and throw out some of the trouble makers. But those who had replaced them weren't any better. His house
had become a den of thieves, and he didn't have the energy to clear it
out.

It certainly was fortunate that the housing shortage was only growing worse. Of course, there was a lot being built, though not for poor

people. Some of the poor were allowed to move into the new houses, it was true, but only for a short while, just long enough to dry the damp cement with their body heat. Then they were thrown out, and they were left homeless once more.

He had suggested to Henning and Matilda that they could share a bed, since they were the only orderly ones in the room. But they were also a little prudish so that didn't go over too well. Then he did more than was expected of him: he had given them each a bed and pushed those two beds off into the quietest corner. And the rabble got the rest and spread themselves out over the floor and the remaining bed as much as they liked.

Both Matilda and Henning fled Bigsack's house as often and for as long as they could. Many times they went with each other to a common destination: Lotten's home. Washer-Malin had heard about their situation and was pleased to have them come over. Malin was actually out quite a bit herself. Her work took up a lot of her time and paid badly, and it was necessary for her to be there both early and late.

Malin's and Lotten's room became the young people's refuge, and it was there that Henning felt for the first time what it was like to have a home. Of course, everything was simple and poor. But Malin's capable hands kept it neat and almost free of lice; the smell of soap and newly-scrubbed cleanliness scared a lot of the lice back into the surrounding apartments. And there was warmth and shelter when the snow fell and the wind tore at the trees outside.

Henning had taken it as his task to keep them in firewood. While there had been work in the harbor, he had salvaged a number of broken crates and bits of boards, and when he was out on other odd jobs later he always kept his eyes open. Sometimes he would walk across the ice to the Sickla woods and collect dried branches in a sack. Lotten offered them a room and something to drink. Thumbs came with bread that his mother had baked. Sometimes he had his cousin Anna-Kajsa with him. She was seventeen now and, thanks to her beautiful handwriting, had managed to land a job in an office.

They sat on the two beds, one couple on each. When Anna-Kajsa was along she would pull up a stool and sit close to the stove. Sometimes Lotten would take down the guitar from the wall, and they sang and forgot the cold and everyday worries. They seldom could afford to go out. The cold drove people into wine cafés and taverns and to go out like that cost too much. But Anna-Kajsa had bought a pair of ice-skates, and on a few Sundays the others had also given them a try on Hammarby Lake or on the rink at Kornhamn. Only Anna-Kajsa attained any proficiency.

The evenings when Henning was alone with Lotten weren't many. But once in a while it happened. They sat on the bed then and talked about that day's worries and the possibilities the future held. Lotten would make coffee in the pot that stood on three legs over the fire. They drank and watched the dying embers. She would light the oil lamp if it wasn't already lit. When mother came home there should be a light on in the room. Lotten turned the flame low to make it as small as possible. Actually she would have liked complete darkness.

The lowered flame, the sign of their love. It threatened constantly to flare up, to capture them totally, to do away with all caution and common sense.

Henning felt like crying over how rough and hard his fingers were. How could they dare reach out to her? But she kissed his hands and whispered that they should be just the way they were, there were no better hands, no other ones who could touch her.

He would have liked to fall asleep with his cheek against her breast and the scent and warmth of her so close. But her mother might come home or else he had to leave soon to meet Matilda. Matilda never dared go alone to the room at Bigsack's ever since she had been attacked by two boarders one evening. Even though those two had moved she never felt quite safe anymore.

So Henning always went from time together with Lotten to bed-time with Matilda. Matilda had become like a sister. For almost five years, Henning and Matilda had lived in the same room. Evening after evening he had followed her in, and they had whispered together while they had undressed, lain down and talked softly until they had fallen asleep.

Every winter when work in the harbor ended, Henning was gripped by the same anxiety. It wasn't just that he had to support himself. No, mainly it was the awareness of his being totally defenseless: being unemployed was punishable by law.

He felt like a hunted escapee, an outlaw. He understood, and almost envied, those of his comrades from the harbor who hurried to the workhouse and could be there in safety over the winter. Ordered around, under the constant surveillance of the supervisors, packed into enormous wooden dormitories, uniformly dressed in easily recognizable homespun and wooden clogs, numbered with numerals engraved on the brass plates of their hats, classified as "drudges." But safe in port for the winter.

To accept that security was still to give up, to recognize his inadequacy. Now that he had Lotten, it was more impossible than ever to imagine that way out.

It was Henning's workmate and Lotten's neighbor, Fearsome, who came upon a solution that winter. He had heard that one of the herring importers at the harbor was going to use the winter to expand his warehouse space. The work was poorly paid but didn't demand any great skills, no fine carpentry or such. Only taking down the old rotten shelves and building new ones.

They were to begin at six o'clock in the morning, at first only to help the warehouse assistants roll the herring barrels that had to be moved out of the way.

The whole warehouse stank of herring, and the odor clung to their clothing and skin. It was especially troublesome now in the winter when the chances of getting a bath were so slim. But even in this respect, Fearsome turned out to be of aid: he arranged it so that the two of them could take a Saturday bath in a washhouse. That way the stench of herring wasn't totally overwhelming when Henning saw Lotten and the others on Saturday evenings and Sundays.

The wholesaler, Bodin, first came down at nine o'clock, and an odor of shaving lotion suddenly blended in with the herring stench. He didn't stay very long inside the warehouse, but satisfied himself with giving some quick instructions before retiring to the well-insulated but still mildly herring-scented office. His bearing and expression, his detachment and haste, all signaled that he belonged to another world, a world where one shouldn't smell of herring. With raised eyebrows he looked at the two dock workers he had employed and at his old, known packers, as if he always was equally surprised each time he caught sight of them. Maybe he wondered if they, too, were people.

But his conscience was clear, he was a member of the Society of Friends of the Destitute. If no poverty existed, then charity would disappear and along with it something of great value to mankind.

He despised those who clamored and were demanding, but felt moved when he saw pictures of small, well-dressed girls who came with food and gifts to the poor. He had two small daughters himself.

The older of the two dock workers had something surly, actually importunate, in his demeanor. The younger appeared to be more pliant, grateful for having a job. Someday Leonard Bodin might call this Nilsson in to him and try to get some insight into the life of the poor. That would be good for him if he became a director on the board of the Friends of the Destitute.

It could be good for several reasons. The wholesaler had a younger brother who caused him some worries. This brother, who was employed in the herring firm's office, could have been a partner in the business by now if he had managed his conduct from the beginning. But instead, Fredrik had been a real party man who had stumbled, hungover, into the office one or several hours late every morning.

It had continued this way for several years until now, when something had suddenly happened. And the wholesaler had trouble deciding whether this new development was something even worse, or a blessing in disguise. Fredrik had now become sober and industrious and was doing everything to reactivate all the old talk about his becoming a partner.

But the reason was the worry: he had fallen in love with a poor girl from the serving class. The girl apparently was a good influence on Fredrik. Still, the situation was demeaning, and the wholesaler had barely dared hint at the affair to his wife. What would Margareta say to having such a person for a sister-in-law?

As the elder brother acting in place of a father, Leonard Bodin had prevailed upon his brother to ask the girl up to the office. He was obligated to form an opinion. He had hardly liked her. She wasn't one of the humble and needy. There was no doubt that she was hard, that she ruled Fredrik and didn't intend to allow herself to be governed by Fredrik's brother. She was one of the demanding ones and had taken a wrong turn.

The wholesaler knew all along that he should have been stronger, harder. But he defended his weakness with the thought that she was probably what Fredrik needed.

He put down one condition: her previous work had to end. The girl had to at least be able to be presented as an office worker. She would become an assistant to the old cashier.

So it came about that Henning was handed his wages by Annika. At first he only thought it was a new face. The girl had become a woman, much of the slender childishness was gone. But the small, dissatisfied expression was still there, and it was this that first led him to recognize her.

He was the same, she someone else. He understood that it was she that had to decide if they knew each other or not, he wasn't going to unmask her.

He took the money she handed him and wrote his name in the space she pointed to with her well-manicured finger. He felt ashamed of his dirty hand with chilblains and split nails. He thought it took an unbearably long time to write.

She read the name, looked up and nodded, bewildered, at him. He said thank you and left.

But a few days later he met her on the stairs and she stopped.

"Are you still living there?" she asked.

He nodded.

"Is Mother alive?"

He nodded again.

"Both are alive," he said. "But Augusta and Nils moved out after a fight."

"Wait," she said.

He waited while she ran up the stairs. Then she came down again and pressed a bill into his hand.

"Give that to Mother," she said. "But don't tell her anything, just say that you bumped into me on the street."

He nodded and started down the stairs. She stood where she was and another question came out. "And...Thumbs...?"

"Both Thumbs and I work in the harbor," he whispered in reply. "He's together with Matilda now."

She shook her head suddenly. Without saying anything more, she turned and went up the stairs to the office.

One evening he happened to see another one of those who had moved out of Bigsack's house. Augusta, his foster daughter. In a demure black dress with a dark shawl, together with some large women — most likely on their way to a meeting — Augusta seemed strangely broken, as if she was so used to being on her knees that she no longer was capable of walking upright.

She didn't see him.

He had just bathed and was on his way to meet Lotten. He stood a minute in the cold winter evening and thought about how costly life was, what large sacrifices were required. He wondered which cost most, escaping or staying. The revolution that Thumbs talked about apparently never happened, everything remained the same. People were broken, were forced down or escaped without finding any happiness wherever they ended up.

Still, he couldn't give up. Still, he dreamed that everything would be different, that he and Lotten would succeed, that their children would be able to live in a world that they didn't constantly want to escape from.

But how that would happen was what he didn't understand.

THE FROST-BLIGHTED SPRING

Time after time spring tried to come stealing in, only to be driven away. The dock workers at the workhouse became more and more irritated with the daily routine and discipline; they hung out of the windows and wondered if the ice age was making a comeback. Those who had requested to be discharged at the normal time worried how they would keep body and soul together when they could no longer live in the institution. The work team had many vagrants, especially from the rough crowd, who snapped up any extra work.

Earth and people froze. The seeds were coaxed out by the sun in the daytime, but turned black with the cold overnight. The buds in the trees and the flowers in the earth died.

Gradually the ice cracked though, and the first vessels arrived. With frozen, withered fingers the stevedores took hold of tools and cargo, straining until they sweated, and then thought they could feel the sweat turning to ice on their backs. The cold had to be driven away, aquavit was the best known and most readily available means. The warmth of the taverns was enticing and always lay close by; taverns existed in practically all the houses along the harbor. And all the old ailments came to life again and had to be silenced. People coughed and spat and complained of sore backs and aching limbs.

Henning had wanted spring to come for a long time. He had wished himself away from the stench of herring at the Bodin warehouse and out to the harbor with its physically harder work but freer life and better income. At the herring firm it felt as if he had returned to the past, almost to the mill where he had worked as a boy. Wholesaler Bodin was certainly a fine and polished miller. He didn't walk around in a leather apron and blow his nose in his fingers, but he had the same attitude toward his people; he was the patriarch, the only one who

understood anything and the one who always had to be asked anything. Even the oldest and most skilled workers in the firm became
minority-aged children who only worked when the boss was looking,
brow-beaten creatures. Still, the wholesaler wasn't a mean or especially difficult man, he just followed the pattern.

Henning had also waited for the warm evenings and Sundays
when he sat with Lotten up on the hill, and when they took outings
in the boat together with Thumbs and Matilda. Even if Lotten's mother was always kind and friendly, she had to grow tired of having him
sitting in the room constantly. He felt like the cold confined him
everywhere: in the crowded warehouse, in the little room. When the
warm weather arrived, all doors were open, people lived just as much
outside as inside their houses. The courtyards and streets were the
large summer rooms of the poor that had to be closed and left unused
when the cold came. And in spite of the dark shadow of the hill, in
spite of the crowds and the sheds, the harbor seemed liberating in its
openness and light. As if dazzled, he tumbled out to the sun shining
off the water and the winds from the sea.

The long winter had demanded its sacrifices, there were more
empty places than usual when the work team was pieced together. But
many waited, of course, to fill them. The bosses sighed remembering
the old, familiar workers who were gone, and they went through the
candidates, choosing and selecting, weighing strength against depend-
ability, experience against motivation. In the coal yard beside
Danviken the loss was perhaps especially deep: the pride of the coal
bearers' team, the mighty Bigsack, hadn't shown up. Friends who visited him reported that the giant had turned into a remnant of his former self. He would never be coming back. But he still ruled the roost
at home they said, and laughed. He sat in bed and bellowed, ordered
his old lady around and swatted at the children. They decided to take
up a collection for him. And despite it being a difficult time, when all
the holes that had been chewed open during the winter had to be
filled again, the result was better than usual; everyone wanted to con-
tribute. A deputation made their way over the hill one cold but light
spring evening to the house by the lake. Bigsack was moved as he took

each comrade by the hand and thanked them for the gift. And both the receiver and the givers suspected that the handshake was a last farewell, that the fumbling words were not only thanks for a gift but also for long friendship. Silent, the men went back, stopping for a moment at the edge of the lake and looking out over the water, perhaps to avoid looking at each other.

Yes, he still ruled in a way. Yet he had become a weak tyrant and didn't spread any real terror anymore. The children kept away; the wife pretended not to hear if he kicked up too much of a fuss; the boarders laughed at him. Eventually he realized himself how it took too much strength to fight. Then he half sat, half lay in bed and just growled ill-humoredly.

Time after time he asked about Annika. Hadn't anyone heard from her? His wife, who hadn't reported the money she had received from Annika through Henning, answered in the negative. But one day she told him that Henning had run into Annika on the street, and she had sent her greetings. Then she was obliged to intercept Henning when he arrived and make sure their stories coincided, make sure the money wouldn't be mentioned. Since Henning had promised Annika not to disclose where she was, he couldn't give Bigsack any information. But he promised that if he met her again he would give her the message that her father wanted to forgive her and asked her to come home, at least for a visit.

Henning knew, of course, where Annika was but it still wasn't easy for him to send a message to her. He couldn't expose her. Nobody was to realize that Mr. Bodin's fiancée was acquainted with a stevedore. Carefully he tried to keep an eye out for her, pretending that he had an errand at the herring firm, and watching for her on the stairs.

When, after much trouble, he succeeded in getting ahold of her, she just hissed back a bitter reply at the message: she didn't intend to forgive her father. She forbade Henning to come with any other messages. She had severed all ties. When he turned to go she stopped him, however, and asked him to inform her if her father died. Not because her father interested her, but for her mother's sake. Henning, who heard someone coming on the stairs, nodded silently and left. A moment later he saw Annika and her fiancé walk away. She pretended not to see Henning.

Bigsack asked every day if Henning hadn't seen Annika. And Henning felt that he couldn't answer anything but no: the truth was all too bitter.

One May night the boarders were disturbed by Bigsack screaming over and over. Whether it was with rage or pain they didn't know. The screams had no words. In the morning he was dead.

Henning informed Annika as he had promised. And one evening a hired carriage waited down by the winter customs house while a young lady walked out to the dilapidated house beside the dye works.

She stood in the doorway, already regretting her visit, cursing her weakness. She shouldn't have come. Those who moved away from home should be as irretrievably gone as those who had emigrated to America. Wouldn't the smell of poverty cling to her clothes? And it would surely be difficult to leave again. Mother would cling to her, not let her go until she knew everything.

But Annika had already said this to herself many times and yet she had decided to come. Perhaps only because the city, in spite of everything, was too small to hide in. She had realized that when she met Henning. An unprepared encounter on the street could be more dangerous than this cautious visit. She had to overcome her aversion and run the risk this visit might entail.

Annika opened the door, recoiling at the smell and the sight. Was it always this terrible? Sometimes when she thought back she had wondered if her memory painted it black. Maybe it wasn't quite so dark and dismal. But it was worse than she remembered. It hadn't been so filthy and wretched even then. She looked at the dirty men who sat on one of the beds, at the invalid who lay and snored on the rags in the corner, the same corner where she herself had lain at one time. The men were drunk. One got up, drooling, and tried to cross over to Annika, then he plopped down on the bed again.

She hurried past to the bedroom. Her mother stood there combing the lice out of the nine-year-old's hair. The girl was being made to look nice for the funeral. It took a few moments before Annika understood that the girl was her sister. For a split second it had felt as if it were she herself sitting there, a younger Annika. She recognized the scene so well. The smell of vinegar, the tray where the lice fell and were killed. Here in the bedroom everything was the same as before, just as unbearable, just as filthy, poor, inhumanly human.

Still, much had changed. Father was no more. Augusta and Nils were gone. Only two of the children were left. The girl here and the youngest. Was that the little fellow she had seen sniveling and coughing between the piles of garbage in the yard?

And Mother had gotten old, even more worn out. She turned around and looked. The comb fell out of her hand, bounced off the tray. The girl who sat with the rag around her neck gave a little cry of astonishment, wondering what kind of fine lady it was who had come to pay a visit.

"Annika!"

Bigsack's widow struggled against tears.

"You came at last," she said quietly. "But too late — he's dead."

"I know," answered Annika. "Otherwise I wouldn't have come."

The mother grew silent. For twenty years she had gone as an intermediary between father and child, been the one to receive the jabs, blows and the hard words they directed at each other. As if most of their hardness and hate had been taken out on her, as if they believed that she could take it all. Would it continue now as well, even though he was dead? No, she couldn't bear any more. Even though it felt like a betrayal, she had no strength left to defend the dead.

"You'll be at the burial of course?" she asked anyway.

Annika shook her head, a little impatiently. Mother apparently didn't want to understand. Perhaps she believed that it would be like before, that Annika would move back home. But she came chiefly to stop any family ties from being renewed.

That answer wasn't so easy to give, and she expected both reproaches and tears. It might take time to get things straight with Mother, but she shouldn't let the carriage wait too long. Soon people would be gathering there, and all too many would recognize her.

"I'm going to be married soon," Annika said quickly. "And he knows almost nothing, his family even less. They aren't going to learn anything either, that isn't possible. For that reason Mother isn't to go looking for me."

The mother sat quietly, as if she hadn't heard.

"This is my only chance," said Annika desperately. "Otherwise I'll end up like this too."

Finally Bigsack's widow looked up. Without tears she gazed at Annika.

"You can rest assured," she said in a low voice.

Annika would have liked to stroke her cheek, say a word of thanks. But the fear that something dangerously soft and weak might be left inside her and would take control of her held her back. Perhaps also respect, almost fear, for her mother. She had expected an emotional scene and only received a few coldly calm words.

She lay the money she held in her hand on the edge of the dresser.

"I don't have much just now," she said. "Maybe I can send more with Henning if I meet him."

"We'll manage somehow," answered her mother. She didn't look at the bills, but didn't shove them back at her as Annika had perhaps feared or hoped. It was true what Annika had said, she didn't have that much money. It cost money to live the way she did now, and she didn't want to ask Fredrik for money before they were married.

"Good-bye then, Mother." The words came carefully, childishly, anxiously.

But the mother turned her face away, looked out the window and wondered if that was her little boy with such a bad cough. She would buy some medicine when she got money. Those who couldn't leave home, at least not yet, were the ones she had to care for. Those who left disowned her.

Life had beaten her; her husband had beaten her; the children beat her. But as long as someone remained and needed her help, she would stick it out. Then she would pray to God to let her die, let her be free from having to cope.

Henning and Thumbs saw the hired coach roll up the street from the customs house, saw the kids running after it shouting and laughing. It was seldom that a hired coach came to this neck of the woods. Thumbs guessed that some old charity lady was out and about. Henning agreed, until he suddenly realized that it could be Annika.

He stood and stared when the carriage passed by, caught a glimpse of light-colored hair, a young face. But he said nothing to Thumbs, his meeting with Annika was, of course, a secret.

He had expected questions, perhaps also a description of Annika's visit. But Bigsack's widow had nothing to say to him, no questions to ask. Slightly ashamed, as if he had deceived her, he tried to stay around her, give her a chance to speak. But she remained silent.

That same evening she burned up a pair of lace-trimmed pantaloons that she had been saving for several years in a clay pot high up in a cupboard.

THE BLUE HILL

He came at dusk through the summer's dense shrubbery, up from the lake which glimmered softly in the darkness behind him. He gave a few tugs to his belt and tucked the unbuttoned jersey more securely into his moleskin pants. He stopped at the opening in the red fence, stood and saw the yard's piles of fermenting garbage and the rotting wooden house with the smashed windowpanes and gaping mouse holes.

He had lived here for six years now. He could, maybe, have found a better place to live, the opportunities had been there over the past years. But it was really only during the last year that he hadn't been happy. Earlier he had thought the inhabitants were his friends, and he had held off from moving to a rooming house where he didn't know anyone. And then again he had responsibility for Matilda, he felt, and he hadn't wanted to leave before she found something else.

But soon it would be over.

He was forced to find a place to live. It had gotten harder. Now people were even fighting over holes under wooden quays and stairs. It would get even worse in the winter with overflowing bachelor's lodgings and beds that never got to cool down, but were used in shifts instead.

Henning went into the yard and hung up the cloths he wrapped his feet in which he had washed after he bathed. And also the rag that he wore in his belt during the day and used to dry off sweat. Then he sat down on the grassy slope across from the gate and waited for Thumbs. They were going to use that evening to walk around the houses and inquire after a place to live.

Bigsack's wife was going to move with her two children, take up lodgings with her sister. A relative of the landlord was going to take over the apartment and soon the repairmen would begin. Something had to be done if the house wasn't going to collapse.

Henning had three nights left, then he had to be out of here. But he didn't worry about being short of time, he could always make do over the summer. It was fall and winter that cast a cold shadow, that made him shiver in the middle of a warm evening in July with the thought of their return.

They went home with the usual result: nothing. Now they had asked at all the houses along the lake and in the White Hills.

Thumbs toyed with the idea of a revolution again: the first thing the poor would take over would be housing. He talked about houses where he had taken odd jobs over the winters, shoveling snow, carrying wood and collecting garbage. A family of just a few people could have ten to fifteen rooms. Thumbs would like to believe they got lost in there and had to call for help. The maids who lived crammed in some dark cubbyhole would have to come.

Henning listened rather distractedly; he knew Thumbs' talk. Sometimes, when Thumbs was having a hard time and his tone changed, Henning could be scared by the hate that welled up, the sharp look in Thumbs' eye. He didn't feel the same way himself; he didn't hate. For Thumbs there was something personal behind all opposition he met, it was individuals who hindered and threatened him. But for Henning the opposition was faceless. Time and circumstances, good luck and bad luck, it all was like a dangerous but completely impersonal swamp. Something which couldn't be hated or beaten, it possibly could be gotten across or, in the best case, eventually drained. He might naturally dislike factory owner Bodin's condescending ways, or stevedore Lundström's coarse bellowing. At the same time, he could both understand and respect them, and it would be impossible for him to cause them any harm. Nor did he feel any of the slave's devotion or admiration either. But to tell the truth, he was uninterested in the upper-class. It was circumstance and not people he would like to change. In any case, he saw little of the rich in his work at the harbor. The ones who screamed and argued were poor foremen. If one were only allowed to exist tolerably, then the rich could exist as well, and be as well-off as they pleased.

This was blasphemy to Thumbs, but since Henning wasn't any

debater, he preferred to keep his opinions to himself.

Besides, it was by autumn, at the latest, that Henning needed housing and not even Thumbs could believe that there would be time for a revolution before then.

"The revolution will probably be a good thing," said Henning. "As long as some of us get to live long enough to experience it."

"We will, Henkan," said Thumbs. "I promise you that."

Some evenings later Henning moved his few possessions to Lotten's home. But he couldn't and didn't want to live there. He slept in Thumbs' woodshed, and fought off wasps, mosquitoes and rats. He tried to find a corner where it didn't drip in rainy weather and where the stench from the outhouse next door wasn't too bad.

One morning Thumbs came with big news: he had heard about a little ramshackle house that stood empty after a seaman had died. It was the widow of a clerk at the wharf who owned the house, but she was too gout-ridden and miserable to be able to live there. The sea and the wharf, now it should be the harbor's turn.

On their way home they took a look at the cottage that lay perched on a hill across from Tegelviken. A long way to the well and a lot of shoveling when winter came, but it must be wonderful to live there in the summer. The view was as good as from Lundin's outlook on the hill closer to the water.

They looked up the widow and succeeded in convincing her that a stevedore with steady work was not to be disregarded. But the widow only wanted to rent out the whole house: two rooms, an attic and a kitchen. She wanted to avoid the bother with many tenants.

To Henning's horror Thumbs declared that suited them perfectly, it was exactly how they wanted it.

"The house is in bad shape," Thumbs pointed out. Naturally he understood that the widow couldn't spend money on repairs, but that wasn't necessary either: she was getting handy people as tenants. An honest-to-goodness former construction worker, he said, and pointed to Henning. They would put the house in order, she should come down on the rent a little in turn.

They came to an agreement, and Henning took out his savings and wondered how he, in the future, would be able to earn anything above the rent. But his confidence in Thumbs was so strong that he didn't ask any questions. Maybe Thumbs had suitable tenants for the different rooms.

They got the keys, and even though it was getting late, they went back up the hill.

The blue hill of seamen and wharf workers, Åsöberget. It lay encircled by the night sea, a rock where some small gray and red cottages had been stranded. Thumbs unlocked the gate in the low fence. And there: the cottage they had rented, overgrown with flourishing weeds and giant sunflowers. Yet another key opened a new lock, and they found themselves in a cramped hallway. A stairway led up to the attic, a door to the kitchen, and another to the room on the ground floor.

Henning walked into the room and up to the window that shone from out of the darkness. Under him the water spread its pale cloth between black shores.

Thumbs clapped him on the shoulder.

"Now we'll pick up and move in here with our girls," he said. "One room apiece, the kitchen we'll rent out."

Henning didn't know how to reply. He stood there bewildered and thought how Thumbs had come upon a fantastic solution. Here he had gone and looked for just a bed to lie in while Thumbs had laid plans for a double wedding. They were going to get married, he and Lotten, Thumbs and Matilda. Sometime, when they could. It had always seemed so distant to him, so hard to reach. But they might never have it any better than they had it now. They had their steady jobs. They were young, strong, healthy. Was there really anything that prevented them? Lotten's mother? But now, when he had what was hardest to get hold of, a place to live?

"I certainly can't let you move in here alone with Matilda," laughed Thumbs. And Henning felt ashamed, he had almost forgotten Matilda, thought that they were looking for a room just for him.

"But I have to at least talk with Lotten first," he objected.

"Go ahead and talk," smiled Thumbs. "You probably won't need to use so many words."

Henning walked for almost an hour outside the house where Lotten lived, but the lamp was extinguished, and no one heard his careful whistling. She slept without knowing that he had rented an apartment for them.

It wasn't until he was on his way "home" to the shed that he realized he could have gotten the key and slept in the house. But it was perhaps better this way, that he waited until all four had inspected it.

Saturday evening, and they were going to meet the girls. They had decided not to say anything beforehand since Henning hadn't gotten ahold of Lotten the previous evening anyway.

Feeling contented, they walked along with the girls between them. They didn't want to say anything at all about how they had thought of spending Saturday evening. As usual, the girls had packed picnic baskets, thinking they would go out in the boat. But the boys just pulled them farther on, past the dock, up into the White Hills, onward between fences and rocky outcroppings, out onto the hillside above the wharf and Tjärhovsgatan. Up here most of the paths and streets had no name, but the one that they walked on happened to be called, for no reason, Garbage Lane. It ended up on the hill, at a gateway in a fence.

"We're going to pay a visit here," said Thumbs. "But since the hosts haven't arrived yet I've borrowed the keys." And he pulled out two keys that were held together by a piece of string, and swung them in front of the girls' noses.

He opened the gate and invited them in. The girls stepped into the yard, hesitantly, as was proper for guests. They waited while Thumbs unlocked the house and went ahead to open the door to the room.

"Come on in!" he called.

Curious, they entered into an empty house and looked around.

"But no one lives here."

"Now they do!" said Thumbs. "Now the new masters and mistresses of the house have arrived."

It took a moment before they understood. They had to ask and ask again, completely overwhelmed. But neither Lotten nor Matilda had any objections. The only thing they asked for was a little time to get used to the new situation.

"We might as well eat while you decide if you'll have us," said Thumbs. But it wasn't easy to eat. They had to talk, jump up and look: through the windows, in the kitchen, out in the yard. Who would live where? What had to be done, what had to be bought? Why hadn't they been told anything beforehand so they could have brought along buckets and rags?

While they talked, the question of who would get what was solved almost by itself. Perhaps it only depended on Henning and Lotten being alone a moment in the room up in the attic while Thumbs and Matilda stayed sitting down below. That was enough: the feeling of being alone in a room that could be theirs created the wish to have that very room. They burst out laughing, all four, when they realized how conveniently their wishes had differed and been the same too. It was a relief to make a quick decision. And already after a short time, it was so natural to talk about "ours" and "yours" that they felt right at home.

The darkness settled slowly over the city. It eventually reached their hill, too, which captured some of the evening light the longest. While the blue dusk blackened into night, they sat together in the kitchen, lighted a little trash in the open iron stove, and were cheered by the fire's crackling glow. Henning had found a couple of simple wooden benches in what had once been an arbor, and he brought them in so they could have something to sit on. They leaned their backs against the wall, sat in the shadow and were warmed by the fire and their happiness.

Lotten's mother wasn't completely unused to her daughter staying out on Saturday nights when it was warm. The foursome used to sometimes spend the night in Sickla Woods when they took their outings with the boat. There was nothing to make them leave the house, and they didn't want to either, as if they were afraid it would disappear. That they got to rent it was too much of a dream for them to really believe in it.

Small lights glowed in the darkness below them. They sat there in the kitchen while the lamplighters made their partial-extinguishing round, and every other ball of light disappeared. At the same time it got dark inside the houses. Soon the city would be completely asleep.

"We should go up to our place," said Henning, and stood up. And they had to laugh, it already sounded so normal, and they had a feeling these were words that would be said many times in the future.

On the dark stairs he felt Lotten's arm around his waist. He had to stoop in the stairway, the ceiling was low, and he had already managed to hit his head a couple of times.

They walked across the attic where spider webs hung between the rafters. He opened the door to the room and nudged Lotten in before him.

They went up to the window. He stood behind her and saw the last small lights glimmer through her hair. His split and torn fingers rustled against her blouse, couldn't get hold of the amazingly small buttons. She smiled, took his hands away and stroked them, then unbuttoned the blouse herself.

The floor was dirty to lie on. But they sat down, Henning with his back against the wall and Lotten resting against him. The peeling wallpaper hung over them like a bird's wing.

Lotten fell asleep, curled up with her head in his lap, with his hand on her breast. The night was warm and it got light out early. Despite the fact that he was tired, he couldn't fall asleep, he was too happy. He sat and watched how the darkness slowly dissolved, how the first streaks of daylight were drawn across the eastern sky. And the sun rose shining over the windowsill, and the room quivered with light. He looked at Lotten who still slept and thought: I have to be strong, I have to manage, I have to work so hard that I can give her a decent life.

Lotten awoke. She pulled at her blouse to button it, but his hand was still inside it, and his feelings of resolve and strength made him unwilling to give up. Then she had to give in and crept close to him. But when he went to lay her down, she looked around and said, "It's so dirty — can't we wait?"

He nodded silently. He could hear their neighbors waking up, voices, footsteps across the floor down there. And Thumbs' cry, "If you're awake up there, there's coffee in the kitchen."

They went down the stairs, and he bumped his head again and wondered how long it would take him to get used to it all.

SO NEAR YET SO FAR

The city had a strange habit of lifting the houses of the poor up into the sun, onto the highest hilltop. The small wooden houses lay high over magnificent houses and stately towers as if they were pearls on display.

This was due to the fact that the arable soil was found down in the valleys between the hills, and that it was easier to lay out streets and build houses on low land. In the valleys grew berry bushes and flowers, there were green houses there and fruit trees. The hills were bare and sterile and windswept. Windmills were placed there and small houses grew up alongside the roads where no carts could pass, and in the nooks and cracks of the granite cliffs.

In this way the poor lived above the rich, sat in shacks on their hills and looked out over the fertile land and the beautiful, well-built houses. But naturally they had to pay their price, struggle bent over in the wind, lugging their pails of water from the wells in the valley, sliding on rocks which were as slippery as ice, and balancing on stones and boards over deep mud pools in the hollows in the hills. Broken panes rattled in many houses, split clay tiles let in drops of water, and all heat disappeared through the leaky walls.

Thumbs and Matilda had time to live in the house a whole month before Henning and Lotten got married. There was never any question of a double wedding; Thumbs didn't want to have anything to do with priests. He pointed to his parents: they had lived together for almost twenty-five years and had seven children. But they hadn't bothered to curry favor with the priest to do that.

Even if Matilda had wanted to be formally married she made no objection, she wanted Thumbs to decide. But for Lotten and Henning it was different. Lotten's mother wouldn't have been happy if they had satisfied themselves with just moving in together. Besides, Lotten did not want to be in too much of a hurry to move away from home. First she had to make sure that arrangements for her mother's lodgings were taken care of. The room on Nytorget cost too much for Washer-Malin to maintain alone. Klara, who had two children but was still missing a husband, was eager to move in, but Malin wasn't particularly interested. Klara, with all her male companions, would be too much trouble. Malin wanted to stay in the room; it was so conveniently close to her workmate and friend, Johanna. Finally she found the right roommate, a third washerwoman who had looked for housing for a long time.

Henning lived alone in the beginning, therefore, in the room in the attic. Even if he longed to have Lotten with him every night, he had to admit that it was rather practical this way. There was so much that had to be improved, and during the weeks he lived alone the room was more like a workshop than a residence. He half-starved to buy lumber and paint, walking long distances to find clay tiles where a house had been torn down or to bid on a table at an auction. He dragged home sacks of dry branches and pine cones so they would have something to burn when winter came. He changed broken windowpanes and tried to winterize the attic with the aid of old rags and cardboard boxes.

Every time Lotten came there was something new to look at. She took with her the curtains she had sewn and hung them up. Since he had papered the walls and planed the floor in the room, everything looked so nice and new that they could hardly believe it was the same room. They put down the rag rugs Lotten had knotted and lit the kerosene lamp which shed light much better than the rape-oil lamps. They sat on the wooden sofa that they had bought and felt happy, almost rich.

Their neighbors came up and shared their happiness. Thumbs and Matilda had also fixed up their room, but not with the same feverish zeal as Henning. They hadn't bought as much either. Thumbs wasn't one to live frugally and save, and Matilda's salary didn't go far.

Even the kitchen had tenants. Thumbs' cousin, Anna-Kajsa, had moved in with a friend of the same age named Tekla. It was a good solution for the girls to take the kitchen, the stove had to be used by all, and it was important to get boarders they knew and didn't have to be afraid of disturbing.

The six young people sat in the little room which soon got warm. Lotten opened the window, and the late summer evening wafted into the room. Anna-Kajsa ran down to the kitchen and made coffee, and it was late before they split up. As she usually did, Lotten stayed with Henning on Saturday night. She slept together with him on the new wooden sofa which could be pulled out.

She turned down the lamp and made the bed with the bedclothes that were under the seat. A straw mattress, a long pillow that was for them both, the sheet and the knitted patchwork quilt. She had sewn and put together the bedclothes herself, and in the bureau lay extra sheets for changing. She liked to make the bed and looked a little worriedly at the new bedclothes: they mustn't be torn or gotten dirty, everything should be kept as nice as when it was new. She was Washer-Malin's daughter and felt the same as her mother did about keeping everything shiny clean. She had also been so particular as to purchase a sturdy wooden tub. It stood behind the house. Henning washed himself there when he came home from the harbor. In the winter they would move the tub up to the attic. Anxiously she asked him, "You do wash your feet everyday so the bedclothes won't get dirty, don't you?"

And he nodded with a clear conscience. Nearly every evening he hauled a bucket of water from the well down on Bondegatan. If some evening he worked too late and was too exhausted, he lay on some sacks on the floor. But he didn't tell Lotten about that.

He also went out into the yard on Saturday evenings, stood there in the cool darkness and pulled off his shirt and pants. He hung his clothes on a nail he had driven into the wall, washed himself thoroughly with soap and water and dried himself on the jute sack he had split and hung up as a towel. Then he put his pants and boots on again and went up with his shirt in his hand. He knew that those on the bottom floor laughed a little at his cleanliness. No one else was so assiduous with the washtub. But it felt good to keep clean. It kept both the smell of sweat and the lice away.

When he came up, Lotten stood in her long nightgown and

looked out the window. She talked about the white wedding gown her mother wanted to buy. The money was there, öre had been added to öre, great sums which had taken much effort to earn. Of course it would be fun to be dressed as a bride, but still Lotten had asked her mother to be allowed to use the money more wisely. There was so much that was needed just now, and it was better to buy clothing that could be used more than one time. Unwillingly, the mother had given in. Lotten looked in her skirt, took the handkerchief out of the pocket, untied it. He looked at the money that she handed him, the capital that Washer-Malin had saved. And at Lotten in the white nightgown. Of course, it would be fun to see Lotten dressed as a bride. But then he would have to rent clothes, and then they couldn't buy the bureau they needed so badly.

No, they would have to let the white veil and dress be. But if it was fine weather they would dance and eat out in the yard. No big drinking party. But still a party.

She extinguished the kerosene lamp, pulled off her nightgown and hung it over the back of the chair where her skirt had lain before. Pale moonlight streamed in, playing on her skin. Henning remembered the evening they first swam together, the glow of white bodies under the dark surface of the water. Almost like now and yet so different. Then she had been near but unattainable, now he could take hold of her and keep her beside him.

Carefully, she wiped her feet on the rag rug before she lifted the covers and crawled in. He came slowly after, following her example. From out of the darkness her arms reached out to him, pulled him down. So close, skin against skin. And still he thought he would like to light the lamp to make sure she really was there, assure himself that he finally was home.

They got married on the first Saturday in September. The priest had been Lotten's confirmation leader but didn't remember her. But Washer-Malin told him, and he spoke of his dear confirmand and wished the girl and the fine young man every happiness. He was cheered by the fact that in these times of moral decay, there were young people who accepted their responsibility, and he pronounced so many beautiful words that Lotten blushed when she thought of the Saturday nights on the kitchen sofa. But Washer-Malin forgot about the worry of those nights completely and felt her heart swell with maternal pride. Lotten and Henning were truly not a couple like all the others. Now Malin thought that she had never felt a bit of worry, she knew so well that Lotten was a girl who could hold back. The priest had seen that immediately and spoken accordingly.

Washer-Malin was content despite Lotten's leaving her. She didn't feel she could mourn the wedding gown either. The dream of the white dress had served its purpose; it had made her happy and caused her to save. What difference did it make then if they needed a bureau instead? For no wedding for the daughter of a poor washerwoman could be more beautiful and fine than this.

The road between Nytorget and Åsöberget wasn't long. Lotten wasn't going to disappear. But still Malin, for some reason, began to long to have a grandchild on the way. It would be nice if they hurried now that they were married. A child would make the distance even shorter; Malin would be more needed.

They walked from the priest at Katarina parish, taking Östrakyrkogatan, which ran along the edge of Stigberget, all the way to Ersta, the parish of lay workers. From there they had to climb via Tjärhovsgränd, which crossed it, down one hill and up another.

The guests began to arrive and carry out the traditional inspection of the house. The party was not only a wedding, it was also a house-warming. The wharf workers from the neighboring cottage came with their wives. Thumbs' parents and siblings arrived with the house-warming porridge and saltcellar. Klara came together with Fearsome and Washer-Johanna, and two of Lotten's workmates from the glove factory presented a bouquet of flowers. The lanterns which Thumbs and Henning had borrowed were lighted between the lilacs and the gooseberry bushes, while a few steamboats far below drew shimmering strokes of light across the darkening water.

High above the city the bare hillside bloomed in the night darkness until the flowers of light gradually wilted and were extinguished until singing and laughter ebbed into silence. When the guests had gone, the bridal couple stood in their room and watched the morning come sailing up over Djurgården. Lotten bent over and straightened the rag rug. Henning let his hand glide over the top of the new bureau.

"They're probably asleep down there now," said Lotten. And carefully they crept downstairs and around the corner to the wooden tub. There they thoroughly washed the dust from the yard and the dancing off their feet before they went up to the bed with the never-before-used before sheet.

The morning and the light were near. And he felt like happiness played like a sunbeam in his hand.

SOMEONE'S KNOCKING AT THE DOOR

With autumn came hunger. Rumors reached the townspeople of a great famine. They read in the newspapers about the crop failure caused by the cold spring, and about the peasants in Dalarna who had begun to bake bread out of lichen and moss.

Henning thought of his friends at the candle factor; he wondered how things were going with them. But they belonged to a distant past. It felt reassuring now that this was the case: it kept the famine at a distance too.

Then it crept closer. The first ones driven to the road by hunger arrived in the city. Tired, ragged and dusty they stood with cans and crutches and begged for soup and leftovers outside the backdoors of restaurants. Peasant women in enormous shawls and kerchiefs tried to comfort their crying children while their husbands stomped their feet in the lines at the pawnshops with the last of the possessions they had with them. At the harbor, groups of idle men watched the dock workers, ready to step in during any short breaks. The old, usual extras grumbled with displeasure. They considered themselves the time-honored substitutes whenever the regulars took time off to get something to eat or drink. There wasn't any official break between one in the afternoon and eight in the evening, so anyone who sneaked off had to pay his replacement himself.

The peasant refugees were determined and silent, not talkative and quick to act like the rowdies who were mainly composed of drifters and alcoholics. But the peasants were tougher, and their hunger and responsibility as providers drove them harder than thirst drove the hooligans. They were already there at six o'clock in the morning when work began, ready to step in if there should be some vacancy on the team. At the breakfast and dinner breaks, they went along too on the way to the taverns and the cookhouse. They stood outside and watched hungrily, at the same time noting if someone drank so much that they couldn't work.

The dock workers felt themselves watched and followed. They certainly weren't unused to working before an audience. They constantly had groups of loiterers, people who strolled about, and day laborers around. But the starving men became too much of an obtrusive presence. They pushed so close that they hardly left elbow room for the workers. And then much of the workers' compassion would change to irritation, and they would swear at their observers and wish they'd all go to hell.

They also knew one thing: those who were waiting gave the stevedores even more of an upper hand. Wages would go down with so many competing for jobs. It didn't take too long for the first proof of this to appear: the fifty öre they received instead of a supper break when they worked overtime was discontinued. The dock workers groaned, but didn't dare vent their bitterness; a steady job was worth too much, and all too many stood ready as a replacement for any kind of pay.

They couldn't threaten, it didn't help to complain. They had to hang on, could never risk being fired. Those who were sick with fever and coughs dragged themselves down there to protect their rights, and the dock workers had never been as sober as they were that fall.

Despite the fear of unemployment and hunger, despite the misery around him, Henning was happy. He went home to the blue hill and locked the door, washed away his everyday life, tried to forget the jealous eyes that stared at his food sack.

Things were going amazingly well since everything in his leisure time was still so new, life together with Lotten, evenings in the house on the hill. He felt so full of everything that made him happy that there wasn't much room left for worry and sympathy for others. Everything would work out for those who were hungry, he thought. All kinds of charities had been set up; carts filled with flour were sent to the starving provinces from regions that were better off. Soon a new and better summer would arrive, new harvests, new bread. And it felt like things were easing up at the harbor: a number of the many unemployed disappeared out onto the road again, others found work on the railroad. A connecting railway was being built right through town and it was a real work of art with tunnels, bridges and viaducts.

There were also a lot of new industries getting underway and devouring the work force. Factories sprang up and elbowed out the craftsmen. But at Barnängen the silk mill had halted production. Matilda had managed to find work at Almgren's textile mill on Götgatan instead.

It was as if the city had, in some odd way, freed itself from the countryside. The peasants were hungry, but the wheels of the city turned ever faster. Poverty and hope were intertwined — the peasants' starvation and belief in the future of industry. The peasants would become workers in the city's factories. But factory work was poorly paid, worse than work at the harbor. You had to live for the day, taking every opportunity to change jobs to bring in a few more öre. Women had to take in washing and go seeking relief, children were sent out to beg.

In spite of everything the wheels turned, faster and faster. Forward, toward what had to be called new times. The wheels were driven by sweat and hunger, by people who had to nourish themselves with skim milk, potatoes and lean herring. Tired and sick slaves who lived in drafty holes had to move more quickly while their wives begged for credit in the shops, while their daughters prostituted themselves and bore children who were farmed out and died before they reached their first birthday.

Hope and hopelessness. But who had the energy to think about starving peasants? They had to either emigrate or let themselves be drawn into the treadmill. With a kind of joy in others' misfortunes, people watched those who had previously been free put on the workers' shackles. Now they could see for themselves how it felt, now they could drink skim milk themselves, pay their own shamelessly high prices for food.

Tenement houses on the outskirts of town and wooden shacks were filled to the bursting point. People from the fields and people from the highways packed themselves in — were ground down and worn away, became part of the city's gray proletariat.

One December evening someone knocked on the door and Thumbs went to open it. The man who stood outside in the rain wondered if Henning Nilsson lived there, and Thumbs nodded and called Henning down.

At first Henning didn't recognize the man waiting there. Tyrs Olle had grown old, although he couldn't have been more than thirty. He was tired and marked by the work that had only yielded disappointment. He managed a smile of recognition though when Henning came down.

He had been to the candle factory, Olle explained. But it was too late, they had a full working staff. Someone there thought that they had heard about Henning living on Åsöberget, and Olle had wandered from house to house asking until he found the right one.

Yes, he had come too late, held on too long. Thought that maybe he could carry the family over the winter, until another spring. When at last they gave up, they were at the back of the line, didn't reach the city until all the housing was occupied and all the work given out. He had left Kerstin and their two children in a shelter in the Old Town. Maja was in the poorhouse, completely out of her mind now. She had born a child who died after a few months.

They sat in the room on the second floor and talked while the rain lashed at the windowpanes and roof; the city and water disappeared in a gray mist. Thumbs and Matilda came up. Matilda arranged herself carefully on the wooden sofa: she was expecting.

Henning felt indebted to Olle. He told everybody what they already knew to be sure they would understand: how he, thanks to Olle, had gotten his first job and his first place to live here in the city. And the four of them who lived in the house knew too that soon their circumstances were going to be reduced. Another week and the work at the harbor would be over for the season. Perhaps one more month and then Matilda wouldn't be able to walk any longer.

"The attic isn't too bad for someone to live in," said Thumbs.

Lotten gave a start. The attic was a part of their private world. The washtub they used every evening stood there, she hung clothes there, and the cupboard full of china and household things stood there too. There was no other way into their own room either. But at the same time it was a luxury, of course, poor people weren't supposed to live so well.

"While you look for something better," said Henning. "What do you think?" he asked Lotten.

She nodded silently, couldn't say no but not yes either. She opened the door to the attic to take out the cups. They were going to serve coffee, it would be good in this foul weather. Olle followed her, looking around the dark attic. One small window pane gleamed in the dark. It was cramped and dark, but also had a newly-scrubbed clean smell. Cold, but not so bad that they couldn't live there.

Olle didn't stay long, he had to go back to the shelter. But they would come tomorrow morning, all four.

Before they went to bed, Henning and Lotten carried all their belongings into the room. Then Henning held the kerosene lamp while Lotten washed the floor.

When she was done, she stood with the rag in her hand, trying to swallow her tears. Henning pulled her to him, tried to console her without words. He wondered if he had forced her into something she really didn't want, but there was the money to think of too. And what could he do, could he drive Olle and Kerstin out the door?

"It'll work out," he said. "It'll all work out."

But Lotten turned her face to the wall that night.

Early next morning the people from Dalarna arrived with their children. Henning and Thumbs barely had time to do more than say hello, but Lotten had a few minutes before she had to leave. She had to show them around.

Henning was naturally a little nervous about his meeting with Kerstin. Was she going to be the way he remembered her, so like Lotten? She was hardly that. She was no longer a young girl. When he saw her, he knew that she had never really been especially like Lotten. Both were dark-haired and slender, that was all.

But it was nice to see Kerstin again, he felt like he was meeting a friend, more than when he met Olle. So much that he would have liked to hug her. But that wasn't the right thing to do, and he satisfied himself with clasping her hand firmly, then he had to dash to catch up with Thumbs who had gone on ahead.

He came back to a different house from the one he had left. Two children sat on the stairs and played with a rag-doll. In the attic stood one of the benches that had been in the old arbor and in the corner lay some sacks and quilts. Kerstin sat on the bench eating; she had fixed a little supper in the kitchen to be out of the way when the rest came home. Olle was still out, he was looking for work. But when he got back he stumbled on the attic stairs and spoke loudly and roughly while Kerstin hushed him cautiously. Then he started to shout and the youngest child began to cry.

Henning looked at Lotten, how she registered every noise, how hard it was for her to control herself. He understood how she felt. They sat like prisoners inside their room off the attic. When they had to go out to the kitchen, to the woodshed, or to the outhouse, they had to pass through, intrude.

Still they were much better off than many others, of course. Many of Henning's workmates lived in more crowded conditions than he and Lotten, and they sometimes had both children and boarders in the same room. They owned no privacy, no secrecy at all; they lay with their women within reach of the boarders' hands. But Lotten was not used to living like that, and he hoped that she would never have to get used to it.

He brooded about it. Somehow the new situation had to be kept under control. At last he came across a temporary solution: they could make a divider from boards and paper it to create a narrow passage from their room to the stairs. Together with Olle he put up a simple wall, and he saw how happy it made Kerstin to get something to hide behind.

Olle finally got work at Barnängen where manufacturer Hierta had started production of tallow candles since silk manufacturing had shut down there. But it seemed like Olle drank up most of his salary.

He always had trouble paying the rent, and Kerstin and the kids would have starved if the girls in the kitchen hadn't added a little something now and then to Kerstin's half-empty pots.

The snow and ice came, the ships disappeared, and Henning and Thumbs took the odd jobs they could get. For a while they chopped wood at Nybro Harbor and walked the long distance there and back every morning and evening. Then they sawed ice at Hammarby Lake. In January Matilda gave birth to a son whom she and Thumbs named Rudolf after her brother who had died while young. Matilda had little milk, and the baby cried a lot.

Since Matilda and Kerstin were both at home during the day, they grew close to each other. They had a lot to talk about, cooked together, helped each other take care of the children.

Lotten felt a little left out. She trudged home through the snow, slid on the icy hillsides, froze in the wind. She came home to the warmth of the cottage and found Matilda and Kerstin caught up in heart-to-heart conversations. Then Henning and Thumbs would walk in from their work together, with their shared interests. And the girls in the kitchen had their own life.

The first winter in their own home didn't turn out to be quite as good as she had hoped and believed it would. And now the hill showed its most inaccessible side, life here was completely different from the more sheltered Nytorget. At times she thought the whole house was going to lift in the wind and be blown out to sea. In the morning it was often next to impossible to get out. Henning and Thumbs sometimes shoveled for an hour before a path was cleared. Lotten didn't have to carry water, Henning did that. But he fell on the slippery hillside and spilled half the bucket, and they had to conserve every drop that cost so much effort.

She tried not to show that she was dissatisfied. She knew that Henning worked as hard as he could to make everything as good as possible. The only problem was that he was too nice, she thought, he never said no. He thought she didn't see it, but she knew that he often carried water for Kerstin too. And he should have gotten mad and made Olle shovel. Olle never came out anymore until it was time for him to go to the factory. But Henning was silent and worked hard. And Lotten longed for spring, for the day when everything would be like it was before the people from Dalarna and the snow had arrived.

THE FLAMES

The noises of the day quieted down while the evening turned to blue. A murmur from the taverns still rose into the air, but no winches creaked, no foremen shouted. The harbor's workers had gotten a few hours to live their own lives and carry their own burdens.

Henning had gotten his boss's permission to take home some empty crates to patch up the shed in the yard. After his comrades from the work team had left, he stood there, taking apart the crates, and he put together a good-sized bundle of short boards. He tied them together with a rope and slung them over his shoulder. He thought he could hardly feel it, the load was so light compared to what he usually carried. And he whistled to himself as he walked toward Last Farthing Stairs to climb upwards. He felt happy that spring was here: everything would be better now. Winter had been quite a test, and they had made it through. Olle and Kerstin would be moving soon, and once again the attic would stand empty. The provisional wall would be taken down. The washtub and cupboard would be placed outside the room again, everything would be like it was before. And Lotten would be happy, really happy.

As he passed the Bodin Herring Firm he took his usual glance up at the house. Once in a while he saw Annika's face in the second floor window. She never gave any sign that she saw him, and maybe she didn't. He didn't look that different from all the other workers in blue smocks that passed by here. He didn't expect a wave or a nod from her either, maybe only a little sign that they had once known each other.

The window shone, like a reflection of the sun. At first he didn't think anything of it, perhaps it was a last ray of sunlight. But then he realized that it couldn't be so, no sunlight could shine in here. A lamp, someone who was working late? He looked up again.

Then the glow grew larger and flickered.

He stopped. And now he saw the flames.

He threw the bundle of boards down in the doorway and ran up the stairs. But the door up there was fastened shut and no one opened it. He ran down again, to the smaller door below, the back door to the warehouse. That too was latched, but only by a hasp, and he managed to break it open.

He was up the spiral staircase in a few bounds, and could hear the crackling of the fire. The office was beginning to fill with smoke. But he still could see the lamp which had fallen to the floor, the man who lay slumped across the table.

It was the wholesaler himself.

For a moment Henning stood there at a loss, not knowing where to begin. Try to extinguish it, or get the wholesaler out of there? Coughing and gasping he got hold of the large man, finally getting him over his shoulder like an enormous sack. He carried him as carefully as he could down the narrow stairs and outside.

Some sailors came from one of the docks, and Henning screamed at them to come and help. One hurried to sound the alarm for the civil guard up in the Sievertska barracks. The other rushed off to the nearest tavern to bring more people.

Henning bent over the wholesaler, whom he had carefully laid down on the ground. He wondered what he should do. Mr. Bodin was alive, at least for the moment. And now he looked up, as if he had with great effort managed to raise an eyelid.

He said something, slurring his words. Henning couldn't understand. The wholesaler tried again, the words dribbling out from a corner of his mouth. Then Henning caught on: the money.

He nodded and got up. Was there any chance? He remembered the bucket which usually stood inside the door. He grabbed it as he ran past. Now the smoke was already in the stairwell, rolling toward him. He held one arm across his face, and pushed onward, saw the flames which licked the rug on the floor. He threw the water on them. They hissed and the smoke became more intense. He groped for the table, grabbing hold of the cash box sitting there. He felt his arm catch fire and slapped at the fire as if it were a biting animal. He tumbled toward the doorway and fell but got up on his feet again.

When he stumbled through the outer door, he was met by the howling, excited mob who had come storming over from the tavern. But he pushed his way through to the cluster of people surrounding the wholesaler. He kneeled down to show the cash box to the man lying there. Bodin didn't open his eyes.

The drums rolled in the Sievertska barracks. Children and adults streamed toward them, filled with expectation. Now things were cooking! The fire engines were rolled out, hoses were put up on the wagons, irritable men swore at children and kicked at the ones who got too close. The horses were harnessed, and they were off. Barrels of water were drawn on carts, and some of the firefighters hurriedly emptied their bottles of aquavit first, so that no one would steal a drop while they were gone.

"Now the goose is cooked!" yelled the street urchins and rushed down the slopes.

Katarina Church bells began to toll: two times. Pause. Two times. That meant it was on Söder. And a lantern was hung from the north side of the tower. There wasn't much to choose from then. Chiefly the locks at Slussen and the harborside at Stadsgården. People spilled out of every house, the streets were filled, pounding feet and rolling drums. Everybody had to be there, everybody had to see. Would the king come? Was it a wealthy house with a lot to "save?"

The prostitutes in Stora Glasbruksgatan's whorehouse hung out the windows in their dirty chemises and screamed with excitement. A horse reared in the crowd; the wagon tipped over, and a hose began to unwind down the hill. Swearing sergeants tried to rein in the horses and the onlookers. The mass of helpers and plunderers rolled in like an avalanche between Stadgården's buildings and warehouses.

"They're offering fried herring today!" someone cried.

"Look out! Make way for the doctor!" shouted another.

But the fire was a disappointment. It wasn't long before the firefighters had it under control, even though more water ran from the holes in the hoses than came out of the nozzles. A few onlookers thought they should light the fire again; it wasn't right to fool people this way. Gradually interest died out; the firemen rolled up their hoses, guards were posted, the fire was over.

By that time Henning was no longer there. He had handed the wholesaler's cash box over to the captain of the civil guard and been driven by one of the guards to the barber-surgeon's quarters on Hornsgatan. The barber-surgeon slit open his entire shirt sleeve, bathed the huge burn, smoothed on some ointment and bandaged it. It stung, but Henning clenched his teeth together and shook his head when they asked if he wanted to stay there a while and rest. He had to get home; Lotten must be wondering by now.

When he walked home, he met the firemen on their way back to the barracks. They grunted and panted up the hills, and a trail of children followed them.

Henning felt like the road went on forever. His arm throbbed and burned, his head ached. He only wanted to sleep, blot it out, but knew that the pain would keep him awake all night. He wondered how he would manage over the next few days. He had to. He wondered how much had been in the cash box. And what had really happened to the wholesaler.

When Henning arrived, Thumbs was in the yard hanging out baby clothes. He saw immediately that something was the matter and rushed over. Soon the entire household was standing in a circle around Henning, asking questions and commiserating. The last one out was Lotten, who had been up in the room laying out the evening meal. Frightened, she saw his tired face, the large bandage. Then leaning on her, with his good arm around her neck, he went up the stairs.

Everyone had to hear, find out what had happened. They gathered up in the room, and Thumbs pulled out a bottle and almost forced a few swallows down Henning's throat. Olle watched thirstily and finally Lotten took out some cups so that Olle and Thumbs could drink too. But after that she was firm: everyone had to leave so Henning could have some peace, he needed to sleep if he could.

She wouldn't allow him to help her make the bed, nor even wash his feet. Anxiously she watched over him, made sure he got into bed all right, that the covers didn't scrape his arm. Then she blew out the lamp, undressed and crept in carefully beside him.

Her face lay against his chest, his good arm across her back. Of course, he still felt the pain; of course, he was desperately tired, done in. But still happy. The liquor may have helped, he dozed off for a short while. But the pain wakened him again. Then he lay as still as he could and just looked at Lotten, trying to forget his pain in his happiness.

He walked down to the harbor the next morning even though he didn't know how he could be of any use. Stevedore Lundström himself came down for a minute to inspect things and find out what had happened. When he heard that it had nothing to do with a work-related accident, he seemed very pleased and confided in Henning that wholesaler Bodin had had a stroke and would most likely not last many more days. Lundström seemed almost proud that it had been one of his longshoremen who had alarmed the civil guard and saved Bodin from burning.

"Take it easy for a while," he said. "We'll let the Bodins pay for this. That's the least they can do!" he rumbled when Henning tried to protest. And a few days later Heathen Dog gave him the message that Henning had orders to go over to the Bodins' office.

He saw that they had put in a new window. The stairs had no sign of the fire. But in the office there were some carpenters hard at work, and Henning was shown into a cramped little room where some accountants usually sat.

The man who received him was dressed in mourning. Henning recognized him since he had worked there: it was wholesaler Bodin's brother, Fredrik Bodin.

"So, it was Nilsson who discovered the fire," said Fredrik Bodin.

Henning answered in the affirmative. Bodin wanted to know a little more and Henning told him: how he had seen the light, carried out the wholesaler, run into the sailors, retrieved the cash box.

"Nilsson may have heard that my brother has died," continued

Bodin. "We are very grateful, of course, that he had a peaceful death, that he wasn't burned in the fire. Director Lundström has informed us that you will need some time to convalesce, and naturally we will want to pay for that."

Henning, who had been standing by the desk, suddenly felt dizzy. He wasn't well yet. The wound took its time healing, and he probably had a fever, was weakened easily. He would have liked to sit down, but nobody had asked him to; they were probably afraid of getting lice in the fine furnishings. Bodin couldn't know how hard Lotten worked to keep Henning free of lice.

Bodin took the cash box that stood on the table and opened it.

"It was actually Nilsson who rescued the money...."

That evening Henning didn't know how quickly he would make it home. Tired and miserable, but still half running up the stairs on the steep side of the hill, arriving so early that he had to wait a half an hour before Lotten appeared. He set the table and put out the evening meal with the extra delicacies he had taken the time to buy on the way home.

She saw his face shining and wondered what had happened. And he showed her the money, the largest amount he had ever owned, an unbelievable sum: one hundred riksdalers. That was more than he could earn at the harbor in two months. To be sure, he had to give up work for one month, both the doctor and the boss had seen that as safest. And then he had ruined one work smock. But still it was fantastic. And he didn't need to worry, he would keep his place on the team.

The evening meal turned into a party, their own. Olle and Kerstin had moved out, found work and lodgings at the candle factory by the toll gate. Now nobody was close by. It was quiet in the room beneath them. Thumbs' family was already asleep. And the girls in the kitchen were out.

It was as if they owned the whole house, the whole hill. They walked noiselessly down the stairs, now he ducked automatically, and across the little yard inside the fence, out to the edge of the hill. There stood a little pile of rocks there, like a bench of stone. They sat down and Lotten placed his clumsy, bandaged arm on her lap. The spring evening lay in repose around them, blue and silent, an endless sea. But summer lay hidden within the springtime already, small puffs of warm air rustled the moist blades of grass that grew in the cracks between the rocks.

Everything was possible, happiness could be reached even by the poor. Henning told her about how friendly Mr. Bodin had been and how stevedore Lundström himself had come and talked with him, as if with an equal. The rich and powerful could also be people.

He could imagine what Thumbs would say: why thank them when you rescued their money for them? But still, for whatever reasons they had, something of the human being in them had shown itself. Once again, he had to wonder if Thumbs' revolution was the only alternative. What if you could coax life into the petrified, could get them to see to that the poor were people who needed a little security and happiness to get through life. Though Thumbs would probably never have any faith in that alternative.

But hope existed that night. Life said yes.

And that night everything was really just right in a way it hadn't ever been before. They were one, and he was inside her. He didn't feel the pain from his arm anymore, just mounting joy and flames inside that warmed him and didn't burn.

They fell asleep in each others' arms, as if dazed, drunken with summer's happiness out in full bloom. Thumbs had to knock on the ceiling several times the next morning before Lotten woke up and realized that she had to be off to work. Usually she was awakened by the children downstairs. She got up, stepping into the sunlight that poured through the window. He lay and looked at her, and for the first time she didn't want him to turn his face to the wall.

During the month that Henning wasn't working at the harbor, he grew a garden on the hill. He collected soil and planted flowers in the crevices, buying plants cheaply from the gardener nearby. Marigolds and dahlias were soon blooming, shining up at him.

With his good arm he carried bucket after bucket of water and gave it to his flowers to drink since it never rained. The wound on his arm healed eventually, even though it had to be opened up several times when he visited the doctor.

What did a wound matter when he was happy? When Lotten was sparkling with joy and the hillside bloomed.

One evening she made herself very small, crept into his arms and said to the dusk: maybe, not for sure, but maybe. Maybe they were going to have a child.

He felt how he would need all of his strength, was glad that he would soon begin to work again. Now he wanted to work as hard as he could and knew that he could manage it.

He came back to the harbor and threw himself at the sacks. His comrades on the team laughed and shook their heads: Henkan was impossible. But he soon tired. Extra effort earned no extra reward there.

DROUGHT
AND
THIRST

The spring had been unusually beautiful, warm and dry. Then summer came, with mounting heat and without rain. The dust stood in giant clouds over the city's gravel streets and roads. The streets were rinsed down where the new water pipes ran, but on the outskirts the wells dried up, the dust blanketed weeds and hedges. Swarms of black flies buzzed over the piles of garbage and flew in every open window.

The hill was scorched but hadn't turned to dust. Everything yellowed quickly; the flowers in the small garden wilted when they didn't get water; the trees died, and the grass rustled in the wind.

Still, the city dwellers enjoyed themselves. They had crawled out of their dark winter lairs and now had the energy to stay awake and be up all night long. The days were too hot, but the nights were deliciously warm, and the hills and grassy slopes gave enormous spaces to live on. Hammarby Lake bubbled with bathers between schools of rowboats. The rowdies roamed in large bands through the hills and copulated with outdoor prostitutes.

The city's wealthy traveled by boats and carriages away from the city and the heat to rest on the beaches of the archipelago in the Baltic and the islands in Lake Mälar. The newly married and newly appointed wholesaler, Fredrik Bodin, moved with his wife to a summer villa on Stora Essingen and spent an hour every day on the steamer that had to tie up at dock after dock before it finally reached the one in town at Riddarholmen.

But the farmers were worried. The year before, the crops had frozen, now they were drying up instead. Anxiously they watched how their meager sowing shriveled in the fields' cracked gray earth.

Olle and Kerstin had planned to return home to Dalarna but

received a message from home that it wasn't worth it. There wasn't even enough food for those who were still there. More and more people talked about giving up and emigrating. The Swedish earth could no longer feed its people.

The city dwellers listened distractedly to the wailing of the peasants. There was so much that pointed in the other direction. Industry was growing faster than ever. And the blasting with dynamite was enough to make you dizzy. Recently they had conquered Tyskbagarbergen, and soon the defiant rocky hills of Söder would be cut down to size. Dynamite would bring an end to all war and transform all cities into comfortable, flat pancakes.

Something of the country and the tenant farmer's son remained in Henning. He watched his flowers wilt and suffered from not being able to water them anymore. The drought seriously worried him. There was Lotten and the child they were awaiting. An expectant mother had to have enough food; their child couldn't be allowed to starve. They had talked so much about what they would buy with the money that was left. Now he was glad that they hadn't actually spent it all. The money would save them if the fall and winter were difficult. Lotten couldn't really understand him. She had been born in the city and didn't feel the same anxiety over the farmers' harvest.

On the other hand, she was afraid she wouldn't have everything ready before the baby came. She enlisted her mother's help, and they sewed and knitted. Thumbs, who saw some of the supply, wondered how she could know already it was going to be triplets. He sat in the arbor and nursed a glass of arak liqueur while he waved away the flies from six-month-old Rudolf, who was asleep in a basket. Thumbs had embellished himself with a dapper, pointed mustache and taken up smoking. He had a limestone pipe. His movements were no longer nervously, impatiently quick. As if he had softened up under Matilda's mild treatment, he didn't get stirred up as fast, didn't foster discontent as diligently. Or maybe the weather was just too warm.

Lately he had almost felt some sympathy for people from the other side. They had gotten a new man on their work team, only as an extra.

A failed white-collar worker in his fifties who had drunk up his inheritance and finally landed in the harbor's gutter. A lanky and dirty wreck in the remains of a suit from his better days. Thurston Åslund he had introduced himself, as if he were paying a call. "So here's Thirsty," someone had said. And Thirsty he was called.

Thumbs had kept company with Thirsty on the way home several evenings; he lived in a woodshed a few houses away.

Those somewhat choppy conversations had revealed that Thirsty wasn't just an unfortunate case from the upper-class. He had been a friend of the workers and participated in meetings that he now made mysterious allusions to.

Thumbs hadn't been especially interested. He had read and heard about the liberal workers' unions but hardly been attracted; they were too lame. But Thirsty only chuckled knowingly. Most likely he was boasting, wanting to make something of himself.

Thumbs watched Lotten's nimble fingers, waved away the flies, held his glass thoughtfully.

That chuckling, superior and helpless at the same time ... it irritated him. What could Thirsty have taken part in? What was actually happening while he sat here idling in the arbor?

He heard the chuckling again. But that wasn't his imagination, it came from the other side of the fence. He asked Lotten to watch Rudolf a minute while he ran out to see if it was Thirsty.

Sure enough, there was a figure sitting on the hill, a bag of knotty bones under its sheath of worn-out clothes. A figure and a bottle. Thirsty was celebrating his Saturday evening.

Thumbs threw himself down beside him. He forgot about both Rudolf and dinner while dusk settled over the hillside, and Thirsty told his story.

Thirsty was an educated fellow. He had first gone to school in Örebro and then spent four years in Uppsala. He had then become a civil servant for a royal government agency and been seen as a man with a promising future.

"At university we learned to look down on manual laborers," said Thirsty, taking a swig from his bottle.

"But then the French Revolution arrived, 1848. Everyone talked about workers' progress, we banded together for the goddess of freedom and the barricades. Societies and circles were formed. We met together with manual laborers and discussed things."

Thirsty had belonged to a circle. Among the members had been some tailors' apprentices who, during their travels, had lived a long time in Paris and participated in communist gatherings. Two booksellers also entered into the circle. Bookseller Söderman's revolutionary activities had been confined to attending meetings and selling music to the Marseillaise in his second-hand book shop on Köpmangatan.

But that other one, the lively one in the Spanish cape .... He had read the gospel of communism to them all right. Per Gotrek was his name and he was probably still alive. Thirsty had received a book that Gotrek had translated: *The Communist Manifesto.*

"Workers of the world, unite!"

He placed the bottle in his mouth and emptied it. He let it roll down the hill a ways. It glittered in the yellow grass.

"The proletariat has nothing to lose but its chains," quoted Thirsty. "But it has the world to win."

Thumbs felt as if he had received a staggering blow. He sat speechless, overwhelmed. So, what he had dreamed of actually existed. Not just as a dream but as a clearly formulated manifesto.

"Say it again," he asked Thirsty. But Thirsty was asleep.

"Do you still have the book?" he asked and shook his comrade. Thirsty looked up sluggishly and shook his head.

Thumbs could have thrown him down the hill. But at the same time he had to hear more.

"The goal can only be attained through a violent upheaval. May the ruling classes tremble," said Thirsty wearily. The words and the tone contradicted each other, but Thumbs heard only the words.

"May the ruling classes tremble!" he repeated.

"Not for me," said Thirsty, and looked at the sheen on the empty bottle. "I belong to the lumpen proletariat, the passive rotting of the old society's bottom layer. Our position makes us allow ourselves to be bought and used for reactionary purposes."

Thumbs tried to protest.

"The *Manifesto* says so," smiled Thirsty contentedly.

When Thumbs at last went in to his sleeping family, the words still went around in his head. He felt the surge, the excitement. He shook Matilda, had to wake her up.

Wonderingly she looked up, about to ask where he had been. But he cut her off, his message was more important than all these petty little concerns.

"Workers of the world unite!" he hissed. "May the ruling classes tremble!"

She looked at him anxiously.

"Don't do anything dangerous," she begged him.

"The workers have nothing to lose but their chains."

"But us, what about us?"

He looked at her, looked at their child. Surely he couldn't doubt the new thing he had just heard? And still, he did have something to lose.

"It's more like a parable," he whispered soothingly as he took off his clothes. The food would have to wait. He was full of this new, this fantastic idea.

THE BIG DAY

Two years of crop failure had stripped the peasants of their resources. Barns stood empty. Bread was baked from wheat husks and chopped up hay, and hungry children chewed on grass and moss.

Hope pointed toward the west, to a new world that could offer a better future. Over there opportunity still existed.

Every day new groups of immigrants wandered through town. Tired and worn they came, bearing their last possessions. They got off the train at North Station and made their way through the city and up the hills of Söder to the well-hidden South Station where the train for Göteborg awaited.

Some never made it that far. They stayed in the city. Others came back when it turned out that clever immigrant recruiters had swindled them and sold them tickets that weren't good on any boat.

The city dwellers looked at the refugees and shook their heads worriedly, but comforted themselves with the thought that both the politically powerful and privately wealthy had provided large sums of money in assistance.

The farmers sought a future in the west. In the city people were completely caught up in commemorating the past and pointing toward the east.

People were talking everywhere about the statue, the monument, the answer to the Russian czar's challenge. The people's answer: Professor Molin's heroic statue which had been paid for through contributions. People rejoiced to see Karl XII pointing so emphatically eastward but were a little concerned by the four mortar surfaces encircling the base: maybe they were on the obscene side with their immoral bas-reliefs. And there was a great deal of commotion over the offensive grand-stand. A private individual had received permission to build it and rent out seats. The grandstand stretched across Karl XII Square and cut off the view completely from that direction. People who had paid for the statue wouldn't be able to see its unveiling. It was shocking, the grandstand should be torn down.

Thumbs decided he had to take himself into town and see what was going on. He asked if Henning wanted to go along, though he could figure out the answer beforehand: Henning didn't want to leave Lotten more than he had to now.

Alone, Thumbs went on his way the evening before the evening of the festivities. He recognized the signs he met: something was going to happen. Apprentice boys and loudmouths ran through the streets and made a ruckus; drunkards made themselves ready for heroic deeds. From dark alleys came tinkling sounds, the first windows being smashed.

At Kungsträdgården he heard cheering. He didn't know if people were cheering for the covered statue or because boys had managed to remove one of the stairs to the grandstand.

Thumbs kept his distance; the time when he would have gotten in the middle of a gang of boys was past. The police tried to strike out at the street boys, but the boys evaded them and continued to pull off boards, though on the other side now. Then Police Chief Östlund climbed up on the grandstand and read the riot act to the young ruffians. A few small boys were carried away, kicking, by sturdy policemen.

During all this time the crowd of onlookers had been growing. Soon the whole square and the adjoining streets were seething with screaming, whistling, cheering and shouting mobs. But alongside Jacob Church something like a high, dark wall rose up and fear crept into the jeers which had recently been so daring. Hussars in the saddle, the mounted guard. And they had not only their sabers, but also their chambrieres, the long whips used in the riding schools.

A cry of command and suddenly they rushed forward, sweeping the mass of people before them. They forced their way in everywhere, between the trees up on the sidewalks. Women fell, tripping in their skirts. Whips lashed bloody slashes in screaming street-boys' faces, sabers whistled, even over the innocent.

A well-dressed and well-fed burgher's wife panted desperately, crying and begging for mercy. But the young lieutenant who ran her down showed no pity.

"Run, you old witch! Pull up your skirts so they won't stop you!"

"Now you'll be pruned to size, old man! Run, you he-devil! Hurry it up!"

Some people who had gathered to help a man badly injured by a saber suddenly felt the sting of a whip across their backs, dropped the injured man and ran. Blinded by the blood running down his forehead, the wounded man crawled away.

People were rushing everywhere to escape. Shouts were heard that the guards were drunk. People lost their galoshes but didn't even dare turn around and look for them. Hats were knocked off and ground to pieces by trampling feet; canes and umbrellas fell out of people's hands.

Thumbs didn't want to run, it went against his grain. He tried to hide behind a tree, but found he soon had to get away from there. He heard the clattering of hooves behind him, and now he ran, ran desperately. They couldn't ride him down, he had to get away. He didn't want to risk his life for a grandstand and a statue. Matilda and Rudolf — why had he come here?

He tumbled on all fours into a doorway, felt the sting of the lash across his back and was glad he had put on his heavy vest.

Out in the park a raging guard rode around the tree Thumbs had just left, striking with his saber so that bark and small branches flew. High over the rider's head sat an eight-year-old boy clnging to the tree, whimpering.

When the first shock was over, Thumbs looked up. He had landed in a good doorway and in fine company, who probably wouldn't be attacked too badly if a policeman showed up. He could stay here a while and wait until it was possible to leave and go home.

A hysterical young girl was being supported by some gentlemen. She was shaking with sobs. One of the gentlemen had lost his hat, a whiplash had lifted off the cylinder. The other was minus a boot and sucked on a finger which had gotten crushed. They spoke of the theater, and first Thumbs thought they were theatergoers on their way home. Gradually he realized that they were actors. The young man who'd had his hat knocked off was to play Karl XII. They had come from a rehearsal.

Karl XII was enraged over the attack of the mounted guard. But Thumbs grew calmer and was ashamed that he had recently been so afraid. As soon as he saw a chance, he left the doorway and began to take himself back to Söder via a large detour.

He saw how the barber-surgeons' clinics in the vicinity were filled with the wounded. He hid hastily when some of the angry guards came riding by.

"Just go home — otherwise you'll get more!" they screamed at curious and frightened evening strollers who had no idea as to what had happened several blocks away.

Despite all his good intentions, uneasiness drove him out again the next evening, the one of the festival. During that day, Thumbs had heard cannon fire from Skeppsholmen, and cheers had resounded across the water from Kungsträdgården to the wharf at Stadsgården.

But the big folk festival wasn't going to take place until evening. Seven-hundred-fifty students from Uppsala University were going to come singing in a torchlit procession, and thousands of limelights were going to shine around the place of the festivities.

Would there be trouble again? He wondered if he dared take Matilda with him. But she didn't want to leave Lotten either. So he went alone, promising both her and himself to get out of the way if there was any trouble. He had a raised red welt on his back to help remind him of his promise.

He looked around a little anxiously at the police and the military who seemed to be everywhere, large numbers of troops standing prepared. But there wasn't much disturbance. Yet still, there had never been so many people collected in one place in the city before as on that evening. The whole area around the festival place was one churning sea of faces.

He let himself be carried by the stream, listened to disconnected words that floated by, and wondered if he had unknown comrades and like-minded thinkers here, hidden among the many apathetic ones.

Tired after the day's hard work, he just drifted along, feeling no real festive feeling or involvement. He almost regretted coming out.

Then suddenly he woke up, hearing the words:

"August Blanche is dead."

He had to ask. The strangers nodded yes. Blanche had been walking at the head of the student procession as they walked from North Station. Then, on Drottninggatan, he had been taken ill and staggered into the Owl Apothecary. Once inside he had collapsed and died.

August Blanche was dead. The friend and spokesman of the poor. Thumbs had only seen him from afar, had heard a few words indistinctly from his speech that evening when representational reform was being celebrated. Still, it was as if a father, a friend, had died.

He turned around, going against the stream of people. How could they laugh and party? Blanche was dead.

It felt good to get out of the milling crowd, to dark and empty streets. He walked faster and faster, feeling that he had to hurry home and tell them what had happened. That which overshadowed everything else that day.

He hurried in through the gate in the fence, opened the door to the room. A lamp was shining dimly, and he walked over to the bed to wake Matilda. But she wasn't there. Rudolf lay alone and slept.

Then he heard the murmur of voices from upstairs and realized that she was with Henning and Lotten. That was good, then everyone would receive the news. He went upstairs and knocked softly on the door.

Henning opened it. He looked strangely absent-minded. Thumbs almost shouted the news: "August Blanche has died!"

Henning didn't really seem to take it in. He only looked at Thumbs, as if he didn't know who Blanche was.

"He's just been born," said Henning.

Then, for the first time, Thumbs saw the others in the room, Washer-Malin and Washer-Johanna, Matilda, and Lotten in bed. And the bundle which lay beside Lotten.

"Then you must name him August," said Thumbs.

Washer-Johanna packed up. She had done her job, helped yet another child into the world. She was no educated midwife, but she had the right touch and the knowledge which experience gives. She had born four children of her own and had assisted at many births. It was safer to get Johanna's help than lie at the hospital and risk getting childbed fever. Johanna didn't argue and cause a commotion, didn't nervously try to hurry along the contractions. She was calm and decisive and transformed something new and terrifying to something almost routine.

Henning had to go down to Matilda while Malin and Johanna took care of Lotten. Tense, he had sat down there and listened. Every noise had made him jump up and expect the worst.

He had expected violent shrieks of pain, thought a woman must almost be torn apart by that unnatural act of nature. But Lotten never screamed. When Henning heard steps on the stairs, he had rushed out, thinking: someone is coming to say she's dead. But it was Malin who, tired but happy, told him that he could go up, and Matilda too.

He hadn't known just how fast he could get up those stairs and how carefully he would look in the door. Lotten lay in bed, her dark hair damp with sweat. She was tired but smiled. Beside her slept their child, tired out from the strenuous passage to life.

He was a father now. His responsibility had grown; he couldn't give up before he got a really good job over the winter, while the harbor slept.

III

THE CHILDREN

The sunny spheres of dandelions shone from the ditches along the edge of Garbage Lane. The cows that had been let out of the barn down on Stora Bondgatan grazed on the green grass in the hollows, and around the pig house grunted pigs still thin from winter. The bleary-eyed old lady in the dairy hid behind the curtain which separated the store from her dwelling place. She didn't want to be seen mixing skim milk from water and many days' leftovers.

A flock of children came rushing down the steep slope, plowing their way through piles of garbage. At the head were the biggest, the lamplighter's seven-year-old twin boys who had just gotten home from school. They went to "the deaf mademoiselle" in the school for younger children, the crèche, and learned more deviltry than catechism. After them trotted whole rows of little children, runny-nosed ones born out of wedlock or undernourished foster children afraid of beatings. At least six or seven of them called the hired coach driver's hovel home, his wife had industrialized foster mothering. And almost as many came from the house next door, the "cigar box." They were the pledges of love of the girls who sold tobacco.

The lamplighter's son Emil had been asked to run an errand to the accountant at the technical factory and earned two öre. The gang stormed into the dairy, filling the tiny space inside and building a large semi-circle outside the door. The old lady grunted and put down her milk container to deliver a cone of bread crumbs in exchange for the coins. Followed by hungry glances, Emil went off with the cone held high above the heads of the multitude.

The ragged youngsters of the outskirts of town and of poverty: close to half of the city's children were born illegitimate. And of those that were called illegitimate, over half died before they reached three years of age. Their mothers couldn't stay at home any longer than necessary from factories, shops, taverns, and the kitchens of the gentry. They had to quickly wean their children and ask a neighbor's wife to give the little ones some of the dairy's milk when they cried with hunger. And in the dairy they threw together souring dregs and poured water into the milk they sold to the mothers.

In this way children were already cheated from birth. But what could the mothers do? Most of them tried to contract out their unwanted children, get someone to take them as cheaply as possible. The children became bartered goods, foster mothers could make a living by taking many at the highest price and nourishing them as cheaply as possible.

The children cried from hunger, were hit for being bad, hit for wearing out clothes, cursed at for eating too much. Many of them soon grew quiet and good, they died. Then there was an opening for new foster children.

While the mothers worked at the factories, while they danced on at their balls, while they lay with men who gave them a few coins or a little warmth, while they gave birth to new children.

The flock of children raced out across the hill to the rocky cranny where they usually gathered. Covetous hands reached for the cone with the desired crumbs. But nobody got anything before they all could say the verse that Emil had just learned:

> *Shit and Piss are cooking mates,*
> *Scraped britches on their plates,*
> *Best herring salad the king ever ate!*

They stood on the bare hill and bawled out what they just learned, a shrill chorus. Then they finally got the crumbs from the cone and small hands clutched them in cramped fists. Like dogs who had found bones, they sneaked mistrustfully and anxiously away into nooks, hiding themselves from the others while they ate, licking their hands clean.

GAMES AND SHADOWS

A little fellow of three who looked unusually well-nourished and well-dressed for living on the hill, sat at the open gate to the house at the end of Garbage Lane. He hadn't gone along in the wild game, had neither been to the dairy nor out on the hill. There was a sort of invisible chalk line that defined the boundaries of his world. He knew exactly how far he could go and how upset his mother would get if he went farther. But she seldom needed to admonish him, he was a surprisingly obedient child.

He sat and played with pine cones to which his father had fitted sticks for legs and heads. They were cows and had their barn between some stones. Then he watched for his playmate who had abandoned him for some of Emil's cake crumbs and finally caught sight of him.

"Rudde, Rudde!" he called.

The four-year-old Rudolf walked slowly. He still had some crumbs left which he really wanted to finish off before he returned to playing with the cows.

"I want a taste!" yelled August.

Rudolf stretched out his hand resignedly. But before August had a chance to reach with his and take hold of the crumbs he saw the shadow. And waited resignedly as well.

"Let's see, what do you two have?" asked August's mother. Rudolf's fingers crooked carefully, but he opened his hand.

"Yuck," she said. "Your fingers are filthy. You can't eat that. Throw it away."

Rudolf quickly pulled his hand back and licked up what was left. Lotten shook her head but was glad that she had gotten there in time to stop August from eating it. She was afraid of the filth around them. Recently several children had died of typhus. There were always some sicknesses around; there was no real safety. But she watched over her children, a protective shadow, herself shadowed by worry.

Actually she would have preferred to keep August inside the fence. But Rudolf was allowed to play outside and it would be cruel not to allow August to have a look around also. And Thumbs teased her for her fears: kids needed to come out and be tamed in the streets.

But the youngest ones she kept inside. Her Emelie and Matilda's Knut, both two years old, took their afternoon naps on a blanket. And her youngest, three-month-old Gertrud, lay in a basket. Lotten took care of both families' children and in exchange received some of the money that Matilda earned at the mill. It was an arrangement that was beneficial to all and gave Lotten the opportunity to keep their house like a clean pearl in the middle of the filth piled around it. Sometimes her cleanliness irritated Thumbs: you shouldn't spend your time carrying out small private bundles of your own garbage when you should really figure out how best to place the whole old society on the garbage heap.

The boys played nicely with the pine cones again; the smaller children slept. Lotten listened while she made over an old skirt into pants for August.

She wasn't more than twenty-four years old. Six years had passed since she had met Henning.

She smiled at the memories. At that time she had been irresponsible, at times trying to escape her mother's care. Her mother had been so worried the first time Lotten had stayed out a whole Saturday night....

And now she herself sat here with the responsibility and worry, with three children.

Naturally it had been easier to laugh before. When they only had themselves and each other. Those years seemed so light now, as if they had just risen up and flown away. But Lotten wasn't dissatisfied, wasn't disappointed. Only a little tired from the responsibility.

It would be nice when the children were bigger, and she and Henning had time for each other again.

Lotten was awakened from her musings by the squeak of the hinges.

Two little men stood in the gateway. Their eyes twinkled, they had plans.

They really were their fathers' sons, she thought. The cautious and calm August and the constantly lively and fidgety Rudolf.

Rudolf knew that the "goat lady" was going to milk her goats in a little while. It wasn't far away, just down Garbage Lane and out a little way along the grassy slope.

She looked at the small, expectant faces and felt she didn't have the heart to refuse. The boys could surely manage that little distance. But they had to promise to stay together, to take the shortest route and watch out for rough boys. Hand in hand they trudged off. Lotten stood in the door and watched, calling out to Rudolf not to walk through the garbage heaps. August took careful detours around them.

Outside the chalk line, without Mama. This was an adventure and August felt the excitement tingling inside him. He held tightly to Rudolf's hand, Rudolf knew the way and was used to being out.

Wet trash shone in the sunshine and caught their eye. You could find so much. But you couldn't keep it. Rudolf had a hiding place far back in the woodshed, but he didn't dare tell, not even Agge. Almost everything he kept there came from the trash heap.

But one half of a cup lay so far down the heap that you could say it wasn't really on it. Rudolf picked it up, wiped it clean on the seat of his pants and stuffed it in his pocket. Agge stared a little enviously but didn't ask if he could have it. He probably wouldn't be able to keep it anyway.

They went past Kvastmakarebacken which wound its way in along the side of the hill. They hardened themselves against the desire to go off exploring; their promise was still so fresh in their minds. They continued, instead, past the dairy where some wives stood and quarreled with the inhabitants. One of the women became so upset that she had a fit of coughing. She leaned against the wall of the house and looked like she was going to faint. The mucus she coughed up was red with blood.

The women shooed the boys away: they shouldn't stand and

watch, hadn't they seen people cough before?

The boys ran. They knew that grown-ups became dangerous very easily. Not their parents and the young girls in the kitchen, but the people outside. All the drunken old men and angry old women. Dangers lurked all the time like shadows and spooks around them; they could suddenly descend on them without reason. Rudde had gotten to know most of them. A coachman had rapped his knuckles just for approaching the cart where children usually grabbed on and rode along. A drunkard had kicked him in the bottom so hard that he had landed in a pile of garbage. An old woman who didn't like his looking at her had boxed his ear. Big boys had twisted his arms till he gave them everything he had in his pockets, and girls had pinched him and tied him fast with a string to a tree.

Agge had fared better since his mama always sat behind the fence. But old men had kicked down his barns, and children taken his cows. They knew they lived in a dangerous world, but danger also lent excitement to their existence, and they were learning an art they had to know: to be everywhere and yet always remain invisible, to go straight ahead and at the same time slide out of the way.

They slipped across Stora Bondegaten, checked that the street corner was clear, and stopped breathlessly to watch the greasy smoke billowing out of the technical factory.

"I'm going to make smoke when I grow up," said Rudde.

He had looked inside the factory yard once, but been quickly chased away.

"The goat lady!" he shouted, and took off with his friend.

They sat down beside the old lady and her goat. Rudde threw himself down on the grass without looking around, but Agge assured himself that there were no cowpies where he sat.

The goat milk streamed between the goat lady's claw-like fingers. At the hill next to Barnängen, drudges from the Dihlström institution stood by the big hill at the edge of Barnängen meadow and broke up macadam. The mill and the cosmetic factory's high smoke stack sent up their clouds of smoke; beyond the low hills in the direction of

Danviken the candle factory belched out smoke. The outskirts were both idyll and industry, green meadows and tumble-down houses. And for the small boys it was endless — a jungle to wander through and explore, full of exciting games and dangerous shadows.

Dusty and tired Dihlström workers came tramping in their enormous shoes on the way to their tavern break. The boys got up hurriedly; they were afraid of the men. They ran back toward Garbage Lane, but saw the new danger in time. A gang from Gröna gården at Tjärhovsgatan had advanced up the hill and forced the troops of Garbage Lane into retreat. Those who fell into the hands of this expedition could count on a beating; the feud was major and long standing.

Rudde whispered the way. They had to take a long detour around the dangerous area. Agge followed him loyally. They had to go all the way around the cosmetic factory, and then get back to the hill.

They ran as fast as they could, slipping on the edges of ditches, and hiding themselves behind some bushes to spy. They tried to take cover at the factory driveway, but they were driven away from there by the red, drink-befuddled gatekeeper. At the cross lane an angry dog barked, they hesitated a moment, but since their retreat was cut off, they had to be daring and pass by. At Lilla Bondegatan, they sneaked carefully past the house where the girls who made cigars lived. Rudde was afraid of some of the girls there. But those very girls caught sight of them, and, with howling and shrieking, Agge was taken prisoner. Rudde, who ran faster, kept a safe distance and wondered what he should do next.

"You're a bad boy," said one of the girls. "You tried to run away from your mama."

"Yes, you're eating us out of house and home," said another. "Just look at how fat you are! Your clothes barely fit you."

Agge stood between them, whimpering, trying to understand what they wanted and what they meant.

"I was allowed to go," he said.

"No you weren't," hissed the biggest girl. "I'm your mama, so I know."

"No," said Agge sullenly.

"And I'm your papa," said the other girl. "Now come home!"

He tried to resist, but it didn't help much. The girls shoved him ahead of them into the woodshed in the yard. At first he thought it was completely dark inside. After a while, though, he could see a little. The excited, hard expression he sensed on the girls' faces frightened him. He began to cry loudly.

"Quiet," hissed the big girl.

He sniffed and quieted down.

"Now you'll get a spanking, you nasty, fat child!"

Agge didn't dare protest; he just sat there and swallowed his sobs. Then they turned him over.

Beside himself, he tried to kick free, but they held down his arms and legs. He felt how they pulled down his pants, and in his fright he let go a little trickle that wet the older girl's skirt and made her angry. Then they hit him, with the pent-up, exploding fury of the beaten and abused.

"Stop now," urged the younger girl. She began to be afraid. The older one looked around, dazed, as if she had just awakened from a nightmare.

"If you tell, you'll get the same again," said the younger girl.

"You'll get a spanking every day," said the big one.

Agge didn't hear them. He hardly felt them pull up his pants again.

"You can't go until you stop blubbering," said the younger girl.

He tried to bite his teeth together, sniffling and hiccuping, tears plowing furrows in his dirty face.

They put him on his feet and pushed him between themselves across the yard. A cigar-maker who was hanging out a window in the courtyard asked why the boy was crying so hard.

"He's fallen and hurt himself," said the younger girl.

"We bathed his sore with water," said the older one.

They shoved him on his way and ran the other way to be safe.

Half-blinded by tears, he stumbled home.

When Henning got home, Lotten was white with fury. She took him to the bed where August lay and slept, showing him his face swollen from crying, and the red marks left by the girls' hands.

Rudolf pointed out where the girls lived. Henning went there to talk to their mother; they had no father since they lived in a cigar box. Klara had moved there from New Square a while back, and Henning hoped it wasn't her children who were guilty.

As soon as he saw the woman, he knew it was useless to speak to her. No threats were new to her, and probably the girls already received more beatings than they should.

It was hopeless. He felt like he had failed his mission when he returned home.

So there was only one thing to do: watch over Agge even more carefully, keep him even closer. He was allowed to play in Lotten's shadow, but wasn't allowed to go with Rudolf down to the goat lady anymore that spring.

He sat in the doorway again and played with his cows while Rudde went off with a crowd of boys. Rudolf always got by. But any time an older girl walked past, Agge hurried inside either to go to the bathroom or look at his younger sisters or get something.

SATURDAY BROTHERS

Every other Saturday night, Rudolf and his little brother had to move out to their "aunties" in the kitchen. That was when the educational circle, "Saturday Brothers," met in their parents' room.

The Brothers made their way up the rough roads and winding paths to the house on the hill. Some lived close by, others had a long way to walk. All but one were workers and artisan's apprentices; the nine Brothers represented eight different trades.

They sat down on the beds and wooden benches that were brought in for the evening. Matilda had lighted the two lamps they had and then gone upstairs to Lotten. Thumbs leafed through the notebook where they kept the minutes and spoke with the evening's guest, a tailor's apprentice who was going to talk about his impression of the German socialists and their party.

Suddenly there was a pounding on the door. Thumbs looked up quickly, he didn't expect anyone else. Could it be the police? The best thing to say, in that case, would be that it was an educational circle; it couldn't be punishable to participate in something like that.

He went and opened the door, and found a tottering figure. The hired-coach driver.

Thumbs had spoken with the coachman a few times. "Dad," as he was called, because of his innumerable foster children, usually staggered out every morning at around four o'clock, heavy and tired from too little sleep and too much to drink. They walked a little way together, sometimes, and then they talked about the inhuman conditions the coachmen worked under.

Coachmen were the true proletariat, the most extreme of the city's rough element. They hung like dirty sacks on their broken-down and miserable carts, whipping the swollen and pain-ridden wrecks of horses and quarreling with the customers.

They had to be at the stable at five in the morning to wash their cabs before they drove out, then they had sixteen and sometimes perhaps seventeen hours ahead of them on the coach box. There they sat in rain and cold, snow or blazing hot sun. No dinner breaks or days off existed. If you wanted a break, you had to pay for a "pilot," as a temporary replacement was called.

Eight kronor a week was Dad's salary. Naturally he stretched it out by pocketing some of the fares he brought in. That was why his jobber took his coin purse as often as possible and emptied it of every öre, disregarding Dad's protests that some of the coins were his own.

"You should go on strike," Thumbs had said one morning.

That was why Dad had come now. He had talked with some of the fellows as they sat on their bench on Södermalmstorg playing cards while they waited for customers. They had made an agreement to strike for one day off a month and ten kronor a week.

The Saturday Brothers made space for their brother in misfortune. In the presence of the newcomer, they seemed almost prim and petits-bourgeois. Here a true proletarian had stepped into their midst. Dirty and lousy, Dad sat on the wooden bench, letting out a long beer belch before he offendedly spoke of his working conditions and his hopes.

Once before, with two comrades, he had tried to ask a jobber for one day off a month, but he had poured abuse on them and blamed them for spending their days drinking and stealing from the jobber. Of course, they drank and probably stole: he admitted that. But what were they supposed to do?

First and most important, stop drinking and pull themselves together, said the tailor who was a teetotaler.

Strike, was Thumbs' opinion. Such notorious fighters as they were should be able to prevent others from taking their work.

But would the jobbers give in to their demands, wondered the bricklayer. The bricklayers some years earlier had built a union, and thanks to that, had managed to stop plans to lower their salaries.

Not everyone was so successful, said the tobacco worker. Think of last year's strike at Hellgren's tobacco factory. It ended with defeat and the dismissal of twenty workers.

Henning listened without making any contribution to the discussion. He was afraid of conflict, and waited anxiously for Thumbs to prevail upon the dock workers to go on strike next. Henning wouldn't be able to keep out of it then and what could they do? Didn't it have to end in defeat? They would have a hard time during the strike and be left without work afterwards. That meant catastrophe for his family; the children and Lotten would starve. He understood that the workers had to struggle for their interests, that it required struggle for conditions to improve. But he understood, too, that the battle would cost an unbelievable amount, crush so much of the little they had managed to build.

If only work helped, if only fighting wasn't necessary.

"We can only have success through uniting," said the bricklayer. "First strong unions and sufficient funds, and then demands and strikes."

"We can't wait so long," Thumbs interrupted. "We have to make a move first and build unions later. The employers don't understand anything but fighting. They can't be talked down. They have to be beaten down."

"Then the police and the military will come to their aid," said the tobacco worker. "Those who own society also own the means to power."

"And workers have gotten stuck in the liberal syrup," said the tailor. "First of all we have to fight the liberal worker's unions that make pronouncements against any kind of strike."

"Temperance lectures and moralistic sermonizing," hissed Thumbs. "That's the only thing they have to give us. We should become sober and moral, so the rich can squeeze even more out of us."

"Improving the workers' lot is only in their own interest," put in the tailor. "The jobbers encourage drinking among the drivers so they will be easier to suppress. The stevedores give the dock workers liquor so they will keep quiet and work without grumbling."

"That may be so," admitted Thumbs, "but still that takes away attention from what's the most important thing. It's a question of a class struggle: the goal can only be reached through a violent upheaval."

"As Marx says," said the evening's speaker.

But Dad didn't want to listen to a lecture. He thanked them for the words he had received and went out to encourage his brothers to strike. Carefully and as inconspicuously as possible, Thumbs wiped off the bench where he had sat.

At around ten o'clock most of the Saturday Brothers broke up. Matilda and Lotten came down from upstairs, and the girls from the kitchen looked in. Saturday evenings usually ended with a simple supper for the most loyal attendants. These were the bricklayer, who was named Kalle Håkansson, and a tall and thin young man named Pontus Berger. Berger was the only one in the circle who wasn't a worker, but he was perhaps the poorest among them. He earned his living by writing small articles and contributions to *The Fatherland*. He had come into contact with Håkansson during the time of the bricklayers' strike and shown such great understanding for the workers' demands that Håkansson had decided that it was worth taking care of his "education."

Anna-Kajsa and Tekla carried in the herring and potatoes, bread, and beer, and schnapps. Håkansson tried to joke with Berger that it was time for the teetotalers to leave but got no answer. Berger sat deaf and dumb. It was Anna-Kajsa's fault; the sight of her always had a paralyzing effect on the young man.

"What did that awful coachman want?" asked Matilda.

"To strike," Håkansson answered, and took a herring.

"What did you advise him to do then?"

"To strike, of course," answered Thumbs.

"And organize," added Håkansson. "By the way," he continued, "have you tried to build a union down at the harbor?"

That was a difficult question, and Thumbs took his time with the answer. Håkansson looked at Henning.

"Lundström, the stevedore, has threatened to fire those who agitate," said Henning.

"Naturally," nodded Håkansson. "They always make threats. You have to organize in secret and not step forward before everything is ready. It's more trouble to fire a lot of people, in that case employers will more likely meet demands."

"We have a difficult crew," said Thumbs. "Lots of day laborers who take odd jobs now and then, migrant farmers, upper-class drunkards. There are too many unsteady workers, too many uninterested ones."

"You have to begin with the steady ones, the best," said Håkansson. "The ones the foremen and the stevedores want to keep."

"Of course something has to be done," answered Thumbs. "But the ones who do it are doomed."

Lotten looked anxiously at Henning. She hoped he wouldn't say anything. She was afraid of the educational circle, afraid of Thumbs' many ideas. Thumbs pushed Henning, she felt, forcing him farther and faster than he wanted to go himself. Not everyone was made to be a pioneer; some were simply ordinary people that didn't demand more than the right to work and live. Besides, Henning was someone who least fit the role of agitator.

"Something has to be done," said Thumbs. "Let's have a toast to that."

Pontus Berger gave a start as if he had been caught doing something. He had been sitting and admiring Anna-Kajsa's profile which was outlined against the shade of the oil lamp. And thinking the exact same words that Thumbs had uttered.

It had already started getting light out before the two guests left the house. But before this, Berger had had a conversation with Anna-Kajsa about the gainful employment of women. The conversation had been extremely rewarding he assured her when he said good-bye. It was true: he had found out where she worked and what her hours were. Someday he would succeed in mustering up the courage to walk past her workplace by sheer coincidence as she walked home.

He hummed to himself as he wove his way home beside the steady

Håkansson. But the bricklayer grumbled and said that they hadn't drunk enough to make them sing in the street in the middle of the night. Then Berger felt like he'd been caught once again and began a serious discussion on the terrible conditions of hired-coach drivers. He would really like to write something which would support their actions. But Håkansson wasn't as interested as Berger had expected, the bricklayer who had a decent salary and led an orderly life didn't want to include those rowdies among skilled apprentices and workers. To a certain degree the hired drivers could blame themselves, he thought. They were drunken, crude peasants without honor and competence in their work, and he himself would never willingly go and sit in one of their lice-infested coaches.

Then Berger grew silent and thought about Ann-Kajsa instead. And they walked down Stora Glasbruksgatan where the whores hung out the windows and doorways and smiled gap-toothed smiles which they thought were inviting.

"One day those sows will also want to call themselves workers and build unions," the bricklayer muttered angrily.

Håkansson wanted be both radical and respected, but he was no smooth tightrope walker who could glide across the rope. Perhaps the events this spring had also caused him to doubt the possibility of organizing a united workers' movement. Troublemakers of all kinds were a difficult burden for the skilled workers. And now remarkable things were happening everyday. Accomplished workers were receiving appreciably higher salaries. Tailors, cobblers and painters had gotten up to twenty-five percent increases — the painters together with a decrease in their workday by one hour. The brewery workers had received a raise without even asking for it, and in newspaper notices they thanked their employers.

It didn't make sense. Surely Marx hadn't said it would happen this way? Or was it just a question of bribes?

If the artisans' apprentices joined forces with the factory workers, longshoremen and contracted drivers, they would lose a lot, both their standing and the possibility of improving their position.

Solidarity, thought the bricklayer. But solidarity certainly had its limitations, one was together with one group and against another. Against the employers and with the agitators? Or with the employers, the profession, and against the agitators? Or against both the employers and the troublemakers?

He spat at the streetwalkers and grumbled ill-humoredly over not really knowing which way he wanted it.

The hired coachmen went on strike, all except for jobber Westerly's men. On that unusually beautiful and warm first of May there were a lot of people, but few cabs out. A few days later the strike was over. The coachmen had neither the solidarity nor the capital, and their wives and children pressured them to a resolution. The jobbers weren't completely impossible to talk to either; some gave minor pay raises. But they didn't even want to hear of any days off.

Dad was still able to be satisfied with their actions. In his joy he bought an extra bottle and became so reckless that he decided to examine and see which of the two policemen outside the meat-tester's office were free of trichina. It cost him a half-year's salary raise. And his jobber, who advanced him the money for the fine, received new proof that it wasn't worth giving the drivers more pay. They only drank away their money.

A LONGSHOREMAN BECOMES A BAKER

Henning and Thumbs were on their way to the harbor and their daily job. The weather had turned; the stifling July heat was gone, and the August morning was refreshingly cool. They made their way down the sloping hillside among Sågaregatan's low wooden houses and cultivated fields, climbed Ersta hill toward Stigberget and took the stairs down to the harbor.

Thumbs had begun to agitate for the dock workers' own union. The opposition was like gelatin, tough and trembling at the same time, anxiously elusive. People understood that it was risky and couldn't see how a union could be of any use. Lundström and the others weren't going to give in just because some longshoremen had been conspiring. No, the stevedores would tell them to go to hell and then give their work to new people. It might happen that the typographers and masons would make use of their own organizations; their work required a lengthy education which represented a capital investment. But dock workers? The whole harbor was full of people who wanted those steady jobs, and even more could be brought in from the countryside if the city workers caused trouble.

Of course, the working hours, salaries and everything were bad. Of course, they needed a union, solidarity, and common demands. Of course, they would join up, only not now and not before everybody joined.

Thumbs felt bitter at times. He could admit that the risks were great for those who joined. But still, something had to be done, some people had to sacrifice themselves, didn't they? Besides, they could wait with appearing openly; they should wait for the right moment to act. After they had grown to a large number and the harbor was full of vessels. Then the stevedores would risk big losses if the old, experienced workers went on strike. But nobody wanted to sacrifice themselves, they had to sacrifice enough to support wives and children. The most recent years had given them some benefits without their having to risk anything. Salaries had slowly risen and work opportunities increased. Perhaps everything would work out eventually, without a struggle.

A few had still let their names be put down as being interested. Most of them had done it with reservations. Thumbs could not give out their names. Henning belonged to this anxious few.

He was ashamed of his caution. Almost every morning as they walked to work, he felt he had to explain himself to Thumbs. Lotten mustn't be made to worry now, she was expecting again. He had promised her not to get involved in anything, not put their existence at risk. Thumbs had to understand.

Still, Henning had trouble making sense of it himself. It was as if he lived in two countries which both demanded his loyalty. Family, or his private life, versus the group, his class. Both family and class demanded their due, neither could be let down. He had to draw a line somewhere between the two of them and their demands. He hadn't found it yet, as if the outermost edges of each ran over into the territory of the other. The fate of families depended on their class's fate, that much he admitted. If the workers' children were condemned to a life of misery, so were his children as well. Some were going to have to take up the cause to bring about a change, but those who sacrificed themselves would also sacrifice their families. And Henning couldn't sacrifice his family for his class.

It ended up being insoluble, whichever course of action he took he was doomed. But he wanted Thumbs to know how eagerly he was searching for a solution, that he wasn't backing off out of personal fear and disinterest.

Thumbs understood, he suffered from the same torment. But he found it easier to shrug things off than Henning did. Thumbs had no small peasant inside him, he belonged to the rootless, had grown up with their proverb: "Everything will work out." In a way that differed from Henning's he had friends everywhere, secret places, opportunities. Lundström and the stevedores could run him out of the harbor;

he would pop up somewhere else, impossible to beat down. He could settle his family down with friends and find a hundred odd jobs and means of livelihood. But Henning needed a place to live and work, a piece of turf and roots.

"Take it easy and have your children," said Thumbs. "I know that you're here, that we can count on you when the going gets tough."

In spite of everything, Thumbs thought that things had begun to work out lately. He had gotten hold of a dock worker who was truly interested, at least, and was prepared to fight.

Long-Jonte didn't belong to the élite in the harbor, not even to the permanently employed. He was a day laborer, a substitute, a tall, skinny native of Småland, who had been allowed to join the same team as Thumbs while Rags lay in the hospital. Rags had been boss at the hatch, and the load that had been hoisted up had been too heavy. The deck hands hadn't been able to lift it out properly and, instead, had lost their grip. The load had slid backwards and knocked Rags down into the hold. Still, Rags had been lucky; other bosses had broken their backs across the keel. Rags had gotten away with a few broken ribs.

His replacement didn't really have the routine down and the strength that was necessary. But Long-Jonte was tough and stubborn and tried his best to fill his place. During breaks he preferred to stick close to Thumbs and listen to him expound. One day he told them that he had a wife and seven children back in Småland, so he certainly agreed that wages had to be increased. Actually, Jonte had participated before in Trollhättan four years earlier when the paper workers had gone on strike. That had been a real party...it had ended in an all out fist fight with the police. Twelve workers had been sentenced to prison for causing a riot.

Jonte was prepared to join a union if they formed one. But first he wanted to know if any of the steady guys were going along.

Thumbs answered vaguely, he didn't want to name any names. But since Jonte was so interested he was told that Fearsome, Old-Nick, and Stringtie had promised to take the leadership together with Thumbs.

"Henkan must be going to join too," said Long-Jonte. But Thumbs shook his head. They went back to the cargo boat which was to be loaded. Jonte took his place on the deck, and Thumbs climbed down into the cargo hold.

"Attention in the hold!" called out Long-Jonte.

"All set!" responded Thumbs from inside the boat.

While Thumbs received the cargo down in the dimly-lit room, he thought about what was bad and what was good.

The newspapers had written that this was a good year, and everybody said the same. There was work and bread; unusually few sicknesses were prevalent; spring had come early and been warm; the summer had been beautiful; a lot of artisans had gotten raises. Everything had been unusually good. And immediately many of them dropped off, felt like it was both useless and silly to work toward a better society: everything would be fine anyway. Did the poor always have to have the whip of extreme want over them in order to creep forward? Were they prepared to accept the existing order of things if they received some charity?

And did he himself wish for that want, did he wish for the whip over them?

It was there all right, just a little less noticeable when the lash didn't come quite as hard as they were used to.

Certainly the whip was there. Every day human lives were crumbled to pieces under it. And if no one else was doing the whipping, then the poor themselves were.

A few days later, Thumbs received orders to appear in the stevedore's office. Pensively he looked at his boss, wondering what it could be all about. He thought how he had worked at the harbor for ten years now, and that probably one of the old bosses wasn't going to manage working much longer. It could be an offer and then he would land in a difficult situation. Of course, it was good to be a boss, but that would place him in an adversarial position with his comrades.

He didn't stay alone in the vestibule outside the stevedore's office for long. First came Fearsome. Then Stringtie. Then Old-Nick.

The entire planned leadership.

A clerk looked out, cautiously. He counted carefully and saw that it was the right number. He knocked timidly on Lundström's door and opened it a crack when he got a grunt in reply.

"They're here," said the clerk and closed the door, disappearing quickly back into his office.

The four of them looked wonderingly at each other. It began to dawn on them what this was all about. And Thumbs had a feeling that it wasn't just himself and his family who were going to be affected.

The door swung open with a quick push and Stevedore Lundström stood and looked at them.

Old-Nick stared stubbornly and scared at the floor, while Stringtie tried to catch his breath. Fearsome tried to look innocently interested, as if he had no idea why they had been called up to the office. But Thumbs smiled; when he stood face to face with his adversary, he got cool inside; anxiety and fear disappeared. It was too late to regret anything, now he had to take it as it came.

"So," said Lundström, "you think some rowdies can just thumb their noses at me..."

"Who has claimed that?" Thumbs asked calmly.

He received no answer.

"I don't want to hear of any trouble," said Lundström. "You have all been told. We've never had any strike here before and we won't have it in the future either. Each and every one who agitates will be fired from here."

"You have all been informed!" he shouted.

"Yes," sighed Old-Nick gloomily.

"Still, I have learned that you four have built some sort of strike leadership," continued Lundström. "Against my orders!"

"Excuse me," said Thumbs, "but we've done no such thing. We haven't built anything."

"Don't try to deny it," screamed Lundström.

Thumbs thought quickly. He had no chance of getting off himself, but he could save the others maybe. If he shouldered the whole blame himself — and of course it was his wasn't it?

"I have agitated," said Thumbs. "But not for a strike, only for a union, the same as they have at other work places. There the employers negotiate with the workers."

"I don't intend to negotiate with any troublemakers!" said Lundström. "If you don't like it you can leave, there are others. In any case you'll all be leaving anyway."

"I am the only one who has agitated," said Thumbs stubbornly. "No one else."

Lundström pondered this. It wasn't that easy to get capable people when times were good. The three old guys were really decent; there were seldom any complaints against them. But the youngster should be kicked down the stairs, he had been fresh before.

"We haven't said or done anything at all," protested Old-Nick and continued to stare at the floor. He had found a little spot on the rug, and he clung to it as if it could save him.

Lundström looked at Stringtie. The beer-bellied man felt his gaze and began to breathe heavily. He didn't dare do more than shake his head.

Lundström shifted his gaze to Fearsome. The dock worker mulled it over for a minute. Then he said in his rough, booming voice: "I maintain that we need a union. So it's just as well that I finish up at the harbor."

Stringtie and Old-Nick had to return to work with a strict warning to guard against bad company in the future.

Thumbs and Fearsome remained. Thumbs felt how his lips smiled without his finding anything to smile at. He reacted that way, and it usually drove his adversary mad.

Stevedore Lundström promised that he would send the police after the two of them if they dared show themselves at the harbor again. Then he shouted for the office workers. But Thumbs and Fearsome left quietly while a frightened bookkeeper stood and yapped in the doorway.

Silently they walked along the wharf, heard the rattle of the winch-es and the dock workers' shouted commands: Haul the line! Let go! Haul up!

They were no longer a part of it. They had known the cama-raderie, belonged to the harbor folk. Now Lundström would call for the police if he saw them there.

Silently they walked up the stairs to the Brass Pole Tavern on Brunnsbacken to drink farewell.

The following day Long-Jonte was a permanent on the team led by Heathen Dog. The fellow from Småland stared a little anxiously at his comrades and listened nervously at break time when people talked about Fearsome and Thumbs' disappearance. But there were only rumors and no facts. Old-Nick and Stringtie refused to talk about what had happened. Many came to Henning and inquired but he answered cautiously.

Henning felt alone; Thumbs and Fearsome had been his best friends at the harbor. He belonged with them, and when he was left behind on his own, it felt as if he had committed treason.

Long-Jonte came over at the dinner break and gave him a friend-ly grin. Henning, who needed someone to talk to, said it surprised him that he hadn't been fired too. Fearsome and Thumbs had been his best friends.

"Did you participate on that strike committee?" wondered Jonte.

Henning shook his head. No, he hadn't been involved in anything.

"You don't have to worry," Jonte assured him. "I happened to be in the office actually when Heathen Dog told Lundström that you should be fired for safety's sake. But Lundström didn't believe that you had been involved. "You were decent," he said.

Henning had a feeling that the memory of the fire in the Bodin factory had saved him. Still, he felt that what he heard was a confir-mation that he had betrayed Thumbs and Fearsome.

It wasn't until he was back at work again that he began to wonder if the person in question didn't also give confirmation of something else. How had Long-Jonte learned what Heathen Dog had confided in the stevedore? What was Jonte doing in the office?

That evening Henning talked together with Thumbs, and they pieced together what they knew. The picture cleared: Long-Jonte was the informant. Slowly the rumor spread along the wharf. Conversation halted wherever Long-Jonte went, and a certain chill prevailed. And the Småland native who had succeeded to the vacated job looked thinner and more afraid, glancing around nervously as if he was constantly expecting an attack. He tried to complain to the boss but actually had nothing concrete to come up with: nobody had hit him, nobody had said anything. Heathen Dog just sneered scornfully. Anyone who couldn't get along with his comrades had only himself to blame.

Long-Jonte fumbled along in terror, waiting for someone to let a cargo hook swing a little too far out or let a load fall a little too soon. It wouldn't take more than that to leave his seven children fatherless.

Unrest continued to spread. Especially among the temporary workers, the ones who had the least to lose. Some of the guardsmen and other unattached men who had worked on the docks on Lake Mälar demanded better wages for their services and tried to hinder those who were willing to work for the old rates. The police were called in and eventually the rebellious ones were fined "for causing obstruction of traffic." At Riddarholm dock, some of the dock workers went on strike but were sentenced for causing a disturbance. There was ferment everywhere, and Stevedore Lundström gave his office workers a scolding for letting the original perpetrators of all this evil get off so easily, without even a good kick in the backside.

But Thumbs knew a baker journeyman who wanted to go out on his own in these good times. Journeyman Sundberg took over an old bakery that had stood empty for a long time, fixed it up as well as he could, and hired a few journeymen and apprentices. The baker journeymen held tightly onto membership in the guild so Thumbs couldn't become a real journeyman. But he tidied up and lighted the fire and stepped in as extra help. The journeymen and the apprentices lived at the workplace, but Thumbs came and went. He had to reshape his habits. Bakers worked at night, of course. Thumbs didn't mind, he liked changes. The only drawback was that he couldn't continue with the educational circle, the Saturday Brothers. And that he got to see his wife so seldom, they only saw each other a few hours in the early morning.

Perhaps there was too little sleep as well. So much was going on during the day when Thumbs was supposed to sleep. King Karl died, and his coffin was carried on an open railway car from Malmö to its final destination at Riddarholm. One day Thumbs had to go see the endless lines waiting to view the royal corpse, another day be a part of the throngs of people at the funeral. Then he had to help Kerstin and the women from Dalarna organize the first strike at the candle factory. It was short and sweet. After a two-hour silent sit-down strike one Saturday, the women got a pay raise. Thumbs' self-confidence, slightly tarnished by disgrace, shone with a newly polished luster, and he was happy he had left the hopelessly backward harbor.

STORM AND DARKNESS

That fall had been unusually mild and lovely. The people who crammed together and lived in outhouses, drafty attics or damp cellars took each of these days as a gift. But every morning and evening they looked anxiously at the sky and wondered what the weather was going to bring. Henning had to put up the divider again because they couldn't refuse to share the space they had. A glove seamstress that Lotten had worked with lived with her children in the attic.

In the pig shed down on Stora Bondegatan, a factory worker had moved into one of the sties with her three children. When it rained, Garbage Lane's water and filth ran into the dark sty where there wasn't a chink for the sun, but where there were many cracks and holes for wind and water.

Many of the poor and homeless didn't dare think ahead to the winter. Some did and committed desperate acts: one father severed the arteries of his children and himself. The factory worker drowned herself and her three children in Hammarby Lake.

Winter was late in coming. But the storms arrived.

The panes rattled in the wind; it whistled in the cracks; dust and trash whirled through the streets. One morning the storm had torn loose the dock at Ragvaldsbro, it lay and bobbed like a raft far out in the water of Riddarfjärd.

New storms followed soon after, even worse, more brutal, and with them came the cold. Some of the panes in the house on the hill were pushed in; the children awoke and cried with fright when the glass crashed to the floor, and the cold flung itself upon them. Henning tried to nail some old rugs over the open window, but the rugs were torn to shreds and flapped noisily in the room. They didn't dare light the kerosene lamp; it might get knocked over and set the house on fire. Henning groped his way down to the yard in the dark and managed to let himself into the shed and find a few boards. Not until he had nailed them up could they light the lamp, and they sat, frozen and afraid, and listened to the organ-like roar.

The roof blew off of a house nearby. Trees and branches cracked, falling across paths and houses. Fences collapsed, boats were torn apart. When Henning got down to the harbor, large and small vessels had piled up and lay banging against each other alongside the Stadsgård docks. Outside the locks a large barge had capsized; fifteen hundred barrels of coal lay at the bottom of the sea, and the barge was left with its keel in the air.

People everywhere were struggling in the storm, rescuing, repairing, clearing roads. But it was as if all efforts were meaningless, the storm continued to tear down whatever people went to enormous lengths to build.

The hurricane raged for two days and two nights. Then the weather reversed; it turned mild, snow fell but quickly melted. The glass master finally had time to get to the wooden houses on the hill. Lotten tried to carefully fill in the ugly holes from the nails. She had trouble moving around, was large and unwieldy. Her immobility irritated her. She knew that it gave the little boys too many opportunities to escape her supervision. She couldn't have them tied to her and couldn't prevent August from going at least a little way from the house together with Rudolf. But worry gnawed at her constantly, and time after time, she had to go down the stairs and outside to look for them. She was especially afraid that Rudolf would get them to wander down to the lake. One of the families in the Dyer's yard had lost three children by drowning.

Every day, danger lay close by, threatening the children. Lotten was amazed now at how little she had worried about it before. As soon as she got to the dairy, she heard about new accidents. One day a neighboring woman told her that one of the houses on Nya gatan had been ravaged by fire. They had managed to put the fire out before the house had burned down, but three children had suffocated from the smoke.

Now there was a wake going on in the summer house in the courtyard next door, and a teacher from the school at Nytorget had collected donations to aid the parents.

Lotten couldn't get away from the thought of the dead children. And she thought how it would be good for Rudolf and August to see how menacingly close death was, especially Rudolf who had such trouble being careful. More and more frequently he came home with torn knees and a bloody nose, and in the afternoons when the kerosene lamp was lighted, she had to watch him constantly to make sure that he didn't play with the flame.

Lotten washed the boys' hands and faces and tried to make them as neat as possible. She wrapped her large winter shawl about her and took a boy by each hand. But she had trouble walking and they were too energetic. She had to let them go at their own pace, and put up with having them first ahead of her, then behind her.

Slowly, they struggled down the muddy hillsides, following Nya gatan along the slopes of the White Hills where leafless black trees spread their outstretched branches between jutting boulders and the roofs of sheds. Already from a distance, she could see which house it was by the crowds outside and the shattered windows.

They got in line, and the boys squirmed a little; they didn't want to stand still. But Lotten held them tightly by the hand and shushed them when they whined. They had to be quiet here, she explained. It wasn't so easy for them to understand, perhaps, in the middle of that noisy crowd.

They squeezed through the entryway and into the courtyard. Many feet had trampled the path and the grass border to mud. A few lighted candles flickered and shone in the glass panes of the summer house, and in the doorway the old, white-haired teacher stood and held out a plate. Lotten dug out the coins she had hidden in her skirt pockets, unknotted the handkerchief they were in and carefully let them clink onto the plate.

In three small, simple boxes lay the victims of the fire, well-combed and with prayer books on their breasts. Lotten lifted up the boys one at a time so they could see. She had trouble going through with it, but she had to. Weeping, she looked at the three, feeling as if it were her children who lay there.

When they had come out into the courtyard again, August asked why the children were sleeping, and why so many people were looking at them. She tried to explain to him that they were dead, that August had to be careful and never run in front of wagons, and that Rudolf must never again play with fire. If they didn't obey they would also die, just like the children in the summer house. They would never again be able to play. And their parents would cry so terribly, never be able to be happy again.

But the boys had hardly gotten out into the street before they ran off, faster than she could follow.

Lotten walked heavily behind them, full of worry for the living and for the unborn. When she had lifted August who was heavier than Rudolf, she had felt her unborn child kick anxiously.

The day came, sooner than she had expected. Lotten was obliged to rouse Thumbs, who slept in the room below, and ask him to try and find her mother. Dazedly, Thumbs rushed off to get Washer-Malin. Malin said she would notify Johanna, and Thumbs went on down to the harbor to get Henning, without thinking of Lundström's ban.

Thumbs and Henning ran up the stairs together to Stigberget. But when they reached the top Thumbs couldn't keep up. Henning had to run on alone while Thumbs caught his breath and continued more slowly homewards. He gasped and wiped his eyes with his coat sleeve, realizing that he wouldn't get any more sleep that day. Someone had to keep an eye on the younger children, at least.

Henning arrived first, ahead of Malin and Johanna, and he came home to a house in confusion. August and Rudolf sat whimpering on the stairs. Lotten had forbidden them to come in, and now they heard her moaning from behind the closed door. Thumbs had locked the three youngest ones in the kitchen, and they were wailing in there, abandoned.

At first Henning stood at a loss. Then he quickly patted the boys on the head, and they calmed down a little. He told them to try and be really quiet and good, there wasn't anything bad happening. But he felt neither calm nor sure himself when he hurried in to Lotten.

She was sitting on the edge of the bed and crying. Even before the pains began, she had been tired, had felt she was at the end of her rope. Now she felt she didn't have the energy to cope with what awaited her.

He sat down beside her and tried to calm and comfort her. Gradually it seemed that some of her tension eased; she leaned against him, relaxed, thought it felt a little better.

Then Malin and Johanna arrived and Henning had to go out to take care of the children.

Darkness fell. Thumbs and Henning sat in the room on the ground floor, saying a few words, mostly listening to the noises from overhead. It got to be time for Thumbs to go to the bakery, right after Matilda got back. She helped Henning put the children to bed. They had to squeeze in together as best they could. The kerosene lanterns shone weakly. The girls in the kitchen came home and learned what was happening, and Henning helped them light a fire in the stove. After a little while Pontus Berger arrived too, he had overcome some of his shyness and was a frequent guest in their kitchen. The girls made supper. Malin and Johanna had something to eat taken up to them, but Lotten didn't want anything. Henning tried to force something down, but it wasn't easy; it was as if the food got caught in his throat with every noise from overhead.

He heard the cry, the reassuring voices. He hurried up the stairs and listened at the door. But everything was apparently going as it should, Johanna sounded as calm as ever.

And then he heard Johanna's voice change, become more tense. Silent and afraid, he waited. He heard Johanna and Malin's low, agitated voices.

Malin was holding up the kerosene lamp for light. She was wondering if she should ask Henning to run for the doctor. But that would take time, perhaps too long. Johanna shook her head. The large woman was dripping with sweat from her exertions. She grew more and more convinced that all was not right.

The child's head had pushed out. And it was blue, dark blue.

Johanna couldn't understand what had happened. Carefully she tried to help the baby out. Then she saw the umbilical cord around its neck, like the rope around the neck of someone doomed to die.

She tried to loosen the tangle. But this pulled it even tighter. If she couldn't do anything about it very soon, the child would be strangled.

She made a desperate attempt, managing to angle the child upward without the cord cutting deeper into its throat. Then she saw that the cord was also wound around one of the child's feet, that every movement the baby made to come out meant that the knot was pulled tighter. Its little foot had the same blue color as its face.

She undid the cord from around its neck and foot and looked at the deep mark around its throat. But the blue color disappeared slowly, a little spank and the baby cried.

It was a girl, Lotten's third daughter.

But the girl didn't live more than five days. Perhaps the journey into the world had been too difficult. First Henning went for the doctor who couldn't do anything, and then got the priest who performed an emergency baptism.

Lotten was too weak to go along to the cemetery. Malin and Henning had to go alone.

It felt like spring in the air even though it was soon going to be Christmas. But Henning only felt the darkness around him.

Lotten blamed herself for the child's death. What a pregnant woman looked at affected the fetus. Through going and looking at the dead children, she had killed her own child. In caring for the living, she had killed the unborn.

She brooded, walked around in the gloom and looked out the window, down over a dark city and dark waters.

THE RINGING OF BELLS

There were many small bells ringing, giving the city a lighter, cleaner feeling. White snow covered the garbage piles, mud puddles, and ditches. No heavy cartwheels creaked and fastened in the ruts. Instead, sleighs glided easily while sleigh bells and harness bells played from the horses' necks.

The winter was still mild; barges had been able to get in and out of the harbor during all of January. The ice at Kornhamn and Hammarby Lake was treacherous, and every day some incautious person had to be hauled out, and almost every day somebody drowned.

One Sunday in February new snow lay sparkling white over the whole hillside and repainted Garbage Lane into a sunny, shining idyll with decorative cotton wool-covered rooftops, tree branches and lampposts. Henning stood at the gate. He had to put down the empty water pails just to look. Wasn't it the most magnificent winter day he had seen here?

Some of the fatigue and sadness disappeared; a little of the darkness gave way to the shimmering sunlight.

It was too bad about the children, Henning thought. Both he and Lotten had been so depressed and worn out. Children needed happiness and their parents' smiles. He remembered the sled that stood in the woodshed, practically finished. He had put many hours' work into it before the dismal days had come. After that it had stood forgotten. He just had to nail on some planks for seats and then it could be used.

Henning hurried and made his way slipping and sliding down the hill to the well at Stora Bondegatan. He filled the buckets and smiled when he thought of sledding and the children's happiness, maybe even at the memory of how he himself once, many years ago, had sped down the slopes of the White Hills.

But on the way up again, some of the fatigue returned. A few buckets of water were certainly no load for a dock worker used to big loads. Still, he felt their weight. His back broke out in a sweat, cooled

off, and then he got cold. Each step required great effort. He had a
fever, that much he understood. He had walked around with something creeping and lurking inside him for at least a week — something
he tried to blot out by denying its existence. But it gave him reminders
the whole time, weighing down on his forehead or aching in his neck;
it made his back feel broken or sat and bore into his shoulder blades.

He didn't want to worry Lotten by talking about it, she still had-
n't regained her strength after childbirth and the death of their newborn. Now she got agitated so quickly, so easily irritated. Sometimes
when he came home she was sitting in the darkness and crying, crying that she couldn't go on. Luckily he had a fair amount of work, and
they had avoided going hungry. He tried to force nourishing food into
Lotten, even if she had protested and wanted the children to have the
best pieces.

Henning put the buckets down. He called to the children to dress
warmly and come out: he had a surprise. He heard them hurrying.
Agge rummaged to get down his coat and his hat, and Emelie whined
for help. Gertrud was still too little to go along; she was just over a
year old.

"Come to the woodshed!" called Henning and went ahead of
them. And while he nailed on the last plank, the two little ones stood
in the doorway to the shed and squealed with excitement. The tone of
their father's voice had told them that something fun was waiting.
They had waited a long time for that tone. Another tone had domi-
nated for a long time: one that was calming, comforting and silencing.
Now some of the merry ringing of the bells had come into it and an
invitation to adventure.

Their mother stood in the window and looked down over the
yard, a little wondering, a little uneasy. But when she saw the sled pull
out of the woodshed she was infected with the excitement and gaiety.
She picked up the littlest one in her arms to show her, and waved and
smiled.

The sled was the kind that was wide with upward-curving runners and
four posts. Henning had thought that it could also be used to pull

wood home. Now he could let the children sit between the posts while he took his place in the back and stood on the runners. He ran a few steps to get up speed and they were off, down pot-holed Garbage Lane. The speed never built up to what the incline promised; there was too much gravel collecting under the runners. But Stora Bondegatan had more to offer, and was already polished smooth by sleds and kick-sleds, toboggans, sleighs and open-sided wagons.

Agge and Emelie held onto each other tightly while Henning pulled them up the long hill, up to the crest where the street swung out around a spur of the White Hills by the windmill called "The Hat." When they pointed the sled downward a slope of almost a kilometer lay before them.

The children had to get off and jump up and down to get warm first. Then Henning put Agge up front, placing himself against the posts farthest back, and put Emelie in his lap. He pushed off with his heels, felt the speed mount, held tightly onto the children who shrieked with delight.

They passed between the empty white fields, between the small gray shacks which stuck up out of the snow, past the technical factory's yellow stone buildings, over Garbage Lane, through the cholera graveyard, and Senior Rock beside Barnängen, where the old men from the workhouse chopped up macadam on workdays. Here their speed decreased, the slope almost went upwards for a minute. But the momentum that was left was enough to surmount the little incline, and they were off again, down the steep last part of Stora Bondegatan, down to Barnängen's dock and out onto the ice. Henning had to put on the brakes quickly there; he didn't want to take any chances. Only a few days earlier a whole gang of boys had gone down into a hole in the ice.

On their way back up they ran into Thumbs, out with his two boys, Rudolf and two-year-old Knut. Then they had to repeat the run, and all four children got to sit while Henning and Thumbs ran alongside down the hill.

Warm and happy, they got back to the house and Sunday dinner. Lotten and Matilda stood on the corner outside the house and waited, and the children rushed up to them to tell about all their adventures. The happy atmosphere was contagious; Lotten felt the darkness disappear — how life was still there all around her. One of her children had died, but three were alive and demanded living warmth, needed happiness. She felt like she wanted to cry when she thought how easily irritated and impatient she had been lately — how miserable it must have been for them. Even though she hadn't sat on the sled and felt the wind rush past her, it was as if much of the damp and dreary mist had blown away, as if it were easier to breathe.

"Shall we do potluck and eat together?" asked Thumbs.

Nobody had any objections, it was a fine Sunday tradition that they had abandoned long ago. The girls in the kitchen wanted to be included too. While they boiled and fried, Pontus Berger came in and shared news with them that he had recently picked up. Mostly he had stories of everyone who had slipped and fallen and broken something or knocked themselves unconscious on the many dangerous wooden stairs down toward Slussen. But he was also able to give Lotten good advice concerning free smallpox vaccinations, and he encouraged her to take both her own and Matilda's children to Doctor Ekekrantz on Sankt Paulsgatan. They could expect a new epidemic, and the small children, especially, died like flies if they hadn't been vaccinated. And Lotten felt once again a prick of conscience about everything she had neglected when she had gone around as if paralyzed with weariness and sorrow. Now what had been lost had to be won back; now she wanted to and had the strength to live and protect the lives of her loved ones again.

The children played on the stairs to the attic while the grown-ups sat in the dusk and talked. Henning had a chance to say a few words to Thumbs. It didn't happen so often these days now that they worked in different places and had such different schedules. He tried to forget the pressure in his forehead, the pain in his back. He felt like the sensations were dampened by the glass of arak liqueur which Thumbs offered him, but it also made him sleepier, and the fatigue crept up on him.

Thumbs looked at him. He guessed that Henning was sick even though he tried to hide it. He had noticed how sweaty and out of breath he had gotten when they ran beside the sled, how tired he had looked. But he knew his friend's gentle stubbornness.

"You should go to bed for a few days," he said in a low voice.

Henning shook his head.

"I can't afford to," he said. "Besides, Lotten would get worried. There's nothing really the matter with me."

"Now, while it's still quiet at the harbor," suggested Thumbs. "That's the best time to be sick."

But Henning didn't want to. Didn't dare? As if it were a question of not giving in, as if once he finally admitted he was sick it would be something serious.

Thumbs knew that it wasn't worth pushing any farther. He made one more and equally unsuccessful attempt to try to convince Henning to leave the harbor.

Now was the time, was Thumbs' opinion. Now while there were good times. He should accept a lower salary in another line of work rather than continue as a longshoreman. For now it was clear, the harbor would come last. More and more were leaving it, and soon only the roughnecks would be left, the ones who were impossible to organize and who the stevedores could treat any way they pleased. The few knowledgeable and responsible ones would be lost among all the drunkards, never be able to make anything of themselves.

Henning felt the temptation, the wish to find something new. But he also seemed to understand that it was too late, he was too old. He had never had the opportunity to really learn a trade. Necessity had forced him to take whatever he could get. Basically, because of this he had always been a carrier, hauling heavy loads: the sacks at the mill, the bricks at the construction site, cargo at the harbor. And he had always known that he really wasn't strong enough for the kind of work he did. His body didn't have the breadth and strength that the loads demanded. He had always been obliged to invest something which cost too much: a kind of tremendous willpower, using his utmost strength.

He was tempted away from the harbor. But he didn't dare. He couldn't take anything that paid less, not even just for a while. He needed steady work, didn't even dare try temporary but possibly better-paying jobs. It was too late now that he had a wife and three children. He had to have the strength, didn't have the choice.

"We have slightly better conditions at the harbor too," he said. "And every occupation has its down sides."

Thumbs certainly agreed with that; he could never quite reconcile himself to the bakery's constant night work.

"We'll probably do something about it," said Thumbs. "We should get one night off a week just like those who work in the day have one day off. But bakery workers don't have any Sunday since people eat fresh bread on Mondays too. We get three nights off in one year: the day after Christmas, the day after Easter and the day after Whitsunday, that's all. That's probably why most baker journeymen are unmarried. What wife can put up with having her husband in bed three nights a year?"

"What are you going to do?" asked Henning, happy to avoid talking about himself and his affairs.

"We're discussing it," answered Thumbs. "And if the bakers don't go along with it of their own free will, you'll see people begin to eat homemade bread for real."

Thumbs felt like a journeyman baker though he actually only haunted the outskirts of that fine, old trade. There were many who were much farther along within the occupation than Thumbs but hadn't applied for certificates of proficiency. They worked there like some kind of overgrown apprentices, and according to the rules they were supposed to politely address the newly appointed eighteen-year-old journeymen as "sir" and be answered back in the familiar you form. But Thumbs, who was an old schoolmate of the master himself, used the familiar form with everyone, young and old, and never asked to see any journeyman papers.

"Uh-oh," he said. "Now old lady Sundberg's ringing the wake-up bell."

On Sundays, as on every day in Sundberg's bakery on Stora Glasbruksgatan, work began at six o'clock in the evening. One hour earlier the master baker's wife would pull on the rope of an old farmyard bell and wake up the journeymen and apprentices.

Yawning and huddled up with cold, they would step into the warmth of the bakery to get a bite of food before work began, seating themselves among baking tables and troughs. The premises were crowded, and there wasn't any room to eat in. They had to take their meals amidst dough and work tools wherever they could find a spot.

The building was old and the bakery situated in a low, dark cellar and a few rooms on the ground floor. The premises could barely be aired out, and couldn't be aired out at all during work hours when the drafts could have an effect on the sourdough and the rising bread. Dust from the flour deposited itself on the walls, ceiling and floor. Gradually a slimy coating built up from the dampness. Dough fell from troughs and tables to the floor and was trampled into a sticky mass that couldn't be removed, neither with a scrub brush nor a scraper.

The journeymen and apprentices lived in a few narrow stalls near the workplace. They lay in bunks, two to each bed, sleeping among vermin, under blankets and on mattresses powdered with white flour. On a wooden crate in a corner stood a wash basin and a water pitcher, but there were far too many using the water pitcher; most didn't bother to wait in line and went without washing instead. Inside the bakery there was a tin washtub to set their feet in. This was used by those who trampled the dough for limpa bread. Before they trampled the dough a few flour sacks were placed over it.

Coughing from the flour dust and scurfy from baker's scabies, the journeymen and apprentices would begin the night's work. One night like the others, one night in the eternal string of nights. They were prisoners of the bakery, living their lives in stalls and on the both damp and dusty work premises. Food and lodging were included in their salary, so how would they ever be able to get out of there — how to get married and make their own homes? A few of them sometimes went to Glasbruksgatan's whorehouses; others made sure they got a young apprentice as a bedmate. Most of them just tried to forget, to sleep, perhaps count the coins they had hidden and dream of the day they would be able to be a master and have their own apprentices, their own slaves.

But among the tired and cheerless journeymen walked that odd man who was neither baker nor stevedore, who both belonged there and left there to go home to his private life in a house on one of the hills. He whistled in the bakery, packed limpa bread and got the apprentices to run out for firewood; he joked with the baker's old lady and took a drink in with the master. And someone had heard him say to the master that soon there would probably be a strike here, and the master had laughed and said they could certainly do that as long as the other bakeries went on strike at the same time. But Sundberg wasn't like other bakers. He was a happy bastard, the apprentices said. It was his old lady who kept them in line and under the yoke.

A long night lay ahead of them. Not until eight o'clock the next morning would they stagger back to their beds, crawl in and feel their backs and their baker's hernias ache. When all the bells and chimes of the city were ringing, they would sleep, heavy and exhausted, gathering the strength that a new night's work demanded.

A little irritatedly they watched Thumbs pull the empty wood cart out toward the yard. When he opened the door, dance music from Södra Salon spilled in and a gay waltz taunted their sluggish and heavy steps.

FREEDOM OR SECURITY

The hillsides gleamed wet and shiny with slush and spring rain when Henning took his usual route to work at the harbor. He walked past the molasses funnel that people called the new church at Ersta, and went on down to what was left of Last Farthing Stairs.

The usual route, but unusually late. His team had worked practically all night, loading a barge that had to depart in a hurry. And even Heathen Dog had understood that those who toiled and hauled had to have a few hours rest in order to have the strength to work again.

Henning's body was still heavy after the night's work; his arms and legs felt stiff and numb; his back ached, and his stomach muscles were sore from all the strenuous lifting. He had allowed himself plenty of time when he left home, had chosen to give up a little of his bed rest to avoid having to rush.

For a second he closed his eyes and felt something like a wave well up through his head, a feeling of faintness. He looked down at the wooden stairs and sat down. It felt a little better then, and after a moment, he continued down the worn and dark steps.

When he passed the Bodin herring factory, he met Master Bodin, Annika's husband. Henning lifted his cap politely and stepped aside. He wasn't sure if Bodin recognized him, but Bodin usually greeted him whenever they passed each other from time to time.

Bodin was evidently on his way to the office. Henning wondered if Annika still worked there. Probably not, now that she was the owner's wife. She probably had enough work with a large home and perhaps many maids to order about. And children? He didn't know, but surely she had children, maybe a whole brood of little, well-dressed, upper-class children. Henning recalled a three-year-old girl he had seen holding her nanny's hand, the dress, the coat. It would have fit Emelie perfectly. He had stopped in the street and stood and watched the child. Or, more accurately, the child's clothes. He would have liked to buy such things for Emelie.

Someone called his name; the sound penetrated gradually and faintly, as if muffled by many layers of fatigue and thoughts.

Slowly he turned around. Fredrik Bodin was still standing outside the entrance to the herring factory: no one else was visible. Could it be him? Apparently yes. Bodin took a step toward Henning who hurried over to meet him.

"So, Nilsson is still down at the harbor."

Henning nodded. He wondered if there was something critical in the question: many of the best had undeniably gone on to better work. It got like that when times were good. Heathen Dog swore every day over the thinning and continually less skilled ranks of workers he had to take stock of.

"At Lundström's wasn't it?" asked Bodin.

Henning said yes again.

"What does he pay?" asked Bodin.

"Thirty öre an hour," answered Henning. "Forty for overtime."

"He pays that well."

"The last few years have been better than before," said Henning.

"But with all day-work it comes out less, of course. Three kronor in the best case."

"And then, of course, there isn't work every day," said Bodin.

"No, that's for sure. We have to go and check every day but can't always be sure of work. But, of course, now that spring is here we can't complain, there is always something every day."

"I wonder how much it comes out to per month?" wondered Bodin.

Henning saw the tally in front of him, Lotten's slightly childish round ciphers in the old calendar where she recorded income and expenses. "Twenty-four in March," he answered. "Forty-two in April. Now in May I might get up to sixty-five."

"We need a man in our stockroom," Bodin said suddenly. "Twelve kronor a week is what we can offer but not more. But it's year-round work."

"Does Master mean that I...?"

Bodin nodded.

That would mean a lower salary during four or maybe five months out of the year. But it would be secure. He would also get an income over the winter and avoid that worry. The hours weren't shorter in the stockroom, but it was a different pace. Henning had seen the fellows who worked there when he had worked on setting it up once. They were three together rolling and lifting a barrel; they knocked the lid off neatly and carefully and looked at the brine. Then they mixed new brine and poured it in with a little wooden pitcher. He had thought they had it pretty good.

"Thank you very much," said Henning and bowed. "When may I begin?"

"We won't provoke Lundström by taking one of his steady workers in the middle of the week," smiled Bodin. "But Monday morning at six o'clock Nilsson can report to the boss."

Bodin nodded and left. Henning stood there and looked at the empty doorway. Then he realized he was probably short of time and hurried off to work. His tiredness had suddenly disappeared and been replaced by a funny, unsettled feeling. But the unsettled feeling was pleasant, very close to anticipation.

As usual they received their pay at the tavern, the "Church" as it was called, where Lundström had arranged credit for his workers. The dock workers gathered at the end of work, took their seats at the rough yellow tables and sat and spat on the sawdust which covered the stone floor. Two bottles stood waiting on the bar: the stevedore's and the tavern keeper's offerings to the faithful. The men glanced at the bottles and some of the thirstier ones went up and bought themselves a drink. They didn't think they could wait until the stevedore and the foremen came and the party began.

The tavern keeper's wife took one of the upside down glasses that stood on the brass tray that was always coated with liquor and filled it, took the money and received the empty glass back. Then she placed it upside down on the tray again, there was always another drop to add to the bitters.

The door flew open, Lundström had finally arrived. The foremen followed their boss like sheep dogs their shepherd. Lundström placed himself at the bar, exchanged a few words with the tavern keeper's wife, pulled the payroll out of his pocket and began calling off names. Man after man had to step forward and drink their schnapps, one from each bottle, pronounce "Aah!" and "Thanks!" and receive what was left of their salary after the tavern keeper's wife took out her part for the week's rations. Some people had only a small sum left over. For Stagger-John it was depleted by more than a whole krona. But then the tavern keeper's wife became extravagant, threw open her hands and said that, for once, it wasn't all that important. And Lundström laughed, roaring with paternal pride over the tremendous thirst of his rowdies, and bought him an extra glass.

But when it was Henning's turn, the stevedore's face darkened. Not because his bill at the tavern was so small, it was good to have some sober fellows on the team as well. Still, you couldn't get away from the fact that the sober ones were often trouble. They thought, planned, and worked not as unwittingly self-sacrificing as the ones that were silenced by alcohol.

"Now we have Henning Nilsson," muttered the stevedore. "Was it a herring strangler he was going to be?"

"A herring packer," Henning answered carefully. "At Bodin's."

"Sure," growled Lundström. "This is the way the Bodins thank me for one of my rascals raking money out of the ashes for them. So! Is he going to have a drink, or isn't it proper?"

Henning took the glass obediently and emptied it. But the tavern keeper's wife let her bottle stay were it was, the herring packer didn't eat at the Church, and this pale fellow had always been a poor customer. If he didn't want a drink during the week, he didn't need one now either.

"Come on, stingy woman, give Henkan a farewell round; he's been a good comrade," said Stringtie. The tavern keeper's wife sniffed but poured one out, and Henning drank though he would have rather avoided it.

Lundström pushed the money, a pen, and the payroll list over to him.

"He's never going to get this much from the tight-fisted herring packer," said the stevedore.

Henning knew this was true; the consciousness of it lay like a cold lump of ice in the middle of his warm feeling over having gotten something secure that he had the strength to do. The work at the harbor paid more during the best months. And the hard work had, in spite of everything, its own special charm. In the midst of its enslavement and harshness there lay some of the freedom of the open water. The opportunities for work and the income were always a little bit of a lottery in contrast to the year-round employee's calm pace and steady sums. At this time of year the profits were manifold, and it left a slightly bitter feeling to forgo them after the lean days of winter. But the stakes were high and Henning understood that he wouldn't be able to manage much longer.

He saw Lundström sway at the bar, a tall man with enormous sideburns and eyebrows like birds' wings, a cane with a silver knob, a gold chain in his yellow leather vest. Still a bit of a dressed-up harbor rowdy, not afraid to drink out of the unwashed glass and stand here in this circle of lousy, dirty slaves.

You could hate Lundström, but you also had to admire him. He had none of the Bodins' snootiness; he belonged to the harbor.

"Cheers, you scoundrels!" shouted Lundström.

"Same to you!" bellowed Heathen Dog and lifted his glass with the drops in it received as a bonus from the tavern keeper's wife.

Lundström nodded and left, his sheep dogs following him quickly. And the noise level rose when their superiors disappeared, people scraped their chairs and banged on the tables, boasting and telling tales. Some were up at the bar sampling the snacks: three öre's worth of herring pieces and one öre cucumber slices. But most satisfied themselves with alcohol. Henning knew what was expected of him and bought a round for everyone on the team.

Some of them got up and left. For the family providers, it was best to be on their way while they still had some wages left. Others moved among the tables, squeezed in with the prostitutes, fingered the watch swindler's bait, gave a few öre to the musician who sat in the corner and sawed on his fiddle.

Henning had stayed unusually long, thinking he shouldn't be in too much of a hurry on his last evening. He felt the liquor rise in waves inside him; he had become light and heavy at the same time and was close to both laughing and crying. But he didn't want to come home drunk and not too late either. He stood up, exchanged hand-shakes and shook his head at new invitations.

Henning walked alone in the twilight, up the steep stairs, leaving the comrades and stevedore team he had worked with for ten years behind. Next week he would be an idler, a deserter, a herring strangler.

The Monday Henning began at Bodin's wasn't a Monday like all the others.

Already at four-thirty in the morning there was activity and com-motion in the house. At five o'clock Malin and Washer-Johanna arrived, and Johanna stayed to take care of the younger children. A few minutes later Henning left together with Malin and Lotten, August and Rudolf.

He had never walked to work with them like this before. But he wasn't alone in doing so this morning, the streets were livelier than usual, and when they came down Stora Glasbruksgatan, the whole street was streaming with expectant people out on their way.

The gutters were streaming with water too. It was raining, the sky was a stormy gray, and the morning was cold. But still people came as if to a party, though wrapped in shawls and blankets, carrying chil-dren and bundles of food.

Henning had plenty of time; he accompanied his family all the way to Slottsbacken, by the palace. Once there he gave August and Rudolf strict instructions not to stray from the grown-ups for one minute. The crowds of people were going to be enormous, and little children could easily be trampled underfoot.

Try to find a place in a doorway, he advised Malin and Lotten. He stood and waved until they disappeared in the throng, then returned to Skeppsbron where all the vessels' flags were waving and the pennants stood out among the masts. He saw a man who was trying to sell the underground newspaper, *Last Rites*, dragged away by two policemen.

It was the big day of the coronation. Oscar II was going to be crowned king, and Henning Nilsson herring packer.

At the Bodin house on Stadsgården, a boy was in the process of hanging a flag from a pole which had been set up outside the corner window on the second floor. Henning went through the stockroom, between the wooden partitions he had helped build. He knew well where the boss had his nook and wondered if old man Törn was still working there. He was, already sitting in his spot, moistening his pen continuously while he leafed through orders and papers.

The smell of herring lay thick and greasy around them. The old man turned his head and nodded.

"So here's Nilsson," he said. "It's a good thing you came even though the king is being crowned. Though all the fellows are off today, but Bodin must have forgotten to tell you? Well, well, come along and we can take a look around."

They went through the stockrooms, walking between rows of barrels. In the section where the newly-arrived and still uninspected barrels stood, Törn broke open a barrel and showed Henning what to do. He had to make a spot check of the herring quality and size and sort the shipment accordingly. Often one had to refill the brine. If it took a long time for the herring to be sold, he had to do another test and pour on even more brine, so it was important to label every section with the date. The salmon tub was used to make brine in. Made of water and Portuguese salt, the brine had to be so saturated with salt that a herring could float in it.

Icelandic herring was not much of a problem; it was already sorted when it arrived. West coast herring, on the other hand, had to be poured out into tubs and then sorted. But the girls took care of that, there were some experienced sorters who were called in when needed. When the girls had finished and packed the herring in barrels, the regular workers poured on the brine and sealed and labeled the barrels.

"There's where we have the corpse chamber," said Törn and pointed to a cellar door. "We don't open that unless we absolutely have to, because of the smell. That's where we keep the rancid herring that the Russians buy. And when we pack it, we have to jump in the barrels with both feet and trample down the herring because the duty on it is calculated by the barrel. Though Bodin is paid by weight, of course ...."

Henning used the coronation day to learn his way around the storeroom and memorize what the symbols and abbreviations meant. It wasn't yet five o'clock when Törn said, "Now we'll go home. We should have a little fun too since the king is being crowned."

Clothes hung drying everywhere, and Agge and Rudde sat wrapped in blankets and shoveled in warm soup to prevent them from catching cold.

They had so much to tell that they barely remembered that Henning had started a new job.

It had been so grand! Of course, they'd had to wait over five hours, but they had gotten a good spot so it was worth the effort. Music, soldiers, courtiers, government ministers .... And the king himself in an ermine mantle: he had walked under a large canopy carried by pages. Fine ladies and the queen in purple ....

Everything had been fantastic. People had hung like clusters of grapes up in the rigging of vessels off Skeppsbron. All the church bells in the city had rung over and over. A drunken man had sat on the roof of the Finnish church and tossed clay tiles down on people, and in the church's funeral shed people had climbed up on coffin supports and hearses. On another roof they had seen a young girl who'd had to hold on tightly with both hands so as not to fall off, and a chimney sweep who had taken the opportunity to kiss the girl until her whole face turned black.

It had been a lively event, a party, an experience that the boys would never forget.

While they talked, Henning sat and smelled the odor of herring, and decided to change his clothes every day when he came home, otherwise the whole house would reek of it.

He pulled out a pair of pants and a shirt, grabbed a water bucket and went down into the yard. The rain had left water in the barrel so he didn't have to go get any. He took the full bucket to the shed, washed himself well and changed, leaving his work clothes hanging. That would be his routine.

When he came up, Lotten had supper ready, and it was a festive meal, a day of celebration. They sat around the table for a long time and talked after they had put the children to bed, listening to the rain drumming on the roof and watching it draw a curtain across the city and the water.

He told her about Törn and his day at the warehouse, and Lotten thought it sounded good. Henning would no doubt like his new work. And it was nice to know that every week provided them with a steady sum.

They felt unusually secure and satisfied, enjoyed sitting in their cozy room and listening to the wind and the rain outside. They felt like they had managed to build up a little windbreak in their life and were pleased that Henning had chosen security over freedom.

SUMMER'S VICTORIES

Henning walked in the garden on the hill on a balmy summer evening and tended his flowers and vegetables. He watered, weeded, lay beautiful round stones around the beds and tied up plants.

August and Rudolf followed close on his heels, and he showed them buds and shoots, let them help with the watering and gave them each a rhubarb stalk to suck on. When it was bedtime, the boys didn't feel at all like going in, the spring evening was so light that it was impossible for them to believe it was already time to sleep.

He shooed them away to their waiting mothers and sat down on the bench to rest a minute. He was ashamed that he felt so tired, now when he no longer had to work himself to the bone every day. He couldn't understand how he had managed to last so long on the stevedore team.

The sun sank behind the hills at Katarina, painting the light streaks of cloud in the western sky an orange red. A freighter drew a dark line across the light blue surface of the water at the bottom of the hill. Henning recognized the boat: Carolus always came on Saturday evenings tended by those who were eager to make extra money on a Sunday. Before, Carolus would have troubled him, created a conflict within him: Sunday rest and family life or extra earnings.

He heard steps on the gravel; it was Anna-Kajsa and Pontus Berger coming. They had gotten engaged a few weeks ago. Keeping company with Anna-Kajsa had changed the previously shy and fumbling Pontus, given him a new confidence. On top of that he had gotten better working conditions; he was a permanent worker at *The Fatherland* now.

"You have to tell Henning," he heard Anna-Kajsa whisper to Pontus. And after making a few bashful excuses, Pontus Berger went up to him, sat on the bench beside Henning and pulled a package out of his jacket pocket. Eagerly he loosened the paper it was wrapped in and held out a sheaf of printed papers to Henning.

The Rose of the Night: A Charcoal Sketch from the Lives of the Wretched by Pontus Berger.

A little pamphlet, big hopes. Pontus Berger's gaze hung onto Henning's face, trying to interpret any expression. When Henning leafed through the pages, Pontus' gaze was drawn to the words and sentences he had read so often that he soon knew them all by heart. Read until every sentence had a melody which he now thought the severest critics couldn't fail to notice.

Henning hadn't ever read any books. With some trouble he tried to spell his way through what Pontus had written, but he had difficulty really understanding it, grasping the meaning. But he read the title page several times and understood that Pontus was proud of having his name printed there. It was certainly something he ought to be congratulated for. Henning congratulated him and Pontus smiled gratefully.

Anna-Kajsa and Pontus were going out to celebrate his book. Dad's coach had been ordered and was going to take them to Hasselbacken Restaurant. Why shouldn't an author on the brink of success indulge?

Pontus sat on the bench with Henning while Anna-Kajsa changed her clothes. It took a while before she returned, but the result would have made an even longer wait worthwhile. She billowed out through the narrow doorway and spread out her magnificent peacock tail. Matilda had helped her tie on the bustle that was meant to give the attractive illusion of a plump backside. In front the fabric was pulled taut over her figure, molded against her body, almost giving the illusion of nudity. But in back, hair and fabric spilled down in great waves.

Lotten had to come down and admire it, none of the others in the house had a dress like that. Matilda got a blanket; Anna-Kajsa shouldn't be allowed to ruin her dress sitting directly on the dirty cushions in Dad's coach.

The young pair sailed out to the wagon which waited in Garbage Lane. Those who were no longer as young and free had to amuse themselves as best they could. They set the table in the garden and drank coffee in the gathering dusk.

Matilda sighed.

They weren't going to get Midsummer night off she said. The master wouldn't give his permission.

In many other trades the employers had given in on various issues. The journeymen and apprentices felt that maybe now it was the master bakers' turn to share a little of the manna from the good times. They had demanded to get Midsummer night off and had seen it as a reasonable request that would certainly be granted. Many were so sure of a yes, that they began to plan their Midsummer festivities. But the master said no, and didn't even want to discuss it.

So the discussion heated up among the bakery workers instead. Now they were indignant. Did the masters think that their employees were animals who had no need of leisure time and human pleasures? Weren't they going to get anything at all of the general increase in prosperity? They weren't going to bow down any longer, now they had to be heard!

Lists began to circulate in the bakeries. They appealed to the masters for a free night every week; anger had hardened their demands this much. And they pointed out that there were bakeries where working hours reached up to eighteen to twenty-two hours a day. Such working hours had to be reasonably reduced, they demanded.

Thumbs had seen the list. But it was only for journeymen. The guild still reigned. Furious, he found out which journeymen had taken the initiative and asked if they had thought the other bakery workers were going to continue to work if the journeymen went on strike. No, they hadn't thought that. Well then, they should include all the bakery workers in everything right from the start.

Unwillingly, the journeymen gave in, they decided that those who didn't have journeyman status would be called to the meeting which had been planned. They wondered anxiously if such steps would bring about a loss of prestige and advantages for the journeymen.

On a Sunday in July the bakery workers assembled in Humlegården Park. They came on foot over the neglected, dandelion-covered hillside, between the scaffolding around the half-finished construction of the library. They clustered together by the rotunda where a band was playing. Many of them came in work clothes, some in their Sunday best. Several had brought along wives and children, some their girlfriends.

The organizers tried to get the participants to line up; they were going to march before the negotiations began. And gradually they started off with the music at their head, parading along Västra Humlegårdsgatan and the road past the cottages along Lill-Jans Park.

Thumbs had brought Matilda and Rudolf with him; Knut was back home with Lotten and Henning. It might be good for Rudde to see how the workers demonstrated for their rights. And fun for both him and Matilda to come out and look at something other than the rocky hills of Söder.

"Do you remember when we walked this way before?" asked Matilda.

Thumbs had to think. Had he walked here? With Matilda? Yes, that was right, once a long time ago on the eve of Pentecost, of course.

"Eleven years ago," said Matilda. She looked at the trees by the side of the road, wondering which one it had been. Thumbs had disappeared under one of them with Klara, and she had gone on with Henning through a calm city at night.

Actually, she didn't want to see the tree again.

They walked silently to the rumble of the drums. Rudolf trotted along, holding onto his mother's hand.

"Klara came by the other evening," Matilda said suddenly.

"Klara?"

"Yes, it's been a while since we saw her last. She has gotten such a good job. She's become a salesgirl for a tobacconist who has opened several new shops."

"Are you sure they have any cigars for sale?" Thumbs wondered.

Matilda shook her head.

"I don't know," she said.

She grew quiet, looking at the large shade tree that they were passing. She wondered if Thumbs recognized it, if he remembered. But he didn't seem to; he lived so much in the present, on the move toward the future. He didn't turn around to look at the green trees of the past.

In front of them the orchestra had picked up and was in full swing again. It had been placed to the right of the speaker's chair and played while the marchers turned onto the grounds.

No drawn-out negotiations were necessary. The chairman of the meeting, journeyman Adolf Lindström, was able to pound the gavel with the decision: Strike!

He informed them that the strikers' meetings would be held every day in the Bergstrahl Building by Munkbron. They should go there to hear information on how the negotiations were proceeding. Whoever breaks the strike shall be viewed as a spineless coward in the future pronounced the chairman and declared the meeting adjourned.

The meeting was over but few thought of going home. Picnic baskets were unpacked; anyone who didn't have provisions with him could always get a sandwich and a bottle at a stand. People circulated, met old workmates and friends from journeyman meetings and their younger days.

Adolf Lindström came over to Thumbs and some of his friends from the bakery who sat gathered around Matilda's well-filled basket. Lindström said a few friendly words to the troublesome bakery worker, who was neither journeyman nor apprentice, but still made demands.

Thumbs got up. "Come over here a minute," he said.

Lindström followed him in among the trees. This Ture Lindgren, known as Thumbs, was a strange character. He remained on the outside, and yet was so involved. Could he be an agent for foreign socialists?

Thumbs explained: he worked for the new master, Sundberg, who had taken over the old bakery on Glasbruksgatan. Sundberg was a boyhood friend and still felt more like a journeyman than a boss. Sundberg had taken part in a meeting the masters had held to discuss the workers' demands and the eventual strike. They had decided to telegraph a string of smaller towns and offer journeymen and apprentices within the profession work in Stockholm, without saying anything about the strike.

"That will break the strike and put you all out of work," Sundberg had said.

Lindström hurried back to call a meeting of the strike committee. They had to take action immediately. What could be done?

There was only one thing to do: telegraph right away to the journeyman organizations in every city in the country and call for solidarity. They had to rush to formulate the telegram, find the addresses and hurry to the new telegraph station at Skeppsbron.

The strike committee had already been elected at the meeting. But Thumbs was appointed as an additional member and asked to keep in touch with master baker Sundberg.

The next few days were hectic. The masters gathered at Mosebacke, the workers in the building by Munkbron. Messages traveled frequently between the two camps, and the masters came over to the workers to discuss things. Baker Sundberg spoke out for going along with the workers demand to have Saturday nights off, but most of the masters didn't want to.

However, when the masters didn't receive any affirmative replies to the telegrams they sent out to the provinces, they began to soften. Without journeymen there would be no bread. Of course, it was humiliating to give in. But there would certainly be times of unemployment again. And, what was lost through having to raise wages, for they had received this demand as well, could be recouped through higher bread prices.

The masters grew eager to reach a decision and invited the workers' representatives to a meeting at Mosebacke. Baker Schumacher welcomed everyone and explained that their conditions would be accepted if the strikers returned to work immediately. They had to be back in their places by six o'clock that very evening so that bread could be delivered on schedule the next morning.

A couple of hours later the strike committee was able to announce that they had scored a victory; that the strike had led to a happy ending. Adolf Lindström encouraged everyone who was sober and able to work to report to their night shift.

Everyone cheered and rushed off to celebrate the victory: the part about sobriety didn't have to be taken too literally.

The bakery workers were wild with the joy of the victors. They felt a strong and sudden urge to have fun, spend some of the higher wages that awaited them. One journeyman decided to start the party with a big cigar. He found a recently opened store on Götgatan and went in to make his purchase.

There weren't many tobacco products in the store, only a few half-empty boxes of inferior brands. But the two women behind the counter were much better. One of them, in her thirties, was dressed in a blouse that gave a generous view of her charms. She came so close when the journeyman was making his selection that his gaze slid down into the cleavage between her breasts and drowned.

He suddenly felt that it wasn't all that important about the cigar; it didn't really matter if it was an inferior brand.

The young salesgirl laughed shrilly. A sixteen-year-old girl, a bit thin and gangly, appearing childishly undeveloped next to the other.

"How much are they?" asked the journeyman, having to struggle to get the words out.

"Only two riksdaler if it's delivered in the stockroom," smiled the shopkeeper.

The journeyman started, after all that was still the price of the cigars he had asked for. He looked over at the curtain that hung in the doorway to the stockroom.

"It's very cozy," she said enticingly and lifted the curtain so he could see the bed.

He nodded and dug nervously for his money.

"Which one of us?" she asked in a business-like tone and placed the coins in the cash box.

He pointed fumblingly at her, and she smiled again as if she were thanking him for a compliment.

"Come along," she said and unbuttoned the last buttons of her blouse as she walked ahead of him. The journeyman followed her compliantly.

The young girl pulled the curtain closed behind them and sat down on the chair behind the counter. She polished her nails and wrinkled her nose when she heard the journeyman's panting and the creaking of the bed. She got up, went over to the window and stood looking out at the street while her boss delivered what the customer had paid for. The street and the crowds out there were tempting, but she didn't dare go farther than the window. She had to stand there, as if tethered. Rumbling cart wheels, the clatter of hooves and heavy shoes. Gratefully she took in the noises, wrapping herself up in them.

A man passing by slowed his step and looked toward the door. The girl pulled herself back quickly as if she wanted to escape. There was another backroom inside the store so they could accommodate two at the same time. But then they had to lock up and place a sign on the door: "Closed, be back soon."

"What's your name?" asked the journeyman when he stood in the corner of their little shop buttoning his pants.

"Madelaine," answered Klara.

"I'll be back, Malena," said the journeyman.

"Then the gentleman can try the girl," suggested Klara a little wearily and brushed the flour dust from the bed and her clothes.

The journeyman looked thoughtfully at the girl behind the counter. She curtsied politely and closed the door behind him. She heard Klara washing herself in the backroom and yawned sleepily. Now it was the girl's turn to present herself to the next customer. She yawned again and hoped it would be some tired old man who didn't have energy to do much. But she was unlucky: it was a rough farm-hand who wanted to get the most for his hard-won coins.

While the bed and the girl groaned beneath the farmhand, Klara counted out the cash box and was happy with the result. She pulled out the bottle she had hidden under the counter, took a swig and congratulated herself over her future. And at having avoided the farm-hand, if he didn't stop soon she would have to go in and demand more money.

THE NEWCOMERS

Henning stood in the shed and sawed wood. He filled the basket, hung up the saw and got ready to go in. He blew out the candle in the old lantern he had in the shed and took hold of the basket's sturdy handles. He saw the kitchen window glowing softly and comfortingly in the misty September darkness. Inside sat Lotten and Matilda helping Anna-Kajsa embroider initials and hem; it was only a week until the wedding.

He guessed that they had the coffee ready in there now. He liked the evenings of warmth and conversation at home; it was then that he could forget the gnawing pain in his back and stomach. He felt the security that he had searched for so long, had worked so feverishly to attain.

The gate in the fence squeaked. Someone stood there and tried to see into the darkness. It seemed to be a young girl. And something behind her, perhaps some children.

He put down the basket and walked up to the gate. The girl started, she had apparently not noticed him. She said she wanted to speak with Matilda. Henning opened the door to the house and the girl stepped inside. After her followed three youngsters like a tail.

The children were Klara's. Nine-year-old and six-year-old girls, a two-year-old boy. They got to sit on the kitchen sofa and each got a rusk to chew on while Matilda and the young girl went into the next room.

The girl was named Susanna and was sixteen years old. She had come with a message from Klara.

Something troubling had happened. A few hours ago a coachman had come to the cigar shop where Klara worked and left a letter from the factory owner, Rosenström. The police had taken too much interest in the cigar shops, and now the factory owner wanted Klara to burn her receipts and papers and clear out a few things from the shop. Klara had understood that she had no way of saving herself; she had stayed and obeyed. But she had asked Susanna to stay away from the shop and take care of her children. Klara had said that surely Matilda would want to take care of the children for old friendship's sake and let Susanna sleep in some corner. The children could no longer live in the cigar shop when there wasn't anyone there to pay the rent or take care of them.

Matilda looked at Susanna, a thin and pale girl in gaudy clothes. She noticed the impudent little glint lurking in her gaze and was frightened.

What could she do? Klara had been Matilda's friend, a good friend many times. She couldn't let Klara's children land in some asylum.

"I can't decide this now, by myself," answered Matilda, "but naturally we'll arrange someplace for the night to begin with."

This was how the kitchen got new tenants. It was as if life couldn't tolerate any empty rooms. Even before those who lived there had time to vacate, their successors stood on the threshold.

While Matilda talked to Susanna, Lotten had sat and observed the three children. They were dirty and ragged. And crawling with vermin. The whole house would be filled with lice if they got to stay sitting there on the kitchen sofa. Worried, she waited: weren't Matilda and the visitor going to come back soon so the children could leave?

They came back, and she learned that the children were going to stay. In that case they had to be washed and deloused, at least. And the women put the sheets and pillowcases aside and put the house's largest kettle on the stove. Henning carried in the tub from the shed. Klara's children stared nervously and crept close together on the sofa. When they understood what awaited them, the two youngest ones began to cry with terror. Matilda tried to calm them: it was nothing bad, it would be nice, and they wouldn't itch so terribly when they got rid of the lice and fleas. But they kicked at her and shrieked with fear. Rudolf woke up and came in, staring glassy-eyed, and was on the verge of tears himself.

No matter how much the children screamed and struggled, they were undressed and placed in the tub while their clothes ended up in the kettle's boiling water. Lotten was the driving force. With red patches on her face from the heat and effort, water dripping from her hair and clothes, she stood bent over the tub and scrubbed Klara's dirty children. She didn't give up until she had combed the lice out of their hair and cleaned out their ears. Finally the three children sat wrapped in blankets, hiccuping and sniveling. But they calmed down when they each got a sandwich, and then let themselves, worn out and with no resistance left, be tucked into bed on the kitchen sofa.

Lotten mopped up the wet floor and Henning carried out the tub with the dirty water. A little charged up, Lotten looked around, as if her energy, now awakened and fired up, needed new tasks.

"Are you full of lice as well?" she asked Susanna.

The girl recoiled, horrified.

"No, no," she said hastily.

"You'd better bathe anyway if you're going to live here," said Lotten. "This is a clean house."

Henning fetched more water. While it was heating on the stove, they drank the coffee which had been waiting there. They tried to ask Susanna what had actually happened with Klara and what kind of work Susanna had done in the cigar shop. But the girl answered evasively, was afraid to tell and was worried about Lotten's scrub brush.

Afterward Lotten made sure that Susanna was properly scrubbed. It was only the girl's hair that Lotten could complain about, otherwise Susanna was almost suspiciously clean. Everyone knew that whores kept themselves cleaner than ordinary people as a protection against shameful sicknesses.

"You'll see that we've got *one of those* in the house," said Lotten when she came up to their room in the attic, tired out from the evening's activities. But Henning didn't want to believe it, the girl was just a child.

On the wedding day, which was a Saturday, everybody in the house woke up earlier than usual. Henning and Thumbs were going to carry in tables and benches before it was time for Henning to go to work. Children and adults flew out of their beds and took part in the general bustle.

Only the one who was neither child nor adult stayed in bed as long as she possibly could. Susanna didn't feel like helping out but hoped it would be a fun wedding with dancing and a lot of good food. Finally she gave in to the children's pestering and the grown-ups' pleading and pulled herself up sleepily from the mattress she had been lying on. She still wasn't dressed when the door flew open and Thumbs and Henning came in carrying the table from the room overhead.

"Little girl, are you still in your shift?" asked Thumbs.

Susanna giggled and laid her hands coquettishly over her breasts which were barely covered by the deeply cut chemise. When the two men came back with the benches from the arbor, she had gotten a skirt on, but no blouse. When she bent down over the bedclothes, it looked like her upper body was going to fall out of the loose shift.

"Sit down," said Lotten severely.

The girl made a face secretly, but obeyed.

When Henning left for work, she was standing washing windows, the rag going back and forth, her polishing turned into a good-bye wave.

He gave her a friendly wave back before he disappeared through the gate.

THE TROUBLE SPOT

It wasn't just that Klara's girls stole food from the pantry, teased Agge and Rudde, and came home from school with fleas and lice. Nor that Klara's boy couldn't be trained to stop wetting his pants and pulling the hair of Gertrud, who was his age. No, most of all, it was Susanna who provoked anxiety. Yet they hardly noticed it in the beginning. Just the opposite, they thought that she fit in quite well. Of course, she was a little capricious and clumsy, but she was still willing to help with the chores.

She fooled them for a long time, masking herself with the fact that they never knew if she was a child or an adult. In front of the women she was an innocent child, or sometimes a rather sensible young woman. But the men who gave a friendly smile to the child suddenly found a woman there trying to seduce them.

Susanna ate and slept maybe more than she ever had before. Her skinny body grew rounder; her arms and legs attained a womanly softness. Her hips broadened while her waist grew even smaller since she was now wearing a corset. Her breasts filled out and were pushed up by the corset.

She wasn't beautiful with her turned-up nose and little rat mouth, but she was unsettling. She swayed her hips as she walked; she liked to stand and hang over a table with her elbows on the edge, with swinging breasts and a bouncing bottom.

And she sneaked around, she was everywhere she wasn't supposed to be. It was mostly Henning she followed. When he came home from work and stood washing in the shed, she would suddenly open the door and look in. She would excuse herself but still hang around, talking as if she hadn't noticed that he was naked.

Since he was not the suspicious type, he never knew what to believe. Susanna reminded him of Klara who had lived at Bigsack's and sat so unashamedly on the edge of her bed, who had such an impudent mouth and impudent hands. But who was also a good friend whom you could never get mad at.

He didn't get mad at Susanna either. But he was disturbed by her, imagined he could hear her step everywhere. It sounded like a threat to his security and home life, as if Susanna were sneaking around to find and tempt something forbiddingly dangerous.

Lotten got angry.

"You should be ashamed!" she would hiss. "Running around like that, that isn't proper."

A child's eyes would look at her, surprised: how, why?

When Lotten spoke to Matilda she didn't really get the support she had expected.

"You've grown up a little differently from the rest of us," explained Matilda. "Close quarters take away so much of people's natural shyness. The girl has naturally lived in a hole with many men around. She has no shame left; they have taken that from her. Can she help it?"

"Maybe not," admitted Lotten. "But I don't like it when she stands and wiggles her bottom at Henning."

Lotten said nothing to Henning. But he felt her worry and became even more careful, trying to avoid Susanna in every way. He put a latch on the door of the shed so it could be fastened from the inside. Finally Susanna gave up. She sulked for a few days, hardly answering when he said hello. Then she turned to Thumbs.

Thumbs didn't have Henning's caution; he also had another view regarding life and women. For Henning every act and every word meant so much. A caress bound you, a confidence brought you closer. Thumbs took it more lightly; he could do and say a lot without meaning so much by it. It had nothing to do with Matilda. He didn't intend to risk having children with others. As a good guest he kept himself to the drawing room and never ventured into the bedroom. No one could deny him a little innocent joking. He tickled the old ladies under their chins at the bakery and put his arm around the barmaids' waists. Sensible people took this for what it was: enjoying life, being friendly, an attempt to make life more pleasant.

Sometimes perhaps a little bit more. But so little that it didn't have to bother anybody. And this was only natural, you should certainly be glad for the good things that came your way and show appreciation for the beautiful. Men were made so that they did this. And women so that they liked it, even if prudish constraints forced them to look angry at times.

Susanna gave him many opportunities to show his friendliness. At first he hardly noticed it, he just thought she was a child standing in the way. Then he discovered that the child was silly, an amusing little woman whom he had to move aside from time to time to get through the crowded house. Sometimes he would pinch her, then she would shriek and jump quickly aside. When he passed her again, she would be standing with her skirts hiked up, trying to find the bruise.

"You can't feel anything through all that fat," he would say. Then she would try to slap him, and he'd have to pin her down and punish her. And then suddenly she might drop all defenses, give in, as if she were making herself fit underneath him. But he would let go of her and leave, wanting her and not wanting her.

The knowledge that she was in the house, that she was there and waiting for him, made him sleep badly in the daytime. He got up earlier than before and would wander around. He would walk past the kitchen window and know that she knew he saw her as she stood there adjusting the laces of her corset or pulling up her skirts to scratch her leg.

He also knew that Lotten saw him, that she watched and wondered about their game. He would mutter to himself that he ought to go back in and lie down on the sofa. But after a while the hunter instinct would drive him out again, he had to at least see what was happening, what that crazy girl was up to.

One snowy winter day Lotten had gone out, taking the children and the sled for hauling with her, and had left the girl at home to do laundry. Susanna knew that Thumbs was lying down, that he was trying to sleep. But she heard him stirring, opened the door and asked if he wanted a cup of coffee.

"Bring a cup in here," he said.

She came in, right from doing laundry. She had taken off her big chemise and her heavy winter undershirt, and was going around in an old skirt and open summer blouse.

"Feel how sweaty my forehead is," she said.

But he saw her breasts with the pale, small nipples and the mocking look in her eyes. Suddenly he got angry: she might as well get what she was asking for.

"No!" she screamed. "I don't want to!"

"Like hell you don't, you little whore," he snarled.

When he went to lay her down, he caught sight of Lotten standing in the doorway watching them.

Quickly she crossed the room. Then she took the time to pull down the girl's skirts before she gave her a box on the ear. Screaming with pain and fear, Susanna disappeared up the stairs to the attic.

"You should get a slap too," Lotten said furiously. "Imagine your not thinking of your wife and children."

She was both frightened and angry. She thought Thumbs was putting their whole situation at risk. They had lived so well together here. Was the house going to become a whorehouse now, and Thumbs' and Matilda's marriage be destroyed?

Thumbs lay on the bed and felt shame. For once he had no words in his defense. He felt naked and exposed and pulled the blanket more tightly around him.

"I'll tell Matilda about it myself," he said quietly. "Don't worry, nothing else is going to happen. But the girl has to get a job so that she's gone during the day."

"I'm still a man, damn it!" he burst out suddenly, and thought he had found a satisfactory explanation.

"Have you already slept with her?" asked Lotten.

He shook his head.

"I was only thinking about the possibility of her being infected," said Lotten calmly. "Has Matilda told you that Klara has been sent to the clinic?"

"Do you mean that Susanna also...?"

"What do you think? What else was the girl doing in the cigar shop? Go out now, and I'll speak with her. She certainly won't get in your way from now on."

"It was my fault too," said Thumbs, hoping that Lotten wouldn't be too hard on the girl.

"I thought you said you were a man," answered Lotten acidly and slammed the door behind her.

He got dressed and went out. The children wanted him to go sledding with them but Thumbs fled. He sat in a tavern with a bottle of beer. He felt ashamed and dreaded what Matilda would say, but at the same time it felt better to have the whole game over with. When he saw Susanna in the future, he would no longer feel any lust and attraction.

Lotten was giving Susanna a severe scolding in the kitchen. At first the girl tried to act disdainful and defiant, but she gained nothing by that. Then she started to whine and blame everything on Thumbs. But Lotten crushed every attempt she made in her defense, and Susanna ended up feeling ungrateful and stupid and shameless. And the girl was made to understand that in the future she would be watched constantly and not be able to stick even her nose out the door without being fully and modestly dressed. If it happened that she tried to tempt the men of the house, Lotten would have the police come get her. After all wasn't it the story that Susanna had avoided registering as a prostitute when she worked at the cigar shop? That was punishable by imprisonment.

She promised everything Lotten wanted. A few days later she managed to find work as a bottle washer in a smaller brewery.

For a while she continued to live with Klara's children in the kitchen. Then she disappeared for a few nights and came back dirty and battered. She had followed some sailors on board a boat, but she didn't say that. She only said that she had been attacked.

She could stay, on trial, said Lotten. But after a week she disappeared again and didn't come back. At that time she hadn't shown up at the brewery for a long while.

They didn't miss her. But if they ever spoke of her, Henning would say that he felt sorry for the girl, you couldn't ask so much of her. As she was probably living now she would soon destroy herself. Could they have done more for her? No, probably not.

No, no one thought so.

One evening when Lotten and Matilda sat alone in the kitchen, Matilda said that she knew what had happened. Thumbs had told her about it straightforwardly. And both she and Thumbs were glad that Lotten had intervened.

Was Matilda grieved by it?

No, she said with some hesitation. She knew Thumbs so well, knew his weaknesses. Thumbs got excited so easily, by a skirt or an idea. But he always came back to her and the children. Matilda didn't demand the impossible. She liked him the way he was and wanted to try and overlook things.

They sat there in the twilight and heard the autumn wind rustling in the trees on the hillside and whistling past the doors. And Lotten wondered at Matilda's ability to forgive and understand. She herself would never have been able to forgive such a thing. Wouldn't she have been repulsed if Henning had tried to touch her afterwards? Wouldn't she have taken the children with her and moved out? Right or not, satisfactory explanations or not, it would have meant the end of all trust and love.

She might envy Matilda, wish that she possessed her gentle tolerance. But at the same time she had to feel sorry for her, because Thumbs was the way he was, and because Matilda was unable to feel love's powerful selfish need to own and be owned without limits and without sharing.

There could only be Henning and her, no one to share any of it with. She didn't even want him to feel sorry for Susanna.

AN ISLAND IN THE SEA

Each day as Henning walked to work, he remembered the past winter's anxiety, the humiliation when he looked for temporary odd jobs. Now he was relieved of that difficulty, went every day to his steady job and received his steady salary every week. He often ran into one of his old comrades from the stevedore team. They were waiting for spring, were drawn to the harbor as if they believed that spring would arrive there first.

During a few winter weeks, Henning even got to get out of the warehouse which stank of herring. The firm's driver was sick and Henning was asked to drive. Together with a comrade he filled the sleigh with barrels of herring, and then they drove out to deliver them to customers. At first Henning had trouble finding the way and had to rely on his colleague's directions, as the city on the other side of the locks was still pretty unfamiliar to him. But he learned to recognize the most important streets and find his way to the largest customers.

Nobody had anything against a pair of boys sitting up on the coachbox. Henning talked Lotten into coming down with August and Rudolf; they were standing and waiting at Slussen when he drove out for the day's last round. He placed the boys between himself and his helper. They waved proudly to Lotten who watched a little anxiously as the vehicle disappeared into the crowd of sleighs and carriages.

They crossed Skeppsbron and the square at Kornhamn where frozen hawkers stood slapping themselves to stay warm, and steam rose from the soup sellers' tented stalls. At Stora Nygatan they rolled the first barrel off while the boys watched the horses who, with front legs tied, stood and chomped in their feedbags.

Then they were off again past the courthouse with its slits for windows in the prison cells, between Helgeandsholmen's jumble of houses and royal stables, out onto the wide Norrbro, down toward Tegelbacken where the sleigh had to wait in front of the closed iron gate at the railroad tracks. They were changing a steam engine, and the boys could hardly sit still on the sleigh, they got so excited. They had never seen a train before. The steam billowed forth hissing, a signal blew, the engine traveled out onto the bridge and stopped. It belched out some smoke once more, signaled again and rolled backwards. Then the guard moved the gate aside, allowing it to swing back and block the tracks. Just as they were going across, the boys could see the engine disappear beneath the giant glass roof over the station area.

The sleigh moved on, over the wooden bridge to Kungsholmen, past the mighty mill belching smoke.

That evening the boys had a lot to say when they came home together with Henning. They swaggered around mannishly with their hands in their pants pockets and boasted about their experiences. And they didn't want to go to bed at all when Klara's oldest daughter, Stina, came and said the beds were made.

Stina had come to them as a little wild creature, dirty and obstinate. Over the course of the first few weeks, Lotten had almost given up hope, the girl was impossible. But slowly she had changed. When she got to eat her fill, she no longer stole. She began to take care of the boys instead of teasing them. And when Lotten made over one of Matilda's old dresses for the girl, Stina was so careful of it that it was touching to see. The new security and the new habits transformed her, suddenly she didn't have to be a wild animal to get by.

Instead she became Lotten's obedient slave. She followed her around faithfully, always ready to help, to lend a hand.

One day when Stina stood in the kitchen helping Lotten dry the dishes she said, "I wish I could always stay here …."

"But your mother will be coming home soon," answered Lotten. "It might be fun to move home with her again don't you think?"

No answer came. Lotten put away the plates and mugs and wiped the counter. It wasn't until she had wrung out and hung up the towel that she saw that Stina was standing there crying.

Lotten stroked her hand over the girl's hair, felt her helplessness. What could she do to console her? Stina knew best why she was standing and crying; she knew what awaited her. In a way it would have been more merciful if the girl had been allowed to remain in filth and misery, then she wouldn't have known anything else.

Klara arrived one spring day, punished and cured. But one could see that neither one nor the other had done her any good. She had aged, undeniably, looked worn out. So much of the cheerful and, in spite of everything, unspoiled Klara had disappeared: the free-spiritedness and coquettishness had grown coarse; become offensive and brazen. If the body had been healed at the cure-house, the soul had been destroyed at the spinning-house.

She came in the evening and had a man with her. He sat in a corner and groaned drunkenly to himself while Klara walked through the house and looked at her sleeping children.

"You have a nice place here," Klara said. "Can't we rent the kitchen from you? It's going to be vacant isn't it?"

Matilda had trouble refusing her in reply, and looked anxiously at Lotten. And Lotten answered quickly that they needed the kitchen themselves.

Klara and her fiancé left soon after. She was going to return the next day and get the children. Henning recognized the man: a professional thief who had been exposed and fired from one of the longshore teams.

Before Lotten went upstairs to bed she looked in on the children in the kitchen. Stina was awake. Troubled, she grabbed Lotten's hand and begged, "Please, don't let her take me."

Lotten couldn't answer. But almost two weeks went by before Klara came back again. The younger ones went willingly, but Stina cried when she left. She turned around time after time and waved to Lotten who stood at the gate.

The kitchen was empty again, finally their own. But at least once a week Klara's two girls came to see her. And to bathe. Stina had asked Lotten if they could: they didn't have a proper bathtub at home. And Lotten swelled with pride over the cleanliness she had brought out in the child and decided that every Monday afternoon Stina and Maria would get to eat and bathe in the kitchen. And they came, were bathed, and then ate with the children of the house.

But Lotten couldn't do much about the girls' clothing. She had to watch the children fall into decline again, grow ragged and thin. She tried to fill them up as much as she could when they were at her house, patch the worst tears. But it didn't help much, one afternoon was so little out of a whole week.

Klara lived with her fiancé on Nya gatan, right next to the house where three children had once been asphyxiated from smoke. One Monday morning Lotten went there; she had been obliged to change the day of the girls' visit.

The house smelled dirty and moldy; the yard was almost filled with filth from the winter which hadn't been carted away yet. Lotten made her way up the stairs to the attic.

She knocked on the door, waited and knocked again. Someone called "come in" and she opened the door. She stood on the threshold and looked around, horrified.

Lotten had grown up in poverty. But her mother's hard work had made their destitution clean, washed threadbare, scrubbed shiny. Even if they only had potatoes to eat, they had eaten on clean plates.

The poverty she saw now she had never encountered before, not so close at hand. The wallpaper that hung in shreds, the spider webs and soot, the broken windowpanes that had been filled with paper, the piles of rags that served as beds, the stench from leftover food and poorly cleaned up vomit, from the full chamber pot and the empty bottles.

Klara sat up, disconcerted. "I hadn't expected such a fine visitor," she said. "We would have tidied up a little first."

The man beside her gave a growl and turned toward the wall. Between them lay the children, naked under the blanket. The youngest, the boy, was clearly sick: he tossed about restlessly, flushed red.

Klara pulled her clothing around her and got up. Lotten said what she had to say, and Klara thanked her for allowing the girls to come. In the foul hole they lived in there was scant opportunity to keep children clean and neat.

Lotten knew: it was an accusation, Klara had of course wanted to rent their kitchen. But Lotten knew it would have looked something like this in the kitchen if she hadn't said no.

The girls came to Lotten the next day. Stina had picked a bouquet of wild flowers in the White Hills and Lotten thanked her for them and placed them in a big mug on the table. Of course, she was happy about Stina's devotion, but still she was sad. She felt like she had to do something to help the girls and knew that the effects of whatever she did would be felt by her own children. Their resources were so limited, whatever they had they needed so badly themselves. She fantasized that she could maybe let them live in the kitchen, keep them as foster children. Though, of course, she didn't even know if Klara would go along with that anyway.

The following week, the bath water was heated in vain as Klara's girls didn't come. Lotten didn't have a chance to walk down to them and ask why; she preferred not to go there either. She waited as long as possible with the bath and the food. But she didn't hear from them.

Later on she found out that both Klara and the children had been taken to the hospital on Sandbergsgatan.

Smallpox.

The epidemic had started just before Christmas and spread, first on Söder and after that down in the city, too. Those most affected belonged mainly to the poor and working classes as well as the serving class. It was as if the disease afflicted the most badly kept houses, going from room to room, from family to family. The houses along Nya gatan were among the worst hit. Klara and her children had fallen sick; the man was the only one left at home, and he filled the room with drinking companions and prostitutes.

Klara and the youngest of the two girls came back to the house eventually. But Stina and the little boy belonged to the more than two thousand victims of the pox.

So the thorn took hold, dug in, was a reminder. Lotten saw Stina's pleading face, heard the words again: "Please let me stay, don't let her take me."

Could she have managed, could she have taken the girl? Was her unwillingness or her powerlessness to blame for Stina's death?

Lotten brooded over it often as spring changed to summer. She filled the old mug with flowers, thought of it as Stina's mug.

A hand had reached out: someone had asked for help. She hadn't done enough. Stina was dead.

Then she felt the hate against the filth well up again, and was freed of some of the sorrow, was able to bury her guilty conscience in hard work. She scrubbed and washed as never before, felt like she had chased dirt and disease out of her house. Like a newly scrubbed little island their house lay in the middle of a sea of filth, hovered over Garbage Lane's piles of refuse and shabby sheds.

But it never happened again that two dirty girls made their way up the hill to bathe in Lotten's tub. Klara and her only surviving child disappeared, and the house on Nya gatan was raided by the police who arrested several wanted burglars and prostitutes.

SUNDAY IN
THE GREENERY

The steamer moved along between the green shores, between Kungsholmen's lush dark green gardens and Söder's meager pale green hills. The picture of the city slipped away and grew smaller; the throng of boats and people along Riddarholmen's pier lost their details. The cluster of house walls changed into a solid wall; the spires of the churches rose above it like strangely insubstantial watch towers.

The water shone and sparkled; the foam frothed and bubbled; the flag with its bright little red union symbol flapped in the wind.

The Bodin herring firm was celebrating a jubilee. Twenty-five years had passed since Fredrik Bodin's father, "the old master," had bought and sold his first herrings in a primitive shed at Stadsgården.

The employees had honored their boss with flowers, a silver vase and congratulatory speeches. In his thank you speech, Fredrik Bodin had promised to invite the personnel and their families on a summer outing. The steamship "Necken" would transport them from Riddarholmen to the Bodin summer house on Stora Essingen.

Now old Törn was standing at the rail and pointing out what they passed. Lotten, Henning and their soon-to-be-six August were his attentive audience. Törn belonged to those few who knew their city, while his listeners didn't know much about what lay beyond their everyday environment.

They saw Eldkvarnen mill's large courtyard, which opened onto the water, the impressive Karolinska Institute on Glasbruksholmen, and the Mint, which was sitting on millions of dollars in silver coins.

"That's where the Cure House lies," said the old man and pointed. Then Lotten shivered and wondered if Susanna was hidden behind the walls.

Kungsholmen's many hospitals gleamed, some stately as castles.

Small, patched wooden houses clung to the hillside above the church, it was almost like at home on Söder. Docks and boat sheds stuck out from the jagged water's edge where tanneries lay close together. Large sheds marked the royal yachtworks alongside the pontoniers' barracks. And soon the light-colored summer houses began to glimmer through the greenery. Rålambshov and Smedsudden, Karlshäll on Långholmen and the houses around the military school beside Marieberg.

At that point the city was already far away and the green islands of Lake Mälar close by. The shores encircled them when they passed in between Gröndal and Stora Essingen Island, and soon they could see the flag waving in welcome from the Värdshus dock.

Master Bodin stood on the dock and received them. Today they were his guests, and he took them each by the hand, said a few friendly words to their wives and asked what their children were called. Lotten curtsied deeply and stammered out a few words; she had always had respect for her superiors, and, for her, Henning's boss stood next to God and the king. She nudged August in the back so that he would bow politely. It was unnecessary since Agge remembered very well the instructions he had received, and he doubled over like a jackknife. He answered the questions: his name was August and he was five and a half.

"What a good boy," said Fredrik Bodin. All day Lotten felt like she could hear those words: "What a good boy, good boy, good boy..." And she thought that Fredrik Bodin must be the kindest and finest boss anyone could have, Henning had really been lucky.

"The master said that August was a good boy," she told Törn when they walked up the hill past the old inn that had been demoted to an alcohol-free restaurant.

Housemaids and temporary serving girls had been at work all morning setting up long tables on the lawn and making everything ready for the many guests.

Annika directed. Calm and assured, she watched over everything, giving quick, decisive orders. No one would have guessed that Master

Bodin's wife was a coal bearer's daughter, a former tavern maid. Among the guests there were only two who knew: Henning and Lotten.

The idea for the outing had been Annika's. She was the one who came up with the ideas. Maybe because she needed them. Idleness irritated her. She drove her workers from morning to night, in the evenings she also drove Fredrik. Something had to be happening: guests coming, activity humming and blossoming in that large, silent house. Actually she was happier in the city, but people in their position had to live in the country in the summertime, of course. And besides, the city was also dreary during the summer, stinking and hot.

Why was she always so restless? Had the bitter years taken such a hold, scarred her? Or was it because they hadn't had any children, was that why their house, home and life felt so frighteningly empty and meaningless? She still had Fredrik, but he didn't fill the void, she didn't love him, had never loved him. He was a stone she had used to climb up on, he was a secure foundation. He had given her the base, but she had nothing to place on the pedestal.

So the many assured commands and gestures hid the anxiety, the many ideas masked the emptiness. She spurred on movement and activity but still felt numbness and death.

An outing for the personnel she had said. Was it because she wanted to see Henning again, meet with something remaining from the time when she suffered but was alive? Or was she quite simply curious about the girl he had married? See if he could be happy, one of Fredrik's herring-stinking and poorly paid employees? Did he have children? Could he have children with his girl while Master Bodin and his wife remained childless?

It would be unfair in some way if Henning had children. And too bad for the little ones, what kind of a future awaited the offspring of a poor worker? She knew.

Weren't the girls going to be done soon? Annika had to hurry them up. The guests might arrive at any time, and then the girls should be standing over by the kitchen door and not dashing about among the tables. Annika would come out to meet Fredrik's employees alone.

Friendly, but still keeping a distance, she would welcome them to Sommarro.

She saw the first guests outside the gate now: the bookkeeper and the clerk with their wives and children, accompanied by Fredrik. The first workers were coming at a respectful distance. But there wasn't any sign of Henning, and for a moment she wondered if he perhaps hadn't come, if he had refrained from the outing so as not to risk making her feel uncomfortable. But Fredrik had said that everyone had accepted the invitation. Among the married ones, only Törn wasn't bringing his wife along, his old woman was all too wracked by pain to go out.

There was Törn coming now. Beside a young woman who was holding a child by the hand. On the other side of the child walked Henning. But now Annika had no time to either look or ponder any longer, she had to go and greet the first arrivals. Quickly she glided across the lawn, her light-colored dress swishing against the lush, dark green grass.

Henning bowed politely to Annika and imagined he saw a brief glimmer of complicity in her glance. He brought Lotten forward. She curtsied deeply and received a friendly nod from Annika. And then it was Agge's turn to bend over double again.

"Is this your only child?" asked Annika and kept the little boy's hand in hers. No, they had two girls as well. But the girls were too young to come along. That wasn't really the whole truth. If Emelie had had a pretty dress she could have come, she was four years old, after all.

Annika watched the boy, his careful answers, the timid look in his eyes, so like Henning. She felt sorry for the boy. A little clumsily dressed in homemade clothing, one could guess that his pants had been a coat or a skirt and that his shirt had been made over from an old women's blouse. Heavy boots on his small feet. But he was polished and shiny clean.

Sorry for the boy. Sorry for Henning and his wife. Henning in a simple good suit, his hands, which were strangely rough against the slender body, hung like clumsy clubs from his coat sleeves. And his wife in a white blouse and dark skirt with a Sunday shawl. But still as if they had nothing to do with the dark and stinking warehouse. If they smelled of anything, it was of soap and not of herring. Annika could imagine what that cleanliness cost. A little unwillingly she felt impressed. As if this clean family tried to prove that the step Annika had taken wasn't so decisive, that you didn't have to give up just because you stayed where you were.

No, Henning and his family didn't spread lice and filth. If all of Fredrik's workers had been like them, they could have had the party indoors if it had rained. Then Annika wouldn't have had to trouble the innkeeper with keeping a dining room ready.

Annika left them, clapped her hands and bid everyone welcome to the lunch tables. And the Sunday continued with games for the children and dancing for the grown-ups, with entertainment by musicians, with punch bowls in the arbors. Some of the bravest men visited the bathhouse; the wives squeezed together on a few benches and talked about housework while they watched the playing children, anxious lest one of them should misbehave. The little ones were amazingly subdued in their play, well aware of what was expected of them.

As dusk began to fall, people gathered in groups, waiting for the signal to break up. A few of the youngest ones were already asleep on their mothers' laps when Master Bodin informed them that Necken was ready to depart.

The employees thanked him for a wonderful day and cheered. And they filed in a line past the master and his young wife, shook hands, bowed and curtsied. Slowly one group after another wandered down to the dock. When they had come a little distance from the house, they picked up speed: now it was important to get a good seat on the steamer.

Annika and Fredrik Bodin stood at the gate and watched the last ones disappear around the bend in the road.

"Well, now that's done," said Fredrik Bodin. "I think they must have had a good time. What do you think?"

Annika didn't answer. She felt tired, let down.

She turned around and walked alone back to the house which shone white against the dark of the greenery. The maids slipped through the twilight under the trees, taking the cloths from the tables, carrying away the benches which had been brought out. In a moment everything would be silent and still again. Empty, lifeless. And Annika longed for autumn, away from here, away from summer, away from Fredrik.

She didn't bother to oversee the serving girls' work, but instead went straight up to her bedroom and locked herself in. When Fredrik came and knocked on the door, she replied that she had a headache.

She went over to the open window and looked out over the water. Necken had finally cast off, gliding with lanterns lighted over the triangle of water between the treetops.

The steamer chugged on through the summer evening's blue mist. Lotten and Henning had squeezed together on one of the benches in the fore, and August had fallen asleep on Henning's lap. Lotten leaned against Henning's arm and felt calm and secure. She thought they'd had a glorious day. And she was proud. Both the boss himself and his wife had praised Agge. She had to stroke the sleeping boy's cheek: he was so good, it really was true. So polite and fine. Some other children had gotten a little noisy, shouting, shoving to get to the table. But not Agge.

The musicians were still playing, they kept it up in the stern and the sound which reached Henning and Lotten was pleasantly dampened, coming as if from across the water, sailing up through the mist.

On the bench opposite them sat old Törn, not as interested in talking and pointing any longer. He was in a hurry to get home; he thought that the outing had lasted too long.

But Henning didn't feel any hurry, as far as he was concerned Necken could travel on all night. He liked sitting here beside Lotten, feeling the weight of the child on his knee. Here they were freed from all duties: they neither needed to nor were able to do anything useful. They had a right to just rest, sit against each other and feel well-being, free of cares for a little while. He was more at ease aboard the steamer than he had been at Bodin's summer place. He'd had to be on his toes the whole time there, had felt like Annika was watching him. In some way she frightened him. Was it possibly because she didn't look happy? He felt the disquietude that surrounded her.

Dim lights flared up from the shore, many small gas lanterns around the rocks and piers. Black towers appeared out of the blue mist, Riddarholmen's buildings rose like a gray wall. They would soon be there.

Necken slid in toward the dock. A little bump when the boat hit brought everyone to life. People began to crowd around the gangway. Henning had to awaken August, just enough so the boy could climb up on his back and put his arms around his neck. August slept this way, hanging on his father's back with his head bumping against his shoulder. They walked through the summer night and the city, up the hill toward Söder.

"Imagine that people like the Bodins, who have so much, don't have any children," said Lotten.

"Maybe they'll have some," said Henning.

No, Lotten didn't think so.

Henning had to stop and catch his breath a minute before they took the slope up toward their own hill. He sat Agge down on a fence and wiped the sweat from his forehead.

Above them rose the hill with its small sleeping houses. The gas lantern on a post on the corner rained a pale light over the resting party, somewhere within the fence a couple of horses rustled among the trees.

"It's such a pity," said Lotten. "Such a pity that the Bodins don't have any children."

She looked at the dozing August. She wondered how the shy and cautious boy would manage, if the soft child would slowly be transformed into a poorly treated adult. She would defend him, she would help him. A warm wave of tenderness and pride went through her. With some of fear's cold grip deep inside, but still mostly joy, in spite of all that might wait.

The boss had said that he was a good boy, a very good boy ....

IV

DESERT
AND
WASTELAND

This was a foreign and unknown land, an area which could be marked by white spots on the map. Or rather black: the home of want and sin.

The Bible ladies came climbing up the slippery path. They walked between collapsing outhouses and old summer pavilions with smashed panes. Old women and children who had bundled themselves up in everything they owned to keep out the cold stared at the newcomers through frosted window panes and warped doorways.

They were missionaries who had come to the wilderness to open a station and spread the Word among the heathens. The deep spiritual and bodily needs in this ill-reputed area had driven them here.

The Bible ladies' home, which was also called the Mission in the White Hills, was a rather small house which had been put together and maintained through gifts from known and unknown donors. But the resources that existed hadn't really been enough. This was why the new home met them with empty coffers, an empty pantry, empty woodshed and incomplete repairs. And she, who was leading the expedition, knew her shortcomings and weaknesses. She felt old and tired; she was fifty years old, and her head had been injuriously affected by many years of working in a school.

A gift awaited them when they opened the door: an envelope with neatly printed verses from the Bible.

Elsa Borg immediately nailed up one of the cards on the wall in the meeting room, it contained a promise:

The desert and the wasteland shall be made a paradise.

The women spent their first evening in the mission station with prayers and song. This was intended to drive away the darkness and the evil which crept outside the house. The Bible ladies knew that they had left safety, light and warmth to go out in the wasteland and find the lost souls. There were wild animals near their house.

One evening at the end of November they celebrated the opening of the station. From far away, as far as the fine houses on Norrmalm, the ladies of the Sewing Society arrived. People streamed in from the sheds and houses of the White Hills: old people, deaf people and the crippled who had been invited. The Bible ladies went off with sleds to get the ones who couldn't get there themselves. At times the sleds almost slid backwards on the icy rocks and almost tumbled down over the precipice. But the women were almost overjoyed at the danger they felt themselves to be in, they sang with exultation. As if in ecstasy, they held on tightly.

Oh, to be a little horse for God!

The poor women moved closer. Suddenly they had been given a glowing fire on the cold hill. At the Bible ladies' it smelled like rice porridge cooking; they passed out clothing; hungry boys were offered sandwiches; dirty girls got the lice combed out of their hair.

The mission station became an opportunity, something to take advantage of. People came and showed their tatters, their needs and their wounds. They went home with a few coins, or a piece of clothing which could be pawned for schnapps if that was what they needed most. If all else failed they could at least get a little warmth during the meetings and a bowl of porridge when the poor were fed.

The inhabitants of the hill called the salvation station the porridge chapel, and the invitations to the poor people's suppers, porridge tickets.

A little mournfully the Bible ladies pronounced the people around the White Hills to be more concerned with their bodily needs than with their spiritual ones. Elsa Borg counted the old ladies who visited them one day and found that eleven had come to get some of the world's goods while only one had come for her soul's salvation. And the missionaries were scared by the motley and rowdy gang at the prayer meetings: drunken, snuff-spitting old men and whiny, foul-smelling old women, yelling street-boys and degenerate prostitutes.

But, they consoled themselves, these pieces of debris and wreckage would be transformed into jewels. Found lying in the mud, formed into ornaments by the hand of the great Master for His royal crown. The desert and the wasteland would bloom one day — want give way, and the wilderness be made a paradise.

A GIFT FOR EMELIE

The new time had come with a roar and violent force. For more than two years, blasting had thundered and the hillside had collapsed with a rumble down toward the wharf. The harbor was being broadened. Three hundred dynamiters and stoneworkers were at work both summer and winter. A couple million cubic meters of stone had to be removed so that a wide new wharf could be laid beneath the hillside which rose up more steeply than ever, cut away and mangled by the blasting.

The visionaries of the future said that now they should blast away all of the troublesome hills on Söder and create a city where the inhabitants and the new horse-drawn trolleys could get around easily and unhindered. Nitroglycerine had given people undreamed of possibilities. The streets were paved with stones; water pipes and sewers extended farther and farther; new bridges spanned the waters. Soon the stately bridge, Vasabron, was going to be opened.

But at the same time as the future thundered in so sure of victory, the old hard times had also crept back. More and more wheels were stopping in the factories. Hordes of people moved to the city, but only some of them could find work. The lack of housing got worse, especially now when so many of the slums were being torn down. New, expensive apartments were being built instead, but those who most needed housing couldn't move there, they had to try to squeeze together in the rubble which remained. In the old cholera hospital on Tyskbagargatan, sixteen families with many children were crammed into one large hall where the homeless tried to pile in their few possessions and sleep close together. Strangers and acquaintances slept in one giant family bed under the clotheslines where rags, smelly from a winter's wear, hung to dry.

In the shacks and alleyways, people fought over space with multitudes of rats which were fed by the fodder from horses' stalls and pigsties and from the garbage in the back yards.

The depression had affected even the Bodin herring firm. At least Fredrik Bodin said so, others intimated that the firm's weaknesses were because of Bodin's ineptness and lack of assurance. In any case, many of the employees had been dismissed and salaries of the ones who remained had been lowered. But lowered wages were prevalent now in all professions.

Henning Nilsson came out into the pale spring evening, stopped beyond the arch over the doorway and took in the cool air. He felt the resistance when he breathed deeply, tried to avoid coughing. But the cough came anyway and he leaned for a moment against the wall while it grew dark before his eyes. The cough wasn't good; it frightened him. But he tried to hide it, tried to forget it.

He walked along piles of sharp stones from the blasting, followed the wharf which narrowed rapidly, and reached the stairs that led up toward the hill at Ersta. He had to take them slowly, they were steep and demanding. He walked like an old man, he thought to himself. He wasn't so young anymore; he was thirty-three, but, nevertheless, he still should have some strength left. He had to. His youngest daughter was barely seven years old; Emelie was turning eight today. August wasn't ten yet. Still it would be several years before the children could manage without him, before they could begin to help Lotten.

Emelie. Perhaps she was his pet after all, though he didn't want to be unfair and place one ahead of the others, not even to himself. Lotten must have looked like Emelie as a child, with the dark hair, the serene gaze.

He searched in his pocket with his hand, felt the rustling paper. The present for Emelie. It wasn't often that the children could get something beyond what was necessary, least of all now. But one of the packers who had just had to leave Bodin's had come down to the warehouse with handkerchiefs that his wife had sewn. She had come across remnants of fine silk and embroidered on them. One handkerchief had some forget-me-nots and a finely embellished "E." It was so perfect, it was like a sign. He had to buy it. He had kept the handkerchief at the warehouse until today, until it was time.

Slowly Henning continued up the steep stairs. And now he saw the face up there, the little figure. Emelie had walked out to meet him today too. He waved, she waved back. And bounded playfully and lightly toward him on the stairs.

Hand-in-hand they walked down Erstaberget to Kilen, the corner where all the smaller streets came together on their way to the customs house. She talked about how school had been, the "crèche" down in Katarina Church's yard. Today they hadn't had to light the stove, that was a real sign of spring. And the teacher had put the kerosene lantern, which usually stood on her desk, in a cupboard.

He felt the warmth from the little hand. And the coolness of the evening around him, like a threatening endless void. Fear took hold, the terror to have to let go of this hand, leave Emelie alone in the world. Once again he denied the certainty, he wasn't sick, it was just a little spring cough. He *couldn't* be sick, he had to go on, move his children on toward safety.

The girl looked curiously at her father. Why was he holding her hand so tightly? He didn't need to be afraid; she walked so carefully when she crossed the street. Though actually there wasn't any horse-drawn wagon as far as they could see, neither on Tjärhovsgatan nor on Pilgatan.

"It's your birthday," he said. She nodded, she'd been feted with a wheat bun and coltsfoot flowers around her morning mug of milk.

He held out the slim package to her. Emelie stopped on the street corner and unfolded the paper. She stood and looked at the handkerchief which was so fine and soft, silky smooth.

"It's an E," she whispered.

"That stands for Emelie." answered her father. "The flowers are forget-me-nots."

She smiled at him, filled with gratitude, as she placed the handkerchief carefully back in the paper again and carried the little butterfly-light package in her hand while she balanced her way between the wheel ruts.

THE THRESHOLD

The gate in the fence had a rounded, worn-down wooden threshold. On sunny mornings it created a border between the yard's heavy shade and the hillside's sunshine. You could step from light into darkness over the same threshold, and from darkness into light. The house's children tumbled out and stopped a moment as if blinded. They saw their friends from the houses next door waiting on the corner and hurried over. And the little band set out on their way to school.

The little children were going to the "crèche" in the church yard, the older ones went to the old factory building on Nytorget, "Malongen." From the crammed housing of the poor, the children went to the crammed schoolrooms. The old buildings had been outgrown long ago, were overflowing.

Agge, Rudde and some of the others were on their way to Nytorget. They jumped over the stinking sewage ditch which followed Stora Bondegatan down toward Hammarby Lake, and then they took the road through the White Hills. They whistled like trains as they steamed past the Bible ladies' white mission station.

Dark and gloomy, Malongen welcomed them, as if the old building still preserved the sweat of orphaned mitten-making boys, the tears of the cholera-ridden and the plaints of the homeless. The windows were dark like slits in prison cells, but outside the trees shone a glaring green and the children played in flocks beneath their treetops.

The school's most feared bullies came from the firemen's barracks. They were drummer boys for the civil guard. Each had a quart of schnapps sticking out of his back pocket and took a swig from time to time. They stole tobacco from the teachers as well, and knew rawer stories and dirtier swears than any of the other children.

The drummer boys shoved aside the other children and swaggered, legs apart, importantly across the schoolyard. They were the last ones to saunter through the door after the schoolmarm had rung the bell long and vigorously.

Agge and Rudde were classmates and were in Master Olsson's class. Olle the Drunk, the boys said in secret, and it sometimes happened that the schoolmaster sent them out to buy him liquor at Nytorget. In the winter the teacher always had a warm beer leaning against the back of the stove. When the old fellow had enough to drink, he became dangerous, hitting hard and blindly.

The hours at school passed drearily and at a crawl. Olle the Drunk half slept at his desk, giving a command now and then. The class's drummer boy stood up and asked to go out for nature's call. He did this every morning, and Olle the Drunk always grimaced with displeasure. Outside the boy would meet some colleagues with the same habit. They would sit for a while on a hill and drink a bracer before they each released their stream on the usual tree. The schools didn't have any toilets.

Finally the long-awaited breakfast recess arrived. Those who could afford to went down to the dairy on Stadsträdgårdsgatan and drank a mug of skim milk for two öre. Most of the children had to satisfy themselves with a piece of bread taken from home. This time of year it was pleasant to sit outside and eat. It was worse during the winter months. Sometimes they could hardly hold onto the pieces of bread with their bare fingers. No matter how cold it was, they had to eat outdoors.

They returned through the long corridors where the wooden rifles for the exercise hours stood lined up in their stalls. They hung up their clothes on pegs which were placed so close that the lice never had any trouble wandering from one piece of clothing to another.

After recess Agge was assigned to go out and buy a new cane; the drummer boy had pinched the old one. He went with a sorrowful air: Rudde was to be the first one to try it out. Agge always suffered from the punishments, even if they didn't affect him personally. He didn't feel any of the curiosity and malicious joy displayed by so many of his classmates; he only felt afraid. And when Rudde lay there across the chair with his pants unbuttoned and cried out, Agge felt bad and looked down hard at the battered desk.

Olle the Drunk grunted and wiped the sweat from his forehead and returned to teaching which was less hands-on.

They didn't learn much in school, and it didn't get much better until the schoolmaster was dismissed for drunkenness and abuse. This happened when he pulled one of the drummer boys' ears so hard that they had to get the barber-surgeon. For the last week of the term, the class got a new teacher while Olle the Drunk showed up as the new mailman in the area. The drummer boy gathered a good-sized gang who followed Olsson unchecked until he was forced to request a transfer to Kungsholmen to get away from his old students.

But that day, while Olle the Drunk was still their daily cross to bear, Agge and Rudde walked home gloomily from school. They stopped by the bushes alongside Meijtensgränd to take a look at Rudde's well-striped backside, and Agge broke off large, juicy dandelion leaves for his friend to place in his pants to soothe the pain. Rudde swore that he would be avenged, and they had an almost pleasant moment while they figured out how they would torment Olle the Drunk. They would put nails in his seat cushion, make the spout of his beer bottle red-hot. Everything suddenly seemed possible. Rudde knew that a girls' class had collected lice that they had secretly put on their schoolteacher, the so-called bearded lady. And the drummer boy had peed in Olle's beer bottle one time, though the old guy never even noticed it. There was a lot they could do.

Still, Agge knew that he could never carry out any of the planned great exploits. He was afraid, of course. But there was something else, too, something simpler and more difficult: *he* didn't do these things. As if something from home prevented him, his mother's eye watched him in the schoolroom as well. He had to read fluently, be well-behaved, be liked by the teacher. There were boys who, in spite of poverty, managed to get ahead. Through a door into another world where they didn't have to walk in constant fear.

If you were going to get there you couldn't pee in Olle the Drunk's bottle, not even be inattentive or rude to the teacher.

This wasn't anything Agge could talk to Rudde about. Hardly with anyone at all. It was just there, in the same way as when he was a little child, and there was always a shadow standing over him. It was a part of his home.

"I'm going to shit in the old guy's hat," Rudde said with satisfaction. But Agge sat quietly, as if afraid of the shadow falling across the threshold.

It was already evening when Henning entered the garden. They ate and the little girls went to bed while Agge and Rudde played out on the hill. Finally Henning was able to talk alone with Lotten, tell her about what had been worrying him all day. Sorrow and joy, the bad news and the good.

He was still stunned. What had happened could be a catastrophe. No, it couldn't be. He had to cope, the strength had to be there, buried within him, to be called on at will. And he had long expected the news that he had received.

He had been fired.

Lotten turned white. She understood, the good days were over.

But Master Bodin had been so friendly. Henning was the only one who had been called into the office to receive the news. This was because he was the only one who had been offered a position in the firm; all the others had applied for work there. Henning could say that he had given up a good and steady job because he had been invited by Bodin. For that reason the boss felt responsible for getting Henning something new. He had spoken with Stevedore Lundström, who was willing to take back his old longshoreman. Bodin hoped that it would only have to be for a while.

"But how will you manage?" Lotten looked worriedly at Henning. He had gotten thinner lately, bent over. A dock worker wasn't supposed to look like that.

"It'll be all right."

What more could he say? What was the use of worrying? What you had to do you had to do. He didn't know how to do anything else. Only carry. And the herring work with other herring firms had all positions filled. And if he went over to a competitor, he couldn't count on coming back to Bodin's either.

Henning knew that Lotten couldn't really understand what the change meant. He hadn't dared tell her about what was gnawing away inside him, his lack of strength. He really knew so little himself, could only guess, fear. Perhaps he couldn't afford to know. If he went to a doctor, he might be taken into a hospital. That couldn't be allowed to happen.

No, it was nothing to talk about. It was better to bring out the good news, let himself be warmed by his pride and get Lotten to forget the bad things that had happened.

"Master Bodin has invited August to spend the summer with them in the country," he said.

Lotten sat up sharply.

Henning nodded. He tried to describe the amazing experience he had just had. Bodin had not just gotten Henning a new job. He had also asked how Lotten and August were and wondered if the boy had turned ten yet. Imagine, the boss had not only remembered August since the outing four years ago, he had also recalled how old the boy was. And then he had wondered if August could come and live with them during the summer. As compensation, to make things easier. And they didn't have to worry about clothes. The Bodins would take care of that. They only had to come down to Riddarholm's harbor with the boy the day after school let out, and he could go with Master Bodin.

Lotten began to cry.

Was she sad? And he had thought she would be happy.

No, not sad, reassured Lotten. Only astonished, confused. She couldn't comprehend. That people could be so kind.

"What if they want to keep him," she said suddenly. "They don't have any children of their own."

Henning felt a chill, felt his vulnerability.

"No, no," he assured her vigorously. "They don't want to do that. And they can't do that without our permission."

"But if ...."

He didn't have to answer; August came in from playing. He had washed up properly in the shed and hung up his outer clothes. Lotten had seldom to remind the boy about anything.

They told him the news. And August sat still and listened, a little afraid and with a lot of anticipation. His mother had often called forth the memory of the large white villa in the green park; he felt he could remember exactly how it looked. Would he get to stay there the whole summer? Just swimming and playing? But he was a little afraid of the strangers, his superiors. Though, of course, it was an adventure, something special that none of his friends would get a chance to take part in.

But when Rudde's papa heard about the summer plans the next day, he muttered angrily that Annika Bodin could get herself a lapdog instead of borrowing one of her workers' children. But then Agge's mother got so mad, you couldn't always mistrust the rich and Master Bodin was one of the finest people she had ever met. But Rudde's papa said that Annika Bodin was a traitor who ought to be sitting in the asylum spinning instead of her ten-room apartment. She had sold herself for money.

Agge listened, fascinated, until his mother recalled his presence. Later she told him very strictly that he must forget every word Rudde's papa had said, and never let the kind Bodins know that anyone had said such things.

"But what if someone comes and takes their house and puts everyone who lives there in prison?" asked August.

"No, no," assured Lotten. "God would never allow anything like that to happen."

Summer vacation began in the middle of June and on his first day of it, August had to put on new clothes after he had been bathed and scrubbed until his skin was a shiny red. Lotten packed a change of clothing in a large paper bag along with a white nightshirt. A little proud over what she was able to do, a little humbled at not being able to do more.

Lotten was eager to set off, even if Master Bodin arrived at the boat very early he wouldn't have to wait for them.

Agge bowed a polite farewell to his grandmother who had come to take care of the girls and Rudde and his two brothers. There were three boys in Thumbs' family since Mikael had been born a few years earlier. This littlest one was called the "night-off boy" by his father.

Grandmother patted Agge's cheek and gave him a whole five-öring piece. And then Lotten left with her son. His sisters and Rudde and Knutte waved after them, and Agge turned around time after time and waved back. Now he felt alone although he still had his mother with him. Singled out, left out. The other ones stayed home in their everyday clothes, were going to run out on the hill and play. He alone was leaving them and didn't really know what awaited him.

The children in the lane stared at him all dressed up; some ran alongside a while and threw taunts at him until Lotten got mad. Then they disappeared into the yards where they climbed up and hung over the fences facing the street.

The way was long, in the hilly district of Söder there were no streetcars, even if they had wanted to indulge themselves in riding. Now they were walking along Renstjärnasgränd out along the edge of the hill, where Söderberg's stairs led down to the harbor. If it was possible Agge was going to say good-bye once more to his father.

Yes, there he was. August saw him from a long way off and ran toward him. Henning was carrying a sack of grain, was stumbling under it. He carried the sack into the warehouse and dried the sweat from his brow and asked one of the many subs available to take his turn for a minute.

He was still breathing heavily when he reached them, had to lean against the storehouse wall. Lotten hadn't seen Henning at work before. Now she was frightened. She thought his eyes looked like they were about to bulge out of their sockets; she felt how his hand shook. She almost forgot why they had come, could only think about Henning now.

He tried to hide how overstrained he was. But it was hard. The words came out a little choppily when he told August to be on his best behavior and write home every week. Master Bodin had promised to bring the letters with him, and Henning would be able to pick them up at his office.

Then mother and son left while some of the longshoremen, who were free, closed in around Henning and voiced their disbelief that such a fine woman could be his wife.

They had to wait almost an hour before Master Bodin came just before the boat was due to leave. For this reason Lotten and Agge's leave-taking was rather rushed when they finally parted. Before Lotten realized it, the boat was untied, the gangway pulled up, and the boat gliding away.

She waved as long as she could see him: she waved until the boat wasn't much more than a speck. Then she turned back slowly. And found that her face was all wet.

AN UNKNOWN SHORE

The boat gently bumped against the dock at Värdshusbryggan, and a few passengers pressed their way forward to the gangplank. Groups of wives and children who had walked down to meet their fathers waited on the dock. A maid came from Sommarro Villa to take care of the little summer guest's luggage. She didn't get more than a paper bag to carry.

Annika stood by the window in her room on the second floor and watched them come. Her husband, prim in a high, light-colored summer hat and long, gray jacket over striped trousers, pointing with his cane. And the boy at his side in short pants and a sailor blouse. He was a little taller, bigger than she had imagined, but of course it had been four years since the last time.

Annika didn't know if she regretted it or not. It was always this way, whatever she came up with. Now she thought about how much trouble it might be with a strange child in the house; she would be tied down. And this child, Henning's son, would never be more than a surrogate for a child of her own. And for those she sometimes felt prickings of her conscience for, her younger siblings. But, of course, they weren't little anymore. Not children who could be influenced and changed, they must have been formed and fixed in the pattern of the lower class by now.

To help Henning's child would be to atone for something. And to return to something in the past that she might miss at times. The memory of Henning, of Thumbs. People whom she liked without calculating, without expecting something from them in return. It was a little bit like deceiving Fredrik. And she wanted to deceive him, be avenged for having deceived herself.

Fredrik was a conceited fool. A failure, stupid. But she would direct him, force him onward. She had been successful in getting him to reorganize the company, and would get him to build it up again. It would take time, but she wasn't afraid of the outcome.

Maybe having the boy would get in the way of her plans, direct her interest along other lines. No, she thought, during the summer, Fredrik could go on being unsuccessful. In the fall she would take over the business seriously.

Now they were going through the gate down below. Annika left the window and walked down the stairs. Lightly, with a summery ease. She had glued a friendly smile in the corners of her mouth. She took the boy by the hand and stroked his cheek. She wrinkled her forehead a moment when she saw his clothing: he couldn't go around looking like that. People would wonder.

Dinner waited.

Three chairs. Two maids in attendance. Agge looked around worriedly and tried to remember all the table manners he had learned.

While he ate, Annika observed him. She wouldn't correct him about anything the first day. But then there would be a little to smooth out, something else to add. The boy was remarkably well brought up though, of course, completely ignorant about certain things. Annika noticed how he stole quick glances sideways to see how she and Fredrik placed their napkins and held their forks; she noticed how he carefully copied them. He wasn't dumb, the little fellow. Good material, she thought, a lot could be done with him. As opposed to Fredrik who was a stiff and poorly-made blockhead, a dimwit who had happened to receive a little money and power.

She was tired of Fredrik, he repulsed her. She didn't like it when he came and stroked her. Now she could place the boy between them: "Not now, Fredrik, we have to think of the boy ...."

"We'll go look at your room now, August," she said and rose. A maid hurried forward and pushed in her chair. August would have to learn to do it eventually, be trained to be a gentleman.

When August awoke he looked around wondering where he was. The sun shone in through a crack in the curtains and the room was lit up a sparkling white. It must be light like this in heaven, he thought, and was frightened for a moment. But he knew that it was the enormous room that Aunt Annika had called his room. So big that almost the whole house on Åsöberget could fit in here. Rudde would never believe him when he told him about it. Maybe Mama would think he was exaggerating too. He would probably have to make everything a little smaller when he told them about it at home.

August got up and the too-long nightshirt dragged on the floor as he walked over to the window. He looked out and felt like he was at a dizzying height. Up among the treetops. The trees too were bigger here than the ones at home. Everything was bigger.

A basin and pitcher stood on a washstand. In a glass was a funny little brush you brushed your teeth with. Aunt Annika had shown him the evening before and said that he was to use it every morning and evening. He filled the glass carefully with water. The rich had funny habits: they brushed in their mouths. At home they sometimes took a rag; Papa might wipe their teeth with his sweat cloth, the large hand-kerchief he carried in his belt. But here they had special little brushes.

August got dressed so he would be ready if they called him to breakfast. He didn't know if he dared leave his room or not. He carefully opened the door a little and looked out into the hallway; the door squeaked, and he looked around anxiously.

"August!"

The call came from down the hall where a door to one of the rooms stood open. He started, frightened, now he had done something wrong.

"Come here, August!"

He hurried over and stopped in the doorway. Aunt Annika sat in front of a low table with a big mirror; she was combing her hair which stood out in a bright haze around her, glistening in the sunlight. Like an angel he had seen in a picture.

An airy, white peignoir rested like a cloud on Aunt Annika's shoulders.

"Did you already get dressed?" she asked.

"Yes," he said. "Is that all right?"

"Of course it is, you silly boy," she said and laughed. "Haven't you had anything to eat yet?"

No, he hadn't.

"If you're not too hungry and can wait five minutes, then I'll keep you company," she said. "Go down and have a look at the garden. I'll call you when I'm ready."

He hurried thankfully from the room and down the stairs. He walked cautiously through the hall and hoped that nobody would see him, not everyone could know that he had permission to go out.

The garden lay like a green sea before him. Green in the greenness and shining red, blue and yellow splashes from the flower beds. He followed one of the gray paths through the greenery, but not too far. He looked at the house and wondered which window was his. Then he returned to the lawn in front of the house and sat farthest out on one of the benches, ready to come when Aunt Annika called.

He had to wait, it took her close to half an hour. But then he got the best rolls he had ever eaten and as much milk as he wanted to drink. The milk here in the country was like cream, he thought, it certainly wasn't skimmed.

"We're going to take the eleven o'clock boat into town and get you a few clothes," said Aunt Annika. August thought that she maybe didn't want him to have his best suit on for playing everyday.

Gradually August got used to all the new things, and adapted. He was like a little sponge, sat in his corner and soaked up everything, retained all the new learning, grew with it. Neither the toothbrush nor the fine clothes he had received for everyday were novelties any longer. At times he wondered what Rudde would say if he saw him, if his friend would be impressed or start to tease him. But there was also probably a lot that Rudde would envy: the swing that Uncle Fredrik set up in the garden, the game with sticks and rings that they had tournaments with on the lawn, the outings in the rowboat when August got to have his own fishing rod.

Still, the biggest adventure lay perhaps in the room just beyond the dining room. It was just a funny little shelf, a pyramid. But in it were books. Some told about travels in foreign lands and had interesting illustrations which showed natives and wild animals. He read, at first with some effort, parts of *The Frigate Eugenie's Journey Around the World* and *The Peoples of the Earth According to Their Own Characteristics*. It got easier to read, and one rainy day he began with a book called *Stories from the Barber-Surgeon*. He became so engrossed that Annika had to wonder what had come over the otherwise so attentive boy. He didn't even hear now when he was called.

These were the first books he had ever held and read besides schoolbooks. And he could envy the rich for these, much more than the big rooms and the good food. Here was where they had adventure, were able to step into an enchanted world.

Annika looked at the boy thoughtfully. Was it good for him to read? It might only distance him from the reality he lived in. But perhaps it was this way with his whole visit here. But she still wanted him to be here, to read.

He had trouble making contact with the other children on the island. It was as if they sensed he came from other circumstances. Or maybe he was too shy. When he wasn't reading, he usually stayed close to Annika. She liked this, it filled the emptiness. And you could talk with him, he gave such thoughtful answers. Sometimes she could be irritated by his understanding: he was still a child after all.

Like Henning, she thought. Quiet, kind, calming. But you could get annoyed with this at times, you wanted to see that there was some fire there too. She had been interested in Henning. So much so that if he had said something, she might have remained in poverty, or would she have? It was as if it was hard to remember how she had felt, as if it was hard to know how she had felt. Words wouldn't have been enough at that time — but if he had dared resort to action. Then she had transferred her feelings to Thumbs. But then it was as if she had already begun to deal with them, divide them up. It came to nothing, everything disappeared. The wish to get away from home had become stronger than what was perhaps not really love.

And now Henning's son sat in the grass at her feet and read. Maybe he was homesick sometimes, he became so serious when he received letters from his mother. He sat and wrote laboriously. She had read his letters. Awkward, childish greetings to his parents and siblings and someone called Rudde, apparently Thumbs' son. Assurances that he felt fine and was having fun. But also a few words about missing them. Missing mother and father, home.

No one misses me, she thought, and forgot about Fredrik's dog-like eyes.

"You won't miss me when you get back home," she said bitterly.

Agge looked up at her, surprised, had to ask what she had just said, he had been so involved in his book that he hadn't heard.

"No," he said thoughtfully, "I know I will."

He looked into her eyes and nodded. And suddenly Annika wanted to cry, she pulled the boy to her and hugged him tightly. He let it happen, without either resisting or pressing closer.

"Why is Aunt crying?" he asked.

"It's just silliness," said Annika. "And maybe because I like you and am sad that the summer is almost over."

"If Aunt would like it, I can come and see her later on as well," said August seriously.

She smiled at his earnestness and felt grateful at the same time.

"That's a good idea," said Annika. "Once a week you'll come to me, and I'll get to hear how it's going in school. But now we'll go down to the dock and meet Uncle."

The evening before August was to leave them, Annika was a little downcast. She was already longing to see the boy again. She walked upstairs from the living room, where she had been sitting and reading the newspapers that Fredrik had brought with him, and opened the door slowly to August's room. He was sleeping: she could hear his calm breathing in the darkness. She went over to the bed, sank carefully to her knees, and let her cheek rest against the boy's until he turned in his sleep.

So empty, she thought. Meaningless.

If.

If she could keep this child. Surely Henning and his wife would understand what it would mean for the boy?

With the interest in reading he had, August ought to go to a real school.

But could she go to Henning and ask for his child?

She felt the bitterness well up, knew who it was aimed at: Fredrik. Incompetent at managing to give her her own child. The poor, skinny Henning had three. The pompous ass down there sat there grunting over his cigar and newspaper. It served him right if she was unfaithful. But at the same time, it was as if she didn't dare do it, as if she were afraid it was really her own fault. A punishment for having abandoned her own mother. It felt that way sometimes.

The next morning August left with Fredrik. Annika stood alone on the dock at Värdshusbryggan. The summer was still green around her; the berries and fruits were ripening; the water was warm. But she felt like fall had arrived, and she longed for the city, would make Fredrik arrange the move back home as soon as possible. There was nothing to stay here for. Sommarro could be closed for the year.

She gave the orders for a thorough housecleaning and hurried the maids along and scolded the gardener's assistants. Then she went down to the bathhouse to cool off. August's fishing rod was still there, leaning against one corner. At first she thought of breaking it to pieces, he was gone after all, had deserted her. But then she regretted the impulse and placed it inside the bathhouse, running her hand along its shiny surface. The pole would still be there, waiting for August. The boy would come back.

August walked home alone after taking leave of Uncle Fredrik at Slussen. In his hand he carried his suitcase. There was a lot more in it than what had been in the paper bag he'd had when he left. His old suit and his new everyday suit, his old nightshirt and his new, his toothbrush and some small trousers called underpants which he had never had before. And *The Stories from the Barber-Surgeon*, those books which he had been given by Uncle Fredrik the last evening.

From time to time he had to put down his suitcase and rest. Uncle Fredrik had wanted to send him home in a carriage, but Agge had assured him that he was able to walk. He was too uncertain about what effect his coming home in a carriage might have.

Everything looked the same. The little house stuck up from behind the fence, the trees were in leaf. He opened the gate and looked in, the door to the house stood open. His mother was in the kitchen.

"August!"

Lotten hugged her son as if she thought she'd never see him again. But then she had to really look at him. Such a fine suit! And he was so brown and filled-out and sturdy. And hadn't he certainly grown?

He had to sit down at the kitchen table and tell her about it while he drank milk and ate a slice of bread. Now he could taste how poor in fat the milk was, how coarse the bread, but he liked it, this is how it had been. This was how it was at home.

There was only joy in seeing it again. The difficulties would come gradually at first. When he would miss the large spaces, the books, the good food. When he felt the loneliness. Rudde had made new friends. The boys in the neighborhood were a little unfavorably disposed toward someone who had lived an upper-class life and wore finer clothes than all the others. They teased Agge who didn't dare fight and play along with the rest of them for fear of ruining his clothes. And they laughed at his love of reading, what kind of upper-class affectation was this?

Once a week Agge went to his summer parents' house dressed in his best suit, gaped at and spat upon by all the kids in the street. He walked carrying a book covered in paper and returned with another; there was a lot to read in the apartment at Skeppsbron. Lotten watched her son, a little worried. How would he manage in life? He read too much, stayed out of sight, kept to himself. But she didn't have time to worry too much about him, she had their home and her concern over Henning.

But when August dressed up and went off every Wednesday, she would stand at the gate and watch him go. She remembered how Klara's daughters used to come walking up Garbage Lane at one time.

At the Bodin's, August would usually find a depressed Uncle Fredrik and an exhilarated and wound-up Aunt Annika. He was never allowed to know anything of Uncle Fredrik's troubles, nor that they in any way had any effect on himself. Annika would have liked to place August in a good school. But before that could happen the Bodins' company would have to be driven until it bottomed out. Fredrik's sister-in-law, the previous owner's wife, and her children could only be bought out in the most desperate circumstances. Indeed, they would almost beg to be allowed to no longer remain a part, to be spared bankruptcy. Once they were gone, Annika would step in for real, then money would begin to pour in again, and the workers be reemployed. And August put in school.

She led Fredrik the way a guide leads the blind. It was just now that he began to understand that the best thing that could happen to his sister-in-law would be for her to be closed out of the firm.

Annika didn't intend to work to support the arrogant Margareta Bodin and her insufferable daughters. She had never been met with any understanding, neither from them nor Fredrik's dead brother. Leonard Bodin had treated her like a hanger-on. Annika hadn't forgotten his tone and manner when she had worked for the firm. Leonard's following would leave if Annika were to take an interest in the company's future. This was why August would have to wait, until they reached their goal they would have to scrimp and save.

She laughed and played with the boy while Fredrik sat and stared at his glass and dreaded the visit he had to pay his sister-in-law. Margareta and her daughters would manage, though probably just barely. And they would blame him and he felt the guilt. He was no businessman, and he despised the firm and its stench of herring. And when he heard Annika laughing in the room next door, he had to wonder if he didn't despise her too.

But he liked the boy, he would have liked a boy like him for a son.

Fredrik Bodin sighed and felt he had been heavily condemned for the sins of his youth. The Cure House doctor whom he had visited in great secrecy had said that the illness Fredrik had gotten from a girl at the Phoenix could have such consequences. And it must be that, Annika had never been sick. But he had destroyed their marriage and driven his father's and brother's fine old firm into bankruptcy.

AUTUMN'S BURDENS

A steam engine puffed along the harborside with rows of empty freight cars rattling behind. The street workers laying stones for the new wharf stepped aside and let the train pass. From the open square at Slussen the alarm signal from a trolley could be heard; the horse trotted inside the curve from Skeppsbron, and the conductor shouted "whoa!" and pulled the hand brake.

The stevedore team came from the Church Tavern, weaving between bales and mounds, bins and stockpiles. Torparsonen and Little Hell were at the head, as usual, and the fat Barge brought up the rear. Henning and Fearsome walked somewhere in the middle, two old workmates who had been forgiven by Stevedore Lundström and now been reunited with the team.

Fearsome had begun to grow old: he had turned sixty. But he still had a lot of strength left, as if time and wear hadn't really taken their toll on him.

Styvnicke came toward them, waving his arms.

"You can go back again, you guys," he shouted. "It'll take at least a couple of hours before we can begin."

They stopped, muttering. The jobs this fall had been uneven, the income insecure. They had whiled away many days waiting at the tavern, with bills mounting. Just now when they had put a little aside to live on over the winter. If it continued this way part of the team would have to band together, and some of the extras who'd had steady jobs before the fall be dismissed.

A few stood doubtfully where they were while the rest hurried back to the warmth of the tavern. The waiting time was hardest for those supporting families, those who didn't feel they could afford to sit in a bar and felt the greatest worry over remaining idle. They felt they could neither stay nor leave; they ought to find another job yet they couldn't leave the one they had. Every hour that they stood there with hands hanging meant less food for their wives and children.

"Let's walk a little," said Fearsome. They walked down toward Slussen, through Fiskarhamnen, the fisherman's wharf, where vendors' stalls stood packed together. At a clothing stall, Fearsome looked once more at a leather jacket which would have been nice to have over the winter, it was used and being sold cheaply. But with the way things were now he would have to hold off. It was the usual: you planned, went and looked, saved. And then you couldn't afford it.

Down by the Karl Johan XIV statue were some benches, one was empty. Henning scraped the edge of the slats with an old newspaper; he wanted to remove as many lice colonies as possible. The benches were the gathering places for ruffians and bums; their empty bottles lay close together beneath the seats and in the patches of grass beneath the trees. Fearsome had seen an old shirt crawl past the statue it was so ridden with lice, he contended. And Torparsonen, who had followed along with Henning and Fearsome, told how the police had made a raid here the evening before and had arrested around ten bootleggers, pimps and whores.

Henning collapsed on the bench, trying to take advantage of the rest time. He heard the voices of his two friends, muffled by the autumn fog. They jabbered on, he himself didn't have the strength to participate in their conversation. It was as if he had to conserve the slightest little show of life to have anything left to give when work began. And then his strength ran from him almost immediately, already with the first sack he felt weak and sweaty.

"I've applied for a job on the trolley line," Torparsonen declared. "It's better there. You only stand and hold the reins and take money from people."

Henning looked up. If he were to... but he still hoped to be able to go back to Bodin's. He had passed Master Bodin on the wharf one day and Bodin had given him a friendly nod. But not said anything. There were only two men left at the herring firm now, and they were waiting for bankruptcy, Henning knew that. He was surprised that the Bodins could afford to invite August to dinner every week and give the boy clothes and books. But the poverty of the rich wasn't the same as that of the poor.

"Let's go back," said Torparsonen who was always energetic. And they walked back toward the eastern bridge of the locks which had just come down after a barge headed toward the sugar refinery had passed through. Some boys ran out onto the bridge and were going to jump across the remaining gap before the two halves of the bridge had had time to meet. One of them was both lucky and unlucky; he didn't make it across but instead disappeared down in the lock-chamber the moment before he would have been sliced in half. Some men in a boat hurried to fish him out.

Something was always happening here at Slussen. It served well enough for killing time. But it didn't earn any money.

They ended up going home in low spirits that day, without having done any work. But the next day Styvnicke's team was called up ahead of all the others and had a full workload the whole day. They carried grain and the sacks were heavy, some up toward a hundred thirty kilos. Henning felt like he was walking in a fog, like he couldn't find his way to the storehouse. He tried to convince himself that he had become spoiled during those good years at Bodin's, that he had been pampered. He had to throw himself into it even harder, train to get in shape. But he knew after the months that had passed that no training helped. He was happy just to manage to hold himself up, keep on going.

It was then that he longed for the offer from Bodin's, the order to come back. Or he dreamed of looking for work on the trolley line. But just now wasn't the right time, possibly in the spring. But by then maybe Bodin's would have gotten going again.

It was break time. He almost fell over onto one of the sacks, trying to smother his cough, but unable to control it. It felt like something had shaken loose inside his body, but it was probably only the pain after the heavy loads and his fit of coughing. Finally he got up and walked slowly after his comrades who had already gone off a long way toward the tavern.

He couldn't eat much. It was cheaper, of course, but how would he have the strength to carry? He thought: I can eat when I get home. And he knew that he wouldn't be able to eat then either, at that point he would just want to escape into sleep.

He carried his sacks almost without knowing how he made it from the barge to the warehouse. Desperation welled up inside him. He felt the fear of work and the fear of having no work at the same time, the wish to just collapse and the wish to be able to work even harder.

Finally he had carried the last sack of the day. He dried his face and chest with his sweat rag. He felt the evening chill come and lay its wet bandage across his back. He pulled on his jacket and buttoned it. He sat a moment in the warehouse to catch his breath. Then he walked slowly toward the stairs.

He sat down there in the autumn evening and felt how he didn't have the strength to get up. He felt fear come creeping along the stairs and throw itself over him. He shook himself. Afraid of what might happen if he tried to walk, afraid to stay sitting there, afraid of life which demanded so much.

He had to, but would he make it home? Now the way appeared endless. First the rest of the stairs ... they were so steep. And then across and up the slopes of Stigberget and Åsöberget.

Now it was autumn and dark, now Emelie didn't wait for him. He crumpled over, his head against his knees. He was sitting like this when Fearsome, who had stayed behind at the tavern, came.

Henning had to lean against his older friend, put his arm around his neck. It was easier then to stumble up the stairs and continue toward home. Fearsome questioned him worriedly. But Henning only answered that he had felt sick, it was nothing.

When they got down to Tjärhovsgatan, they parted since Henning declared that he could manage the last part himself. Fearsome watched him, saw how Henning tottered unsteadily up the cross lane like a drunk. He should have a different job, thought Fearsome. But we all should. Though he was too old himself, he had to be happy with the one he had.

Henning barely had the energy to eat the food Lotten placed on the table. He tried, but then the nausea returned, and he had to rush out to the yard. Lotten helped him upstairs and into the room where the children were sleeping.

The noise from the sleepers: light, steady breathing in the dark, warm room. Summer wind playing through the grass on a short, mild night. Suddenly he felt like it was a night from very long ago, a summer night by Hammarby Lake when he stood together with Lotten at the edge of the water and looked at the stars.

Secure like a child. How could he feel this way now, in all his wretchedness? Didn't he have the strength to worry any longer? He didn't know, he only felt how Lotten led him, how gratefully he allowed himself to be led. The memory of struggle and responsibility lay far away. Now Lotten was removing his burdens, he was being relieved of them. At last he could collapse, dissolve into nothingness.

She unlaced his boots, helped him get out of his clothes and into bed. With eyes half shut, he lay and tried to find her shadow in the darkness. He heard her over by the children tucking them in. Then the rustle of her dress as she undressed. And how she came to bed in her long nightgown as usual.

He pressed against the wall, making room for her. She put her arms around him, protecting him, comforting him. Her hand stroked his back as a mother strokes a little child to get it to sleep. And he fell asleep, strangely happy in his unhappiness.

It felt as if he was better the next morning, healed. He tried to eat a little more than usual and hoped that not too heavy a job awaited him, otherwise he wouldn't benefit much from the food. Lotten wondered if he was able to go but he was insistent. He felt how his will power grew and carried him along. Lotten had helped him through the hard part, now he had to continue on his own. But when he got out into the street, he noticed what an effort every step was.

Styvnicke got alcohol poisoning and had to be taken to the hospital. Henning was obliged to fill in as boss for a few days. Stevedore Lundström was the one who gave the orders; he'd had his eyes on the "Herring Strangler," as he called Henning. The Herring Strangler was a little too weak and good-natured to really garner a lot of respect. But his comrades had faith in him. And he was thorough. He checked the lines of the winches, removed dangerous blocks of wood that they might stumble over, and kept his eyes open and called out warnings when it was necessary. In this respect Styvnicke fell short, he drove his people effectively with harsh language, but there were many accidents. And it looked bad, even if Lundström didn't have to pay any compensation to those afflicted.

Henning was boss for four days and was spared carrying. His stomach calmed down and his back felt a little better. Still he got tired before evening arrived. But he took himself home as fast as he could, home to Lotten. He felt like smiling to himself as he stumbled through the darkness, as if he were a newlywed. He could see Lotten before him, in the dimmed light from the lamp. She was his goal. His longing for warmth could almost obliterate his fear of the cold.

On the evening of the fourth day this longing and love grew so strong that not only fear but common sense disappeared. He pulled her along with him and neither of them managed to check themselves in time, they were united as they hadn't been since she'd had the child that died. It wasn't until it was too late that worry came and cooled them with the fear of what could happen.

But they didn't dare speak of it to each other, to say anything might bring on bad luck. They shouldn't have any more children.

The next day Styvnicke was back. Henning carried loads once again. That evening he couldn't keep down his anxiety despite all his efforts, even though he wanted to protect Lotten so much. He felt anguish when he heard his children's calm breathing in their sleep; he loved them and was so weak that he couldn't provide them with any security. And because he felt his body's pain and the terror of death.

Lotten tried to be calm, to reassure him. Master Bodin had said that maybe by spring ....

Suddenly Henning dropped off to sleep. Lotten lay still, awake, as if keeping watch over husband and children. She knew that she had to be strong now and imagined she could feel a calm strength growing inside her. She thought about what Henning had said before when things were difficult: everything will work out. And about how she and Henning had it better than most others. Indeed, they had something rare and beautiful, a strange foreign bird which could seldom be coaxed into making its nest in the tumbledown houses of the poor.

They would make it through this difficult winter also. She felt the certainty so clearly that she couldn't fall asleep, and instead lay awake until it was time to get up.

"I know we're going to make it," she said to Henning. "Everything will work out."

The words carried him, as well as her certainty. He saw her face, heard her voice. As if she carried part of his burden, he could manage. And he carried everything he was allowed to carry until the ice came and the harbor was paralyzed. Then Lotten forced him to stay home a few weeks and take care of the house while she was out and did laundry together with her mother and Washer-Johanna.

THE CAGE AND
THE BOOKKEEPER

The hill was covered with snow and trampled, dirt-brown tracks formed a slippery pattern between the house and the outhouse. Smoke rose from the stacks of the industries on the outskirts and from the low houses' steel pipes and stone chimneys. The Bible ladies came plodding up with cough drops and hot pads, their tracks were crisscrossed by those of women from the shelter association who passed out proverbs and firewood coupons.

During the weeks while Henning was home from the harbor, he had the opportunity to discuss quite a lot with Thumbs, who renounced sleep so they could spend time together. Thumbs was waiting for a convenient chance to change jobs; he was tired of the bakers' eternal night labor. And a little disappointed: the strike carried out so successfully a few years ago had apparently not been a catalyst for anything new, just a one-time event. The workers were still in hibernation. But the day would surely have to come when the giant would awaken, begin to shake himself and shake off all this which lived off his blood.

Thumbs looked for the first signs of this. Wherever the revolution began was where he wanted to be. It wouldn't be among the dock workers. Apparently not among the bakers either.

Henning listened readily to Thumbs' plans for friendship's sake. But he saw them as fantasies, both beautiful and cruel. He couldn't paint these pictures in his own imagination, couldn't make Thumbs' visions seem like a reality which awaited them. In any case, he was sure that he himself would not experience any of it, nothing happened that fast.

He didn't want to say this to Thumbs. But he could ask: Was there no other route to future happiness? Did everything have to happen so quickly, so bloodily? In the labor unions lowering the voting barrier was being discussed, more and more workers would be allowed a voice in decisions.

Thumbs spat contemptuously. Labor unions! There were no workers in them, that was where literary types and craftsmen played with social reforms. Their task was just to put the workers to sleep. What help was it if they were satisfied with lowering the voting barrier? The employers had only to lower wages to show that the workers remained without a decisive voice. They haggled over everything. In the communal elections, for example, even the workers had voting rights. Maybe there were twelve thousand in the city who had one vote apiece. But those twelve thousand could be outweighed by three bigshots who had four thousand votes each. One bigshot was worth the same as four thousand workers, that was the upper-classes' view of human worth.

And besides, every postponement meant suffering for many. The slow, non-bloody resistance was perhaps the cruelest, the one that cost the most and hit the workers hardest.

That day Henning didn't have time to discuss more; he had been promised temporary work. The caretaker at the cosmetics factory had gotten sick and Henning had a chance to fill in.

He stepped out into the lane and squinted at the sun; it hung like a giant red lantern in one of the bare trees on the hillside.

He slid down Garbage Lane and walked up the slope toward the factory. The entrance gate opened for a fully loaded sleigh pulled by two horses. The man who guarded the entrance stuck out a bushy snout and wondered what Henning wanted. Then he pointed: the big office, bookkeeper Melinder.

The office shone with dark brown wood varnish. Four distinguished gentlemen sat perched on their stools at large, high writing desks with sloping tops. The visitor was prevented from entering farther by a railing which was supported by lathed wooden posts. A large kerosene lamp hung from the ceiling, and between the two windows behind the clerks a tall grandfather clock swung its little brass mirror.

Mr. Melinder nodded, so this was the substitute caretaker who was to replace Jacob. He noted down his name and address which was so conveniently close by. He pointed out how important it was for the factory to have honest employees. There was a lot to tempt them. Fine perfumes, sweet-scented soaps. But the checks were thorough and Nilsson had good recommendations.

Melinder called for an apprentice who was to show Henning around the factory so he could learn where the different departments were. They walked through the warehouse where wicker-encased demijohns, barrels of soap fat and sacks of snail shells for making toothpaste competed for space. Henning felt one of the sacks a little suspiciously, it seemed unmanageably big to him. But it was so light that he almost fell over backwards when he lifted it.

They continued through the factory buildings, entered the soap-making hall where the open fire crackled beneath enormous cauldrons, and passed through the packaging rooms with their supplies of colorful flower-printed boxes. Then they looked at the coachhouse, the woodshed, the stalls and the cages. There was a little zoo within the factory grounds. Henning had heard the children talk about the bear that was supposed to be there. But the bear was hibernating in a hole inside the cage and wasn't in sight. It was half mad, said the apprentice. The foxes, on the other hand, were playful and fawning, and as tame as dogs. Peacocks, owls and falcons were also among the animals that were to be fed by the caretaker.

"Be glad you don't have the bear," the apprentice said. "Jacob barely dares go near it."

It was Melinder who was the assigned boss for the caretaker. Every morning Henning received his orders from the bookkeeper, who sometimes put on his top hat and overcoat and went along with him into the yard to show what he wanted taken care of. Melinder was very glad to talk, Henning soon noticed. The bookkeeper was a philosopher and a moralist and interested in what was happening in the workers' world.

Practically every day Melinder took the opportunity to warn Henning against both socialist ideas and liberal labor unions. It almost sounded like Melinder considered poverty an inherent defect that workers had to accept. They had learned over the generations to suffer, starve and keep silent. They had imbibed work and poverty with their mothers' milk.

Nilsson had never asked for poverty assistance had he?

No, he hadn't.

There, you are! Melinder could see it written all over him, otherwise he never would have given him the position.

"I am a friend to workers," Melinder said, "but an enemy of crude behavior. Labor unions attract people with ideas of dangerous utopias and clear the way for socialists and the reign of terror. But the people of the Nordic countries must stand guard over their ancient freedom. Honorable and industrious workers are worth their wages, but trouble makers and beggars should be put behind bars."

They stood in front of the fox cage, and inside it the clever foxes swished their tails ingratiatingly, hoping to be petted. Melinder stretched out his hand and scratched the vixen under her chin.

"Today Nilsson can give the cages a thorough cleaning," he said. "Don't worry about the bear, it's sleeping. You only have to remove any trash that may have blown into its cage."

The work as caretaker for a cosmetics factory was relatively easy compared to work on the docks. Despite Melinder's talk he wasn't an especially demanding boss; he was impressed by rather small achievements and always took a good-willed interest in his caretaker. If he happened to see Henning carrying something heavy, he would send an apprentice out to help and then flutter around them like an anxious hen: "There, now we can put it down, now we'll take a little rest."

If it was a really cold day, he would say to the gatekeeper's wife that she should offer the caretaker some coffee. If he heard that there was a load of boxes to be sent out for pasting, he would ask if Henning's wife wasn't interested in the work. And Henning would carry home a large stack of them and, Lotten would earn a much-needed extra income.

Dirt and poverty had made their way into the house on the hill. The rent had been raised recently, now so much that it was impossible to keep the whole house to themselves. Once again the space in the attic had to be used, and the kitchen rented out. In the kitchen they fortunately got some quiet and orderly girls. The man they rented to had seemed nice but had turned out to be a slob. And his wife bickered and quarreled, and the neglected children cried. Soon the tenants began to rent out in their turn and gradually seven or eight people were squeezed into the little space. Often there wasn't room for all of them inside the temporary wall, and, instead, one or some of the lodgers would lie in the passageway that Henning's family had to use to reach their room.

Both Henning and Thumbs tried to talk things over with their tenants, but that only led to more fighting. After countless run-ins Thumbs managed to at least evict the ones who were subletting. Things got somewhat better, but it was still hard. Especially for Lotten who felt like she had gotten a source of infestation in the midst of her clean house. It would be different in the spring when Henning earned more and the tenants could find housing. Then the Franssons would have to move.

For a while Henning thought he could understand Melinder's reasoning. These people could be called slaves; they could be despised. They drank up everything they earned, and the children had to starve and run around half clothed.

The Franssons belonged to the lumpen proletariat, explained Thumbs when he and Henning spoke about it. They were as impossible to figure out as the upper-class: this is what Thirsty had said once, Thirsty who had fallen in the water at the harbor and drowned. Thirsty had read a remarkable book which Thumbs had long looked for but never been able to find.

Was it the case that both Melinder and Thumbs condemned the Franssons to eternal poverty? Melinder's slaves, Thumbs' lumpen proletariat. Not even foxes, only lice. He himself knew what the Franssons were like: helpless, useless. Other poor people could have hope. The Franssons had nothing to wait for, nothing more than alms every day. They drank themselves down deeper, sinking.

After a few months the regular caretaker came back. Henning had to stay a week to help Jacob, then it was time to return to the harbor. He felt unusually rested, healthier than he had for several years.

He said good-bye to those he had worked with, particularly Melinder and the gatekeeper. The bookkeeper promised that Lotten would get pasting work in the future as well; the packaging supervisor had expressed himself very positively regarding the careful work she turned in. And the bookkeeper took out a farewell gift: a bottle of "Stolen Kisses" brand perfume and a tube of "Aromatic Amykos — Toothpaste for the Cleaning and Conserving of Teeth and Gums," and a soap called "Bust of a Woman." Henning also received a soap for his children called "Chimney Sweep."

Before he left the factory with his package, he went one last time to the fox cage and patted the red dogs who had become his friends. But he hadn't gotten to see the bear; it was still hibernating.

Shortly after this the bear had to be shot, it had tried to attack Jacob in a fit of madness.

For this reason the cage was standing empty when Lotten came to leave a basket of finished boxes. She had the children with her, and the gatekeeper let them come in and look at the foxes and the birds. However, they didn't get to see the bookkeeper. And Lotten was just as pleased, she was in her seventh month and didn't feel especially presentable.

THE REVOLUTION
THAT WENT AWRY

The little girls were playing a game in the lane; they were taking the opportunity before the older children got home from the big school. They placed two flat stones on their sides, and Emelie, who was up first, hit the stick. The stick flew out in a high arc, easy to catch, but Gertrud didn't make it in time. Now Gertrud was to knock down the stick which Emelie had placed across the stones, but she wasn't successful. Emelie was successful with her second try also; the stick went farther and was harder to catch. Gertrud was supposed to throw the stick between the stones from where Emelie hit it, but once again didn't manage. Now it was time for the most difficult part, the main strike. The strike was a double hit: first you had to knock the stick which stood leaning against the stone up in the air, then with another forceful strike send it into mid-air. The point was to send it as far as possible; every foot's length between the stones and where the stick fell was worth one point and they were competing to one hundred.

Now! Emelie struck and the stick rose up. But she missed the decisive second strike and the stick fell dead to the ground.

A little resignedly, Emelie stepped out of the square she had drawn around the stones, leaving space for her sister. Far away, past the crossing of Tjärhovsgränd, came a dark figure of a man half-running. He wasn't usually in such a hurry. What could have happened?

Emelie and Gertrud stood and watched Thumbs; he was in such a hurry that he didn't even have time for a word in their direction. The newspaper he held in his hand fluttered; the mud splashed around his boots.

"Hurry up," whined Gertrud. "Soon we'll have to go in and paste."

There was no use in worrying about what the grown-ups were up to. They had to get going now, otherwise, the game wouldn't be over before they had to go in.

Emelie managed to knock down Gertrud's stick which was lying across the stones. They changed places again. And now Emelie was lucky, she made just the right hit the second time when it was the main strike and was able to rack up fifty-seven points.

He took the stairs in a few leaps, knocked and heard Lotten's reply. "It's happened!" shouted Thumbs.

He saw her turn pale, and remembered that she was expecting and shouldn't be upset.

"No, no. Calm down," he said quickly. "Not here, in Sundsvall. The revolution!"

He spread the newspaper out on the table, told her about it and read. There, as here, the workers had gotten their salaries cut. But in Sundsvall they had called a strike. They marched by the thousands on the town from the sawmills outside it, with banners at their heads and cudgels in their hands. The leaders of the uprising were traveling vendors of newspapers and other literature, prohibitionists and religious evangelists. The strike meetings began and ended with prayers and hymn singing, and the workers had demanded that all taverns and establishments which sold liquor be kept closed while the dispute was underway.

Maybe it had happened a little differently from what Thumbs had imagined, but he would have to think about it some more.

He had to go around and hear if something wasn't going to happen in Stockholm. Now was the time to do the same thing!

He hurried out again. Lotten sat down heavily. If it was as Thumbs said ... but Henning had never really believed in it. The newspaper may have exaggerated: it was *The Fatherland.*

But if .... Then she would have to say that the revolution came a little inconveniently; it could have at least waited until she had had her baby. She should have stopped Thumbs.

She thought she could hear the cries, see the flames rising up from the city below. And the water would swell into enormous waves and crash against the hill. The last day. Then it would be both safe and unsafe to live up here, up above everything.

She heard a cry and rushed out and down the stairs. But it was only the children playing and a few drunken old men fighting. She called the girls in. Even if the revolution was at hand, they still had to think of their daily bread. It was time to paste boxes.

The newspapers continued to report on the strike every day. But in Stockholm no one was prepared to take action. People couldn't afford to take risks when times were hard.

And the military had been sent to Sundsvall where the strikers, by order of the provincial leader, had had to throw down their cudgels. But the strike still continued, the strikers spending the nights together out under the open sky. When asked if they wanted to return to work they had replied that they would rather die.

But after a nine day strike, the opposition was broken. Troops had marched in and the small ship, *Ran,* controlled the workers' camp from the sea. The employers had demanded and been granted permission to turn the strikers out of their company-owned housing. Without work and housing the strikers were compromised. Now they could be condemned as vagrants.

They were called in according to their place of work. All night long, while the rain poured down, the rounding up and questioning went on. The next morning the leaders sat in prison. Out of necessity, the rest had gotten work and housing back and avoided the vagrancy law.

Then it was all over. The revolt which had been triggered by despair and hunger had only yielded even greater despair. Many of the Sundsvall workers prepared to emigrate — wrote the papers — they no longer had any faith in a decent life in Sweden.

Thumbs had his own theories about the reasons for the failure. He had distrusted the pietists the whole time. What was it that Thirsty had said? *Let the ruling classes tremble.* They weren't worried by prayers and hymn singing.

When the workers read their prayers, the provincial leader read out the vagrancy law. He hadn't even needed to utilize the uprising law, only the most degrading law had been put to use.

Thumbs talked a lot with Henning about the events in Sundsvall. They ought to be able to launch a revolution in the entire country thought Thumbs.

Henning had to smile. Thumbs' voice, his words. Thumbs had talked like that on the very first day they met, soon it would be twenty years ago. Thumbs was just the same, just as young. Henning felt like he had aged. And he had come to the city so fearful and insecure, he had never really conquered the provincial boy's anxiety at anything new. But he had transformed it into habit and behavior: he tended to stand to the side, hold himself a little apart.

August had inherited his caution. He was standing where Henning had once stood himself: hesitating at the customs house. Unsure as to where his home lay. The Bodins had said that they wanted to pay for the boy's schooling in the fall. But Henning didn't believe that his son would ever become an enemy, standing on the other side of a barricade. The boundaries weren't as easy to draw as Thumbs believed. It could turn out that the boundary line went right though Henning's own family.

"You know that August is going to go to school at the Bodins' expense," he said quietly. "Maybe you think this is a betrayal?"

Thumbs shrugged his shoulders.

"It depends on the boy himself," he answered. "We need educated people. But naturally the risk exists that he'll become a lackey to the upper-class. You have to give August a sense of his class, a hatred toward the oppressors."

"I don't know if it can be called a sense of his class," answered Henning, "but I would like to give him a good memory of us, of home. Something that would make him remember where he came from. And to never despise us for not being able to go farther than we could."

Thumbs had the protest ready but kept silent. For someone else he might have had bitter words in reply, accusations. But not for Henning, not for the Henning he saw before him. Marked by hard work, coughing, hunched over.

But he was happy that no one had thought of putting Rudde in any fine school. Thumbs wanted to keep his hatred; it warmed him and kept him alive. He felt healthy, strong, ready to fight. But Henning was sick. For his friend it felt most comfortable if everything went along in its same old tracks, if the Bodins took care of August, if no revolution disturbed Lotten's delivery.

Thumbs stayed sitting where he was when Henning went upstairs to sleep.

It was like he was saying good-bye, thought Thumbs. He knew that Henning would not walk beside him when they went out and marched.

Comrade. Friend. And still they had to go their separate ways. He felt like he wanted to and would be able to but wasn't allowed to understand Henning.

The emancipation of the proletariat must come about by their own actions.

That was what Thirsty had said. One thing was certain: that Rudde and his brother would become part of the proletariat. If that was any consolation for a father who knew what it meant. But that was surely one more reason to hope for a revolution.

Summer came, clad the hillside, spread her greenery along the roadsides. Every evening the little girls sat out by the new pump down on Tjärhovsgatan and waited for Henning; they each had her empty bucket with her. Henning filled the buckets and carried them up the hill. The water in the pump was much better than that in the old spring beside the barn. It came in pipes all the way from Årstaviken. And it looked clean and good even if some sewage ran into the inlet which had railroad beds on either side.

August had left for the Bodins'. This summer Lotten hadn't been able to accompany the boy to the boat; she was too heavy now. But August had arranged everything with the Bodins himself. This time he wasn't going somewhere unknown and strange, instead he was going back to a place that had seemed like a dream to him at times during the winter.

But the girls stayed in the city and spent a large part of the day gluing soap cartons. Now Emelie was the one who both picked them up and dropped them off. She wandered in and out of the cosmetics factory as if she belonged there.

One day she got to see the new bear. It was completely unlike its predecessor. A poor wretch who begged for sugar and had belonged to an animal trainer. He had been taught circus tricks and traveled around the country. The pads of his paws were strangely scarred, deformed. The animal had been tortured, the tricks burned into it. Now the bear sat down prettily as soon as anyone approached the cage.

"This one is nice," said Jacob the caretaker.

Emelie felt like she ought to tell her brother about the bear since he was so far away and didn't get to see it. She wrote on a piece of brown wrapping paper and got to put it in with her mother's letter.

Annika came down the stairs. She had looked in August's room, the boy had fallen asleep. A light twilight had settled like a veil upon the treetops outside. Down in the big living room Fredrik had lighted the kerosene lamp.

"You have to read this letter he has received," said Annika, and passed over the wrapping paper that was covered with Emelie's large, childish letters.

He read. About the nice bear that someone had treated so badly and about the boxes that the boy's sisters made.

"So, Holmström has gotten a new bear," said Fredrik.

"It's a touching little letter," said Annika. "I'm thinking about how there is something that we can't give August. Siblings, little childish confidences, this warmth."

"We are so cold, Fredrik," she mused aloud. "So without life." But in saying it she was accusing herself. Or causing him to come closer to her, asking for his damp hands, his flabby body. She didn't want to have him; she wanted something else. The warmth he couldn't give that she, herself, didn't have.

"We have something else perhaps," answered Fredrik. "We can give him an education, for example."

She smiled quickly, a little scornfully. They certainly didn't have much. Fredrik couldn't fool her so much anymore. The sister-in-law with the daughters had been bought out at a cheap price. But the bankruptcy that Annika played with, like a spook to scare her sister-in-law with, wasn't so unreal. Maybe they had gotten through the worst. In any case there wasn't any over-abundance just now.

"She's expecting a child again," said Annika.

"Oh, really."

"They won't be able to say no," she said. "And it's bound be a relief for her."

"How do you mean?"

"When she has one more child how will she have time for everything? It must feel good for her not to have to think about August, at least. Especially if he is going to begin at a better school and has to be well dressed."

"But we should probably wait a little while still," put in Fredrik. "Let him begin at the school for now. Maybe there will be a little more business activity over the winter."

Annika kept quiet. More activity, she thought. There was no activity in whatever Fredrik took care of. Henning and his wife might not want to go along with it.

She sat there feeling gloomy, at the mercy of others. Then she turned the brown paper that still lay on the table toward her and read about the bear who sat so prettily on his burned paws.

Suddenly, she got up without saying anything. Fredrik looked up, wondering, but picked up his newspaper again. He was used to his wife's little whims.

Annika walked out into the garden, the gravel crunching under her white boots, her light-colored skirts sweeping across the flower borders which curtsied and swayed. She stopped where the dusk was densest, under the heaviest linden trees. She stood and looked at the lights from the villa glimmering between the trees. They became more and more blurred, trembled and were blocked out by her eyelids blinking back the tears.

A TIME
OF
CHANGES

Autumn came. The trees yellowed and the leaves fell between red and gray fence planks, swept into piles by the wind. The paving in the lanes was churned to mud; smoke rose from the chimneys, and the windows were sealed again for the winter. Small groups of people sneaked out in the darkness to steal wood from the construction and demolition sites.

Lotten sat on the wooden sofa in the room in the attic and gave her newborn child the breast. Olof ate poorly and cried a lot; they said that the child had inherited his father's upset stomach.

The crying scared her — it felt like an omen. Her worry for Henning returned. How long could he manage? It was strange that they hadn't heard from the Bodins by now! As long as Olof was little she couldn't go out and get work. Otherwise, she would have liked to make Henning stay home and rest for a time.

Soon August would be coming home. The boy had been allowed to enter the second year at Katarina School. He would be an educated man. Yet it still made her feel a little bitter: those fine suits alone which August was given …. That money could save Henning. But no one wanted to help an adult.

I'm being unfair, she thought. The Bodins do so much for August. If Henning only had the strength to get through, until he found something easier …. Then they could really rejoice at August's good fortune.

The child at her breast had finally gone to sleep. But when she tried to put the boy down, he started to cry again immediately. She had to pick him up and walk back and forth, trying to quiet him so Thumbs wouldn't wake up downstairs.

August walked home from school together with Valle, a thin and serious boy from the orphanage out by Lugnet. A couple of the best boys from the home got to go to secondary school, and Valle was one of them.

August got along with him best. Valle was the one closest to normal. They usually played together under the pyramid poplars in the schoolyard or between the graves in the church yard. Often the classes played war, and the raised grave slabs served as forts. But then August and Valle would hide and go balance on the stonewall. There they looked for tracks: people said that Sten Sture's horse galloped along the wall every night. It haunted the place ever since Kristian the Tyrant had dug up Sturen's body during Stockholm's blood bath and in an all-consuming rage taken a bite out of the remains.

Agge and Valle came walking along between Östra Kyrkogatan's low houses. They talked about how different the new school was: there were no teachers who hit and no drummer boys. Of course, you could be frightened by Headmaster Björling's booming voice during morning prayer, but the headmaster never hit them. And their class's teacher, Master Eurenius, was a kind and refined gentleman who had received some prize from the Swedish Academy. That was a real change from Olle the Drunk.

The lane curved and descended toward Renstjärna's hill and the new school for commerce beside Söderberg's Stairs. Somewhere far away down there August's father toiled with his sacks and down there sat Uncle Fredrik in his quiet office. But the two boys didn't dare stay and look down, here was where the "rats" from Malongen usually lay in ambush. Agge and Valle had their school insignia on their wide-brimmed caps and were called "pissers." They had to fight hard battles with the elementary school "rats" and Maria School's "growlers." It didn't matter what they felt or thought; the boundary was real all the same, and those who lived on opposite sides were enemies.

The two friends passed the dangerous spot hurriedly and continued toward Ersta where the district lay workers were based. From here the steep cross street sloped toward Tjärhovsgatan, dividing into stairs and an incline. They chose to take the incline. Soon they would part.

Outside the grocery store in "Kilen," they nodded farewell and continued, each in his own direction. Valle took the way down toward
Danvik's Customs and twisting road while Agge climbed up toward
the hill.

Crouching down he ran through the lane. A few stones landed on
the ground behind him. At the Cigar Box a drunken girl stood and
hung out against the fence. Agge took a careful detour around her.
Elvira had once dragged him into the woodshed and beaten him. Agge
was still afraid.

"I didn't tell," he tried to protect himself. "I only cried and I could-
n't help it."

But Elvira didn't even look at him.

At the harbor it was time for a break and the longshoremen
squeezed in at the Church's brass counter. It was the day after payday
and many felt they could afford to eat an extra bite. Torparsonen
shouted for longshoreman's fare, boiled sausage. But most of them satisfied themselves with taking a drink, a good stiff one.

Henning and some others waited on the stairs; they didn't allow
themselves a visit to the tavern during the afternoon break. The cold
crept along their sweaty backs, the breaks were both dangerous and
necessary. Someone had asked if the company couldn't set up a little
space for breaks but received the answer that Lundström didn't want
to be disloyal to the tavern keeper at the Church.

Besides, you might need a drink and can afford to take one was
Lundström's opinion. He had been considerate and fair: set up credit
for his rowdies. Why were they making a fuss then, wasn't the tavern
good enough any more?

As usual, Henning's stomach gave him trouble, and the paper cone
with the bicarbonate of soda didn't help much. Every now and then
he was forced to pay a few öre to a substitute who took his place on
the team while he himself hurried to the outhouse beside the steep
wall of the hillside. In this way he still paid his tribute to the tavern:
the substitute's remuneration corresponded to the price for a little
schnapps and was transformed into one as a rule.

He returned, exhausted and miserable. The pain, the aching, the strange feeling of fainting. There had been blood in his stools again. There were small streaks of blood in what he coughed up as well. He didn't dare tell this to Lotten; she would get too worried. It would surely be better if he got lighter work. He counted on taking Styvnicke's place. The boss had had alcoholic seizures several times and surely couldn't have much time left.

He heard his name. A thin little voice was calling. Henning gave a start, afraid that Emelie had walked down to the harbor. But it didn't sound like Emelie.

A girl was sitting between two bales, apparently it was she who had called. His first thought was to walk on past: it was so obvious that she was a little whore, it showed just by her clothing. But she knew him. Susanna he thought. But Susanna should be bigger, older.

Then he saw who it was: Klara's daughter. She could easily be twelve years old now and there were younger girls than her who sold themselves. Still it gave him a bitter feeling.

"Help me," she begged. "A dillshark ripped off the old lady and gave her a shiner."

During his years in the city, Henning had learned some of the argot. Enough so that he understood that Klara had been cheated out of some money and been hit by a worker from the Dihlström Institution.

"Where is she?" he asked and looked around.

The girl pointed in between the bales and he hurried over. A fat and swollen woman lay groaning on the ground in front of him. When he tried to pull her up, she resisted, and then suddenly she sat up and stared at him.

"Henning!"

It took a moment before he recognized her, before he found the young Klara hidden behind the pasty and swollen flesh. Her hair was gray; her features blotted out from beer and hard liquor; her clothing was in tatters. Klara couldn't have been much more than thirty-five but it was an old woman he saw.

"That damned bastard, that scum," she swore. "Ripped me off just because I was a little drunk."

He didn't know what he could do for her. But he went and got Fearsome and together they led Klara a little way up the hill. There she could lie and sleep off her intoxication in a rocky nook without the police finding her. They scraped together a few coins even though they knew Klara would immediately send the girl off to buy aquavit.

"Where do you live?" Henning asked the girl.

She shook her head.

"Mom's old man kicked us out. He doesn't have a steady job anymore," the girl said.

So Klara was now without a "provider," homeless.

But what could he do? It was still warm enough to sleep outside, and Klara would soon find a "job" again.

"There isn't much left of her," Fearsome said when they were on their way back to the team. "Do you remember ...?" And he thought of the Klara who had once glided around in the blue dress at his wedding. And Henning remembered the girl who had sat on the edge of the dyer's bed and shown her white legs, who stood leaning against the railing down at Fiskarhamnen and joked with two boat rockers.

"And the kid," Henning said. "What's going to happen to her?"

"She's already a little whore," said Fearsome. "Though she's not cut out for it, really."

Maybe the Bible ladies could help, they had their emergency station after all. The two pooled a little more of their meager funds and sent a substitute up into the White Hills.

A few hours later the reply came back. The Bible ladies had gone down with him and taken both Klara and the girl.

"Determined ladies, those ones," said the substitute. They had pulled Klara up the hill to a waiting wagon and gotten the girl to go with them too even though she had kicked and resisted. But Klara had been thankful to be picked up.

Henning walked over to the Bible ladies one evening and asked how it had worked out with Klara. They had sent her to the hospital but didn't place much hope on her getting better. But Klara's daughter was turning out well and rather happy at the home for fallen girls.

He had worked for sixteen hours, carrying sacks of grain.

Was he getting sloppy because it was the last sack of the day? He didn't know; he only knew that the sack had slipped so that he was about to lose hold, had to hike it up again to get a better grip. He felt the nausea coming on but hurried, wanted to make it over with the sack before he threw up. But he had to put it down and stumble to the side. He saw, as if in a fog, how Torparsonen who had just put down his last sack now took Henning's and carried it over.

The vomiting came on with more force than ever. As if his stomach was being turned inside out, he had to cling to the boom so as not to fall over.

And then: the taste of blood in his mouth.

He finally managed to see and saw the blood, dark as if clotted. He had the idea that people with tuberculosis coughed up foaming and light-colored blood.

Fearsome hurried over, helped hold Henning up.

"It looks like it's bleeding from your stomach," he said thoughtfully. "You've overstrained yourself."

In the middle of all his misery, Henning felt some sort of gratitude. It probably wasn't consumption after all.

"You have to go a doctor," said Torparsonen who had also come over to Henning.

No, he didn't want to. What could a doctor do? Only suggest things that he couldn't afford.

"It's usually better when I'm not carrying things," he said. "And soon it'll be closed here for the winter."

"You probably shouldn't carry anything these next few weeks," counseled Fearsome.

Henning insisted on walking by himself. But on the stairs up toward the hill, he didn't have the strength; Fearsome and Torparsonen had to take him between them and carry him up. It wasn't hard for them. Henning was a small load, a light sack.

They waited a little while he emptied his stomach a few more times. Now it was just a little blood and phlegm which came up: he didn't have any more food left to bring up.

Slowly they continued across Stigberget, leading Henning between them. But when they got closer to home, he wanted to walk on his own. If Lotten saw them coming this way, she would get too worried.

His comrades obeyed against their will. But they stood there and watched him. And he didn't take many steps before he fell.

Then they had to carry him the rest of the way, no matter how anxious it might make Lotten. Fearsome pushed open the gate; he who knew the way went first. Lotten heard them coming up the stairs and hurried out. But Fearsome shook his head at her unasked question.

"He's only fainted," grumbled Fearsome. "He had some bleeding from his stomach."

They lay Henning down on the wooden lid of the kitchen sofa and he opened his eyes and saw he was home. Then he sat up carefully in spite of their protests.

Torparsonen reached out his hand to say good-bye.

"When you come back to the harbor, I'll probably be gone," said Torparsonen. "Next Monday I'm starting as a streetcar conductor."

Lotten made the bed for Henning and then went to see if the poor doctor could come. The baby, lying in a drawer, cried when she left.

WAITING

The day was gray, a thick fog hid the city and the water. Whoever came to the houses on the hill could imagine themselves farther out in the archipelago. From out of the mist, a steamboat called and another answered.

Five-year-old Mikael, Thumbs' and Matilda's youngest, was standing alone and hanging out by the fence when he saw the strange-looking man coming. Dressed in dark clothes with a little box in his hand. What could this guy be doing here?

The stranger looked at the houses next door, and came closer. Mikael sneaked into the yard and hid. But the man came after him and opened the gate. He stood there a little while and let the gate swing, as if he was testing to see if the hinge was well-oiled. Then he looked at the house they lived in, poked at a joint, looked through a windowpane. But he didn't go inside, approaching Mikael instead, who ran away hurriedly. The man went over to the shed in the yard, looked in the woodshed, and opened the door to the outhouse. He even lifted up the cover and looked at the barrel.

"You, boy!" he shouted to Mikael. "Do you live here?"

"Yes..."

"Is it your papa who's sick?"

"No, he's sleeping," answered Mikael. "He always does that in the daytime."

"Isn't he working then?"

"Only at night," said Mikael.

"So, maybe he's a lamplighter," said the stranger.

He looked around: the yard was free of garbage. Amazing, he had to make a note of it. It had been a long time since he had done an inspection here on the hill.

"But there is a sick man living here?" he asked while he wrote in his notebook.

"Yes, up in the attic. He has a pain in his stomach."

The stranger put away his notebook and walked toward the entrance. He looked around in the little vestibule; it looked tidy, and he couldn't see any mouse holes. He began to walk up the stairs.

Before he had even reached the top, a door opened and a woman looked out into the dim light of the attic. When she saw who it was, she curtsied politely and opened the door all the way.

"I wondered just now if it could be the doctor," she said.

He nodded and continued the inspection before he answered her. Very well-kept, surprisingly so. The wood of the floor shone white; the table and benches were clean; a spittoon stood beside the sick man's bed.

"Well, how's the patient? No, lie down, lie down," he admonished Henning when he tried to sit up.

Lotten hurried to pull up a chair. The doctor handed her his hat and coat, then he sat down beside Henning.

Observer, exposer, judge. Henning squirmed a little uneasily under the doctor's gaze. But the questions which followed were calming, seemingly safe. Henning answered as best he could: no one in his family had been consumptive, as far as he knew. His mother had died of cholera and then Henning had come to the miller's. Yes, he had worked at the mill and slept there too. And then? Yes, then he had come to the city, worked as a brick carrier at first and then as a long-shoreman and herring packer.

The doctor nodded, taking notes at times. Henning had to sit up, and the doctor placed an ear against his chest and listened. He rapped with his knuckle on his chest and asked Henning to cough. Then he squeezed his stomach: did this hurt? And this?

How long had Nilsson been coughing? Had he had diarrhea a long time? Was there blood when he coughed or blood in his stools?

A little embarrassed, Henning had to make his confession. Lotten looked at him horrified.

"I didn't know ..." she said, "that it had been going on for so long."

The doctor only growled. He had listened and knew: tuberculosis in the far advanced stage. Stomach and intestinal ulcers meant that the tubercular process had spread to his intestines as well.

It wasn't his duty to rob his patients of their will to live. But what could he prescribe? If it had been a merchant ... a long-term visit to some foreign spa could help ... but a dock worker ...?

"You only have this one room of course?"

"Yes. We have to rent out the space in the attic."

"Do you have any tenants in here as well?"

"No."

"It would naturally be better if Nilsson could sleep alone," the doctor said. "So that he isn't disturbed by the children. If you could rearrange things it would be better."

"Is it serious?" asked Lotten.

"Well," said the doctor. "The lungs aren't exactly strong. Nilsson will have to be careful with them. And his stomach isn't what it should be. But we will have to see with time ...."

"Rest," continued the doctor. "Don't carry anything. No spicy food, no herring. But milk. And eggs, especially soft-boiled. Meat and fresh fish."

"Does he have to go to the hospital?" asked Lotten.

The doctor looked up, waited with the answer, then he gave her a friendly smile.

"To be honest," he said. "Nilsson could hardly be better off than here. I don't think we'll undertake any operation. But the children...do you have many children?"

"Four. Three in school and then the little one. He cries a lot; it's probably his stomach that's giving him trouble too."

He took a look at the child. Well cared for, clean, it wasn't his care that was causing it. As clean as this room was kept, maybe it wasn't so dangerous for the children, if they aired it out so the sick air disappeared.

"There's nothing wrong with the child," said the doctor. It'll surely go away in a month or so; it's probably just infant colic. It can help sometimes if you put him on his stomach when he cries."

He walked over to the window, looked out and wrinkled his forehead thoughtfully.

"You live very exposed to winds from the east," he said. "Easterly winds aren't good for Nilsson. The room should be aired out from time to time, but never when it's blowing from the Baltic."

The doctor stayed there a little longer than he usually did, or should have, considering the number who were waiting. But this family interested him. It wasn't this clean many other places.

"Nilsson has a good wife," he said to Henning. "But how are you going to manage without an income?"

Lotten told him that she and the children usually pasted boxes for the cosmetics factory. It didn't give them much of an income, but it was still something. If only she dared leave the house, she would go out and take in washing.

The doctor wrote out a prescription and packed his bag.

"Something soothing for your cough and stomach, laudanum. With a sugar binder to help with the diarrhea too," he said. "It will make Nilsson sleep more peacefully. We'll put this on the communal tab since Nilsson doesn't have an income. But in exchange I'm going to use you as proof that people in the poor quarters can live cleanly and comfortably."

"Let me know if Nilsson gets any worse," he said.

The doctor left, and for many weeks afterward, he scolded people angrily over all the filth he encountered: he had seen how it could look if people only tried. But even as he preached, he had to wonder: how did that person manage? With a poor sick soul for a husband, four children, almost no money. Want caused most people to crack in the end. A few were really tough, fought against it for as long as they could. Was it meaningless or not? He didn't want to try to answer that question. Still, it irritated him so much that he almost disgraced himself during a discussion at the medical society. He spoke for more radical measures to come to grips with the problems of the working and poor classes. Over the last hundred years, the average life span had increased by ten years from thirty-five to forty-five for men. But he firmly believed he could state with confidence that the difference between classes was so great that the average age for men in the working class was still not more than thirty-five. Something had to be done. To begin with, society had to build housing worthy of people.

Someone had called him a socialist, that was bad. He had to try to calm himself down.

Sometimes he thought he would go over to the sick dock worker on the hill, take along a gift, a little food. But it never happened. And it wasn't just a question of this single case, but one of principles. Something had to be done whether they called him a socialist or not.

Henning and Lotten didn't hear any more from the doctor and didn't send for him either. There wasn't anything else to do other than try and follow the doctor's instructions. Henning had to rest and try to eat the food he ordered. But they were never able to afford any eggs.

The illness gave them new habits. The children gathered around the table by the sick man's bed and pasted boxes. Lotten went out washing together with her mother, and Emelie saw that the family was fed and the little one cared for. August sat in a corner with his fingers in his ears and did his homework. Thumbs came up for a little while every day. The medicine helped pretty well with the cough and the pain and made Henning comfortably drowsy.

But this idleness, not being able to work and earn the money they needed, this still worried him. As if he was waiting to be called down to the harbor, had to be always prepared to answer yes and step in.

Gray days and black nights. In spite of the medicine, he often lay awake and stared out the window, waiting the way dock workers usually wait for the first ship in the spring. Anything at all, as long as it was a boat.

He half sat up in bed sometimes and tried to help with the pasting. It was the season for the cosmetics factory now, and they were using Christmas packaging for the soaps and the perfumes. But it was hard to work in bed, especially when he was afraid of getting paste on things. He wasn't much help, the children did it much better.

Especially Emelie, he never tired of watching how quickly she worked. She discovered new methods, spread paste on six or seven boxes at once, folded, cut and glued like a machine. She could do two to three times as many as the one-year younger Gertrud; she was even quicker than Lotten.

He wondered what kind of work Emelie could get: pastry chef, seamstress, lacemaker. But it would probably be in a factory or a spinning mill. Gertrud was a little harder to fantasize about; she didn't really have the same abilities as her sister. A good wife he thought: that wasn't the worst thing.

Lotten came home late from the laundry where she had been working since early in the morning. But she forgot her tiredness, she was growing as a person. Before she could be a little tired and out of sorts at times, her tone sound a little sharp when the children were noisy. Now she showed neither tiredness nor worry. And he was amazed, didn't understand how she had the energy. He thought: I help her best by neither complaining nor becoming impatient. Things are the way they are and no amount of crying helps.

He waited. As quietly and patiently as he was able.

One day Anna-Kajsa came.

Her husband, Pontus, was still working at *The Fatherland*. His book had not been a success; his attempt to talk about the life of the poor had been a failure; everything had remained the way it was.

But that fall something had happened which Pontus Berger had experienced like an explosion. It was a book. It swept away all the veils, spat all the gods in the face. And it prophesied a revolution. Yes, it said there that people from the hills, from the White Hills too it said, would stream into the city and demand their rights and freedom.

The author's name was August Strindberg.

"Now something's happening," Pontus had said. "Things are stirring again — now the waiting period is over."

Anna-Kajsa had the book with her, really so that Thumbs could read it. But since Henning was lying sick in bed maybe he wanted to borrow it first?

She left soon after. Henning lay and looked at the book. *The Red Room, Descriptions from the Life of an Artist and Writer.*

He leafed through it. He read the first few pages with a certain amount of trouble. He leafed through it a little again and tried once more, farther on. But he couldn't really understand what it was all about. It felt as if life in the outside world couldn't engage him now. Now only those who were closest to him were left, his worry for Lotten and the children, his dreams to be able to take a job again, his wish to work hard for his own. Everything else was unimportant.

The book lay unread on the table beside his bed. It was written for those who had the strength to live and hope, for Thumbs who read and enjoyed it, cursing with joy and anger.

Henning was waiting for another message. He listened inside himself for the rumblings in his stomach, for the whistling in his chest. He listened for footsteps on the stairs: would Lotten be coming soon?

One day he received a message which made him very happy and made his waiting easier.

It was also an August who gave it to him, his own son. Uncle Fredrik had said that a position in the warehouse awaited him in the spring. He had only to manage until then, rest his way to health, survive.

DECEMBER DAYS

The darkness came early; their only window let in so little of the December day's gray light.

He lay in the twilight, the kerosene lamp burned only when they took care of their chores. A person lying sick didn't need to waste light. Besides, he liked it best this way, the darkness muffled things, was merciful. Sometimes he could drift off, then he would lie and look at the window and try to guess how long he had been asleep — how much of the day had gone by. If the children would be coming home from school soon, how much longer Lotten would be. Emelie would have their youngest with her when she came; the little boy was with a neighboring woman when Lotten was working, and the girls went to school.

The doctor had said that Henning should lie in bed. To get well and regain his strength. He had a right to lie there, he had to. But as he lay there, he felt how his strength and life crept in the wrong direction, out of him instead of in. He felt even weaker and felt like his feet were swelling up just from his lying there. Rest became meaningless. In that case shouldn't he try to work anyway?

He coughed. Spat into the cup, which he kept under a plate, closing his eyes to avoid seeing.

Time after time he had to drag himself out to the bucket that stood in the attic; he didn't have the strength to go down to the outhouse. He felt ashamed at times in front of the children. What must they think of a father who lay almost as helpless as an infant?

But he never felt ashamed in front of Lotten. They had gotten so close that everything was theirs together. When she was in the room, his worry diminished; he could almost feel content. Her nearness was enough.

The Lotten that he saw and loved was already worn out, marked and bent prematurely. She arrived carrying pails of water, which she lugged up from Tjärhovsgatan: she had never been able to skimp on water. She woke up first and fell asleep last, sat at the kerosene lamp late into the night so the children would be neat and in one piece when they went to school. She toiled at home and then went out to toil for other people. She didn't dare count the hours in her workday; they were closer to twenty than fifteen.

When she was younger she had complained sometimes. But not any longer. Sometimes she left in the middle of the night around two o'clock, he could hear how her cart rattled over the bumps in the lane. She transported the washing to the laundry with the cart, and then she lay on the jetty by the harbor and rinsed. Her hands split open from the ice-cold water; she had to rub them with fat and wrap them with rags in the few hours she was idle.

He imagined he could see her pale face shining from out of the darkness, even when he was alone. It was bitter knowledge that she was working so hard while he just lay here. He who was supposed to support them, who wanted to, who had to.

Luckily they got bread cheaply, through Thumbs who bought left-overs from the bakery. Henning lived mostly on soaked bread; his stomach couldn't tolerate the salty herring. At times Lotten was able to come across a little cheap meat. Then she made sure that Henning and the girls got it. She felt that she herself could manage without, and August had a meal at the Bodin's every week.

Things would be better by spring; he had received the promise of work at Bodin's again. He lay and thought about the dark warehouse that stank of herring; it seemed like a paradise to him. A good job, a steady income. It was just a matter of hanging in there, having the strength to wait.

The girls arrived from school and a beam of light and life filled the attic room. The kerosene lamp was lit while Emelie changed the squirming Olof and Gertrud, set out bread and skim milk. Henning got a mug to dip bread in, but couldn't get much down: all food made him nauseous. The girls talked about the day's events in school, then they brought out the boxes and began to paste. It was the last batch before Christmas; in a few days Emelie would go down and hand it in.

They whispered while they worked, but he wasn't sleeping as they may have believed, he just had his eyes closed. He heard when August came and looked up and nodded. The boy sat with his lessons; he was going to study before he went to the Bodins as he did every Wednesday. One time he'd had a basket of food with him when he came home, then they'd had a party. But Henning had heard that Bodin's business affairs were still going badly, and when he tasted the good things from the basket, he had done it with a guilty conscience: what if Bodin was being so generous that he couldn't afford to hire him?

August left after a while; the girls were still working. Henning slept a few hours, when he woke up it was dark. The girls were probably downstairs at Thumbs' place. Henning lay and looked out into the darkness, heard the breathing of their youngest child. He wept over his helplessness — he wept until he sank into a daze and slept.

A week before Christmas he received a visit. Kerstin from the candle factory had come, and she had a white candle with her. He hadn't counted on their being able to afford any Christmas candles and was cheered by the gift, for the children's sake. Kerstin couldn't stay long, but she sat a while at his bedside and talked about her children and Olle who was often sick. Henning knew: Olle drank too much, Kerstin didn't have it easy. But they had housing within the factory grounds, and the children were big now and had work.

Kerstin got up, a little stiff and wracked with aches and pains. Work was waiting, the candle factory had hectic days, and they went on late into the evenings. She had taken the opportunity to stop by during the afternoon break since she had heard that Henning was sick.

The candle lay where it was on the table. Emelie came and placed it carefully in a holder. A beautiful and white shining candle. He remembered the hall with the polishing machine, the terrace for bleaching, the room where the girls stood and packed candles. So long ago, so distant. And yet so near, the years had gone quickly. Kerstin and Olle were still at the factory, and Henning lay and wondered why he wasn't still there, what a mistake he had made.

The candle shone from the dresser, unlit but still gleaming. They would have a lighted candle this year, too. But what more would they have? There wouldn't be any Christmas presents, and still less Christmas food, unless August got a basket from the Bodins. Henning both hoped for and dreaded it.

He lay and looked at the candle. Alone. The girls had gone down to the factory, August hadn't come back from school yet; the little boy was at the neighbor woman's, Lotten was out, washing.

One candle. Nothing more. He couldn't support his own family any longer, couldn't keep want at a distance. He only lay, lay like a burden on them. And now he understood that he wasn't getting better from lying there. The doctor's medicine didn't help, nor did rest.

Then he got up.

A drizzling rain hit him in the face; the snow in the lane had been transformed into a dirty slush. He gave himself a shake, pulled his coat tighter around him and stumbled forward in the wheel tracks.

He didn't actually know where he was going. It was as if habit led him toward the harbor. Maybe he would be allowed to join the team for a few hours if some boat had gotten through the ice. Maybe he could find out at Bodin's firm if there was anything he could do. The main thing was that he had now gotten moving, had made up his mind to work again. He would surely have time to earn something before Christmas.

But it was already late in the day, he had to hurry. He didn't have the strength to think that he might go back empty handed, that he had gone out in vain.

The closest route to the harbor went over Erstaberget, up the four flights of steps on the lane crossing Tjärhovsgatan, toward the lay workers' institute.

As long as he was going down, he was propelled as if from behind; he thought it went more easily than he would have believed. He tried to increase his pace. He passed Pilgatan and the dark back of Kilen and tripped in front of a wagon which came driving down Tjärhovsgatan. But he managed to escape the horses' hooves and the creaking wheels. He reached the stairs and took the first step up. Perhaps he should calm down now, slow down. But he continued nonetheless: what if he were to get there too late!

The children and Lotten and Christmas, which was so close, he should be able to do something, have time to earn something.

He had to.

Then everything disappeared, there was just a wave swelling over him, and it lifted him up and threw him.

He collapsed on the stairs, fell down the few steps he had managed to climb up. The old hired coachman was on his way home with his coach. He saw the people gathered around and braked. If it was a fight, he wanted to have a look.

Then the crowd broke up and some people came along carrying a man. Dad looked, surprised: he had heard that Nilsson was bedridden for good.

He climbed down from his coachbox and stopped the people who were carrying the man. "Lay him in the coach," he said. "But wipe off the blood first so the cushions don't get ruined."

Light, foaming blood. Well, well, that was nothing unusual.

The coach drove slowly, swaying in the potholes; it was on the verge of getting stuck in the mud. Dad let the team stop, climbed down from the box and wrapped the reins around the horse's front legs. Then he walked calmly through the gate and banged on the door to the house. Thumbs looked out, surprised.

They carried Henning up the stairs. Thumbs got the many curious onlookers who had followed in the coach's tracks out of the house, and tried to settle Henning in bed. Dad nodded and left.

"It's probably best if I try and get the doctor," said Thumbs when Henning opened his eyes.

Henning shook his head.

Still Thumbs asked again, shouldn't he?

No.

Henning stayed sitting on the bed until Lotten came.

"Lotten," whispered Henning, "forgive me."

She held him carefully while she washed his face, loosened the blood which had dried in the corners of his mouth.

"I want to live, Lotten."

She nodded. "You'll be better soon," she answered. "And in the spring ...."

"I have to. I can't die now, not yet."

"You're not going to. You'll see that you'll be better soon. If only you'll be careful, don't do this again."

She got up to put away the water basin, took a few steps toward the counter by the window. She heard a bubbling noise and hurried back. She saw a little stream of blood glimmering in the corner of his mouth which she had just wiped.

"Henning!"

He opened his eyes and looked at her: he was alive.

She saw that he tried to say something, but it strained him — carefully she guided his head back to the pillow.

His eyes which had just shone at her in the twilight became duller, as if their light had gone out. His face sank inward, toward the pillow and toward his skull. His skin grew smooth. A slight tremor passed through his body. Then he lay still, quiet.

She fell to her knees by the bed and prayed: Dear God let him live, dear God help us, don't let him die.

But when she at last forced herself to understand that no prayers helped, she lit the little white candle that hadn't been in the room when she left that morning.

She heard the girls on the stairs, pulled the sheet up over his face.

She met them at the door.

"Father is dead," she said.

BREAKING UP

The dark year ended, went out in the December night. A new year came: a new decade. People wrote 1880.

That was the year before Robert Koch discovered the tuberculosis bacterium. And the year before August Palm came to Sweden to preach Socialism.

One Sunday in January, Lotten was expecting visitors. Annika and Fredrik Bodin had sent a message that they wanted to come and talk to her. Worried, she had a presentiment as to the purpose of their visit.

August was to go out and meet his benefactors: it had been decided. Even if Annika ought to be able to find her way to Åsöberget, it was perhaps simplest if someone pointed out the street and the house.

The boy had to put on his best suit, and Lotten combed his hair before he left. Was he going to leave her now also?

But August ran off happily. He thought it was exciting to have Aunt and Uncle come to visit Mama; it brought his two worlds closer together. And he, who knew both, would be at the center.

Lilla Bondegatan was nice, and even after the last snowfall, the coachman would probably be able to get all the way to Garbage Lane today. The snow hid the piles of garbage and covered up the flaws on the little houses, the street looked very inviting. August bounded along with his school cap bobbing up and down over his protruding ears. For once he wasn't cautious and afraid, but instead almost daring.

He got down to Pilgatan and followed along the endlessly long shed that housed the rope maker's track; he had to wonder if it wasn't the city's longest house, and if Aunt and Uncle had ever seen such a long building. He would ask. He could tell them how it looked inside: the big wooden wheel which went around slowly and the ropemaker who walked backwards while the rope seemed to glide out of his hands.

August was going to wait on the corner of Renstjärnasgränd. Now when it was slippery out, the coach would probably not be able to make it up Glasbruksgatan, maybe not up Götgatsbacken either; they would probably have to take a large detour around Maria Church.

Naturally the boy was there too early, he had time to get really frozen before the coach came, and he could crawl inside. The windowpanes were icy, and he completely forgot to show them the rope-maker's track.

August opened the gate. His summer parents looked about curiously in his winter world. Annika breathed carefully through her nose, as if looking for the stench of poverty. She looked around, but the snow hid any secret the yard might have.

Far below them lay the city, beyond it the water and inlet shone. Such an unrestricted view, what a vista, they didn't even have that at home on Skeppsbron.

The door to the house opened, and Lotten came toward them. Older than they remembered her, more angular, more bent over. Worriedly Annika thought: she's younger than me, am I already so old?

Fredrik Bodin had to stoop carefully, the ceiling was low on the stairs. The door to the room stood open. Surprised, Annika saw how clean everything was, how polished. The youngest child lay in a drawer and slept, a six-month-old.

Somehow Henning had fooled her, she thought. The world of poverty he had stayed in wasn't the same as the one she had left. She could have guessed it from August, now she saw it clearly.

"Our visit is really to ..." began Fredrik Bodin fumblingly. He probably wished the boy weren't there when they spoke about it.

Lotten understood, and sent August to get his sisters who were out playing. August went, obediently but unwillingly.

They wanted to adopt him, make him their heir. Just now there wasn't so much to own and inherit, the firm had been having a rough time. But it looked like it was slowly starting to progress again.

Lotten nodded, but lowered her head without looking up. Yes, of course, she wanted what was best for the boy. She was grateful. For the schooling, for everything.

They wanted to help her, too. They couldn't do so much, as they had said the firm ... but something. She must have big expenses just now.

The sum which Fredrik Bodin named was large, Lotten thought. The same amount which Henning had once received after the fire. One hundred. They had been called riksdaler then. Now they were called kronor.

"Will I be allowed to see him?" she wondered. "Ever?"

Fredrik looked quickly at Annika; this was for her to decide. There certainly couldn't be any daily running back and forth; the boy was going to be their son, their own.

Annika hesitated a moment. She herself had left everything, wiped everything clean. Wasn't that what you had to do?

But she thought of her own mother, the bitter parting, the constant feeling of being unappeased. She couldn't decide for August; he had to make up his own mind when the time came.

"Of course, he can come and visit you," she answered smiling. "He can come once a week — the way he's been coming to us now."

Lotten nodded, still without looking up. She felt like she was sitting closed inside a fog, couldn't see out through her tears. August. Once a week. What would Henning have said?

Luckily August and the girls arrived. Emelie and Gertrud had to curtsey and say hello. Fredrik Bodin thought the girls looked oddly clumsy beside August. The boy had another style, was another strain. They had chosen the right one. But when he talked with Annika afterward, he understood that it was only the clothing that made August seem different.

Annika would have really liked to take one of the girls with her too, thought Fredrik. But there had to be some restraint, business wasn't that good. Though, of course, they were sweet, well-brought-up children which that poor Nilsson had left behind. It was tragic about that fellow who had gone and worn himself out in the harbor. If they had known things were so bad, they could have arranged something.

Fredrik Bodin nodded to August, and the boy smiled back happily. It was pleasant around the boy, August was a little person who didn't demand anything, just gratefully took what he was given. It would be nice with the boy in the house, more alive, more of a home.

But August's mother apparently wanted them to wait a week or two. And Annika wanted to clean and put a room in order, they had to buy a bed and a few other things. Two weeks, Annika said. Of course, there was no hurry.

The visitors thanked them for being allowed to come see them, and Lotten and the little girls curtsied. August went along in the coach down to Tjärhovsgatan.

After the children had fallen asleep, Lotten sat and looked at the large bank note, examining it as if she believed it were false. Somehow she had sold August. But it was for the boy's own good, he couldn't have a better life than with the Bodins. Should she deny him the life they could offer?

Oh Henning! If only I could talk to you, if only you could give me some advice. It's so hard to be alone, to decide everything alone, to part with August alone.

It was Sunday afternoon, the last day in the house on the hill. Not only for August but for his mother and his siblings.

The snow had melted away, and the hill lay dark and slick, unveiled and naked. Trash blew in the wind, mud spattered from the cartwheels on the sides of the houses and fences.

When Monday morning arrived, Lotten would also be moving along with the girls and Olof down to Grandmother in the "mahogany house" on Nytorget. It was too expensive to rent in both places.

She looked at the furniture. They didn't have much, still it would be terribly crowded in her mother's room They had to take the dresser and the fold-out bed the girls slept on. And Lotten wanted to keep the sofa.

She stood still a moment and looked around the room. She remembered how it had looked the first time she had come there: the wallpaper in tatters, the insulation hanging out of the cracks in the ceiling. Henning had almost rebuilt the entire attic; it was a nice room for those who followed after them.

It was hard to leave. It was like leaving a part of her life behind. Leaving the memories of happiness and pain, of everything that had meant something. She had made love, given birth to her children. Henning had lain sick and died here. They had lived twelve years in this room. It may not have been so long, but she knew that they were the twelve most important years of her life. She wasn't much more than thirty, but still it felt as if time had run out, only old age and death remained.

She walked through the room which already seemed empty and silent, abandoned. She stopped before the two packing crates, on top lay a little finely wrapped package.

In Emelie's childish hand stood printed:
Gift from my Father on My Birthday 1878.
It was the handkerchief with an embroidered E.

How much does a child remember? How much are they able to grieve? The little one whimpered in his sleep. He wouldn't have any memory of a father. But the others?

August was ready for the journey. Yes, he should leave; it wasn't good if he was late and the streets dark.

But it was hard to part. She held him tightly, sniffing in spite of trying to be calm.

"But Mama, I'm coming on Wednesday."

"Yes, yes. That's fine." She nodded, tried to smile. He was coming on Wednesday. But then he would no longer be hers.

"Take care of yourself," she said. "And behave so that you bring us honor. And ... don't forget us."

He looked at her wonderingly, couldn't understand that she was so upset, that she could believe that he would forget her.

Lotten followed him to the gate, stood there and waved. She saw him go, grow smaller, disappear into the dusk. The street lay empty and silent, the wind blew some papers past her and banged the gate.

CITY
OF
MY DREAMS

The city waited, shone palely out of the dusk: walls and towers along the water.

The twilight had dissolved the contours of the shoreline, erased the borders between land and water. But towers still stood black and sharp against the lighter gray of the western sky.

With all its dirt and its poverty, for those who were born there the city was still home. They felt it when they moved through the narrow passages of the streets. Rotting wooden houses and fireproof gables with crumbling plaster were safe, and well-known landmarks became beautiful in the twilight.

But most people knew only their part of town, their quarter. They walked in a pattern and seldom went outside it. Only a few hundred meters from their worn-in tracks were houses and streets as unknown to them as if they had been parts of foreign cities, distant countries. And while people led their lives there, the known quarters also changed, became unfamiliar.

For the city grows and grows constantly: so much becomes new, so much disappears. Before we have even noticed it, we are walking in another city; we have had time to be turned into strangers.

So unfaithful is the city. And still we don't abandon it, still we love it as only he who has been betrayed can love.

It waited for him, pulled at him from below the gray hill of his childhood.

Men with magic staffs walked down there in the darkness now; light after light flared up in the wake of their path. In the gathering dusk the city was a pile of embers that someone blew to life: it blazed up, flickered like a dream castle in the firelight.

The city which plays and sparkles, lifted on a tray, extended like a gift. There, below the hill, in the wealthy quarters, there lies opportunity, the future. In the good soil of the valleys everything grows which doesn't exist in the bare hills. Both magnificent flowers and weeds grow more abundantly there.

The city and life awaited. For the eleven-year-old boy, too.

He stopped just where Stora Glasbruksgatan opened onto the area by the locks. A train chugged through in the old iron yard, spreading its mighty cloud of steam when it throbbed on into the tunnel.

In the billows of smoke, in the glittering street lights, in the mist over Strömmen, he saw the promise everywhere. A few more years — then he would be grown, ready to succeed where others had failed. He knew he had been given great opportunities. He belonged perhaps to the chosen, to those whom life and the city smiled upon.

The boy dreamed. The city waited.